Argument and Inference

Argument and Inference

An Introduction to Inductive Logic

Gregory Johnson

The MIT Press

Cambridge, Massachusetts

London, England

This book was set in Stone Serif by diacriTech, Chennai. Printed and bound in the United States of America.

Library of Congress Cataloging-in-Publication Data

Names: Johnson, Gregory S., author.
Title: Argument and inference : an introduction to inductive logic / Gregory Johnson.
Description: Cambridge, MA : MIT Press, 2016. | Includes index.
Identifiers: LCCN 2016017246 | ISBN 9780262035255 (hardcover : alk. paper)
Subjects: LCSH: Induction (Logic)
Classification: LCC BC91 .J64 2016 | DDC 161—dc23 LC record available at https://lccn.loc.gov/2016017246

10 9 8 7 6 5 4 3 2 1

Contents

Preface

This textbook was written for students taking my Critical Reasoning course. Searching for suitable material, I landed on inductive logic. This, I found, not only met the needs of the students and provided a coherent theme to the course, it also complemented the standard introduction to deductive logic course and connected nicely with other areas of philosophy, especially epistemology and the philosophy of science.

In the early stages of thinking about this textbook, I had in mind a simple primer that would only state the structure of each type of argument and list the rules and guidelines for making each type of inference. But once I began writing, that no longer seemed practical. Explanations and examples had to be added. I have tried, however, to keep the emphasis on the application of inductive logic. Hopefully, with the provided exposition, the reader can get to the heart of the material rather efficiently, and once that is done, the emphasis can shift to practicing the material. To that end, each chapter includes practice problems, plus the answers and, in many cases, explanations for how to work through the problems.

The scope of inductive reasoning is vast, and I have not tried to capture it all here. A range of different types of inference are included, though, and, throughout, there is an emphasis on representing the inductive inferences as arguments. This, I think, helps the reader see that, although the rules and guidelines for making the inferences may differ quite a bit, they all serve the purpose of generating a conclusion that is probable and thus less than certain.

Chapter 1 begins by explaining what an argument is and the difference between deductively valid and invalid inferences. In the second half of the chapter, I introduce several types of arguments: modus ponens and modus tollens, then the inductive generalization, proportional syllogism (sometimes called *direct inference*), induction by confirmation (i.e., the hypothetico-deductive model), and analogical argument. The exposition here is quick. The purpose is only to introduce the reader to some different argument forms and the notion that arguments with different content can share the same form. After chapter 1, the textbook can be divided into two parts.

First, chapters 2, 3, and 4 are about inferences that do not require precise probabilities or the probability calculus. Chapters 2 and 3 focus on the induction by confirmation and variations of this argument. Chapter 2 examines the basic induction by confirmation and how the evidence determines the appropriate conclusion about the hypothesis. Chapter 3 covers, first, the crucial experiment: the inference that is made when one set of data can be used to determine which of two hypotheses is probably correct. The inference to the best explanation is also covered in this chapter since it shares some features with the induction by confirmation. Chapter 4 is devoted to Mill's five methods. Necessary and sufficient conditions are discussed at the beginning of this chapter and used in the explanation of the method of agreement, the method of difference, and the joint method of agreement and difference.

The second part of the textbook comprises chapters 5 through 8. These chapters focus on inferences that are made using the probability calculus. Chapter 5 introduces some terminology and definitions, and then chapter 6 begins with the probability calculus. That is a natural introduction to the proportional syllogism, and the material developed while explaining the proportional syllogism is the basis for the inductive generalization, which is covered in chapter 7. To explain the inductive generalization, I use the probability rules to develop an interval. This interval is not that flexible and its application is limited, but this chapter does illustrate, step by step, how an interval is created. Once it is established, it is used to demonstrate the role that an interval has in the conclusion of an inductive generalization.

Bayes' rule is explained in chapter 8, the final chapter. To some readers, the rule may look a little bit daunting at first glance, but once the probability calculus has been mastered (and with a calculator handy) the material here is straightforward. One idea discussed in this chapter is that Bayes' rule can effectively be used in cases where the induction by confirmation seems to be inadequate. Updating probabilities as new information becomes available is also covered, as are cases where prior probabilities do (or should) have a moderating effect on one's assessment of the likelihood of some event.

The textbook concludes with two appendixes. The first extends the coverage of deductive logic from chapter 1. Some of the basic rules of propositional logic are given (not, however, any rules that require making an assumption or involve the biconditional) and categorical syllogisms are explained. The second appendix covers a few more topics on probability that may interest some readers but which did not have a natural place in the chapters. The first is odds and how to convert odds into probabilities. Next is expected value. And last is a discussion of some different ways of establishing probabilities.

I must thank my students at Drexel University and Mississippi State University who have read many, many drafts of this textbook. Thanks also to Tuffer Hammons and Lin Ge for help with chapters 1 and 7, respectively.

1 An Introduction to Arguments

1.1 Premises and a Conclusion

Among other things, Jeff knows the following. *He and his next-door neighbor live a few blocks from the campus of State University. The next-door neighbor looks about twenty years old, and the neighbor often wears State University T-shirts and sweatshirts.* On the basis of this information, it is quite reasonable for Jeff to generate this new piece of information, although he does not have any direct evidence for it: *his next-door neighbor attends State University.* This sort of process, using a certain set of information as a basis for generating a new piece of information, is what this book is about.

Together, all of the information in the above example is an argument. The term *argument* has a technical meaning, and, of course, it has a colloquial meaning as well. Here the technical meaning is what matters. In its technical sense, all arguments have two parts: a premise or set of premises, and a conclusion. The premises are that first set of information—the information that is used as a basis for generating the new piece of information. The conclusion is the new piece of information.

To clearly identify each premise and the conclusion, we can write the above argument this way:

Premise 1   Jeff and his next-door neighbor live a few blocks from the campus of State University.

Premise 2   Jeff's next-door neighbor looks about twenty years old.

Premise 3   Jeff's next-door neighbor often wears State University T-shirts and sweatshirts.

Conclusion   Therefore, Jeff's next-door neighbor attends State University.

argument (1)

Notice that each part of the argument (each premise and the conclusion) is a statement that can be true or false. Right at this moment, there is no way to determine if Jeff and his next-door neighbor actually do live a few blocks from this campus, if the next-door neighbor looks about twenty years old, or if the next-door neighbor often wears State University T-shirts and sweatshirts. Nevertheless, even without knowing if these sentences are true or false, it is still the case that each of them is the type of sentence that *can* be true or false. Some sentences cannot be true or false, for instance, questions ("Is the door closed?") or commands ("Close the door!"). Only sentences that can be true or false can be parts of an argument.

But leaving aside whether they actually are true or false, if the three premises are true, then they provide reasons for thinking that this sentence is also true: *Jeff's next-door neighbor attends State University*. In other words, the three premises support the conclusion. Preserving truth is the core notion behind support, but a more intuitive definition will also work, something like *the premises back up the conclusion* or *the premises provide justification for believing the conclusion*. In short, that's what an argument is.

> An **argument** is a set of statements, one or more of which are intended to support another in the set. The statements providing support are the *premises*, and the statement receiving support is the *conclusion*.

And an *inference* is just the process by which an argument is created: generating a conclusion on the basis of a premise or set of premises.

For comparison's sake, here is short passage:

(i) Usually, Kate gets to school an hour before her first class. Most mornings she takes the bus, but yesterday she walked.

Although (i) is composed of statements—sentences that can be true or false—it is not an argument because it does not have a conclusion that is supported by premises. Instead, it is just a description of an event.

Often—but not always—an inference is indicated by words such as *therefore*, *thus*, *hence*, *so*, *since*, or *because*. Either the conclusion will follow *therefore*, *thus*, *hence*, or *so* or the premises will follow *since* or *because*. For example, (ii), (iii), and (iv) are arguments. In each, the final clause is the conclusion, and what precedes it are the premises.

(ii) Because all men are mortal and Socrates is a man, Socrates is mortal.

(iii) Since no man is immortal and Socrates is a man, Socrates is not immortal.

(iv) All men desire glory and Socrates is a man; thus, Socrates desires glory. But an inference can still be made without one of these words. For instance,

(v) All men want respect and Socrates is a man; Socrates wants respect.

Perhaps it is somewhat subtle that *All men want respect* and *Socrates is a man* are supporting *Socrates wants respect*. But compare that to a case such as (vi) where an inference is not being made, and you should be able to see the difference between an argument and just a description of, in this case, Socrates.

(vi) Socrates is mortal, he desires glory, and he wants respect.

Before moving on, it is worth looking at two qualities that, although not desirable, do not prohibit a set of statements from being an argument. First, sometimes premises are meant to support a conclusion, but they fail to do so. For whatever reason, they provide little or no justification for believing the conclusion. Nevertheless, as long as the premises are *intended* to support the conclusion, the collection of statements is still an argument. Here are a couple of examples:

P1 Jeff slept with his chemistry textbook under his pillow last night.

P2 He slept for seven hours.

 C Therefore, he will do well on his chemistry exam today.

argument (2)

P1 Denver is the largest city in Colorado.

P2 Colorado is the twenty-fourth-largest state in the United States.

 C Therefore, Denver is the twenty-fourth-largest city in the United States.

argument (3)

These are both arguments, but they are not very good ones, because the premises provide little or no support for the conclusions. In argument (2), the inference is based on a folksy and false idea about how information is transmitted. In argument (3), the inference is based on an assumption that the size of states and the size of cities are somehow directly connected such that the largest state will contain the largest city, the second-largest state will contain the second-largest city, and so on. But since the sizes of cities and states are not connected—at least not to the degree that this argument requires—the premises provide very little support for the conclusion.

Second, it is also sometimes the case that an argument will lack premises that it really needs in order to be considered complete. For example,

P1 This summer, Derek and Megan are getting married.

C Therefore, Joan will buy them a blender.

argument (4)

This would be a better argument if it had a premise stating that Joan knows the couple, and even better would be a premise indicating that they have some sort of friendly relationship. Plus, a premise stating that Joan has a tendency to give blenders as wedding presents would help.

When evaluating an argument like (4), it is generally preferable to be charitable, at least up to a point, and fill in the information that is missing from the premises, rather than judge the argument a poor one. While ideally, all—or at least most—of the information that is needed to support the conclusion will be explicitly stated in the premises, sometimes it may be assumed that an argument will be understandable without all of the details, and so some of the information that could be in the premises might not be included.

Whatever the case may be, to identify an argument the important thing to look for is this relationship of support. If there is a statement or series of statements that are supporting (or at least trying to support) another statement, then it is an argument.

1.2 Deductively Valid and Inductively Strong

Consider argument (1) again.

P1 Jeff and his next-door neighbor live a few blocks from the campus of State University.

P2 Jeff's next-door neighbor looks about twenty years old.

P3 Jeff's next-door neighbor often wears State University T-shirts and sweatshirts.

C Therefore, Jeff's next-door neighbor attends State University.

argument (1)

Notice that even if the three premises are true, there is still a chance that the conclusion will be false. The next-door neighbor might live there and wear State University clothing, but not attend the nearby university. Nonetheless, if the premises are true, then there is a high probability that Jeff's next-door neighbor does attend State University.

Whereas Jeff does not get to be absolutely certain, in some arguments, if the premises are true, then the conclusion has to be true. Consider these two simple arguments:

P1 Mary is either in the library or in the cafeteria.

P2 She is not in the library.

 C Therefore, she is in the cafeteria.

argument (5)

P1 All men are mortal.

P2 Socrates is a man.

 C Therefore, Socrates is mortal.

argument (6)

These two arguments have a feature that argument (1) lacks. For these two, if the premises are true, then there is no way that the conclusion can be false.

This distinction between a conclusion that is certain versus one that is only probable is at the heart of the two most basic standards used for evaluating arguments: the deductively valid standard and the inductively strong standard. These two standards are defined as follows.

> An argument is ***deductively valid*** when it is the case that if the premises are true, then the conclusion has to be true.

> An argument is ***inductively strong*** when it is the case that (1) the argument is not deductively valid, and (2) if the premises are true, then they make it probable that the conclusion is true.

When evaluating an argument, it is important to figure out if it meets either of these two definitions.[1]

---

1. There are different ways of stating these definitions. Alternative ways of defining *deductively valid* are

   (a) an argument in which the truth of the premises guarantees the truth of the conclusion; or

   (b) an argument for which it would be contradictory to assert the premises and yet deny the conclusion.

(footnote continues on next page)

If an argument does not satisfy the definition of deductively valid, then it is *deductively invalid*. There is no in-between; every argument is either deductively valid or deductively invalid. And when an argument is deductively invalid, even if the premises are true, the conclusion is not guaranteed to be true.

With respect to being inductively strong, the situation is somewhat different. An argument that is invalid can have any amount (or degree) of inductive strength from strong to weak, and then even down to worthless. The issue here is this: How probable is it that the conclusion will be true if the premises are true? The more probable the conclusion, the higher the argument's degree of inductive strength. Table 1.1 outlines different degrees of inductive strength.

To see how the degree of inductive strength can vary, compare arguments (7), (8), and (9).

P1 Paul is twenty years old.

P2 Paul is on his university's cross country team.

Table 1.1
Inductive strength

Relationship between the premises and the conclusion	Degree of inductive strength
If the premises are true, then that makes it probable (i.e., very likely) that the conclusion is true.	The argument has a high degree of inductive strength, and so the argument is inductively strong.
If the premises are true, then that makes it somewhat likely that the conclusion is true.	The argument has a medium-to-high degree of inductive strength.
Even if the premises are true, that does not make it very likely that the conclusion is true.	The argument has a low degree of inductive strength (i.e., the argument is inductively weak).

Inductively strong may be defined as

(c) an argument in which the truth of the premises supports the truth of the conclusion, but does not guarantee the truth of the conclusion; or

(d) an argument in which the premises are about what has been observed and the conclusion is about what has not been observed, but what is likely to be true if the premises are true.

P3   Paul runs six days a week.

C   Therefore, Paul will complete the race, consisting of 1,576 stairs, up the Empire State Building.

argument (7)

As it is, (7) has a pretty high degree of inductive strength; if the premises are true, then they (the true premises) make it very likely that the conclusion will be true. The same cannot quite be said for argument (8), however.

P1   Tom is forty years old.

P2   Tom runs four to five miles twice a week.

C   Therefore, Tom will complete the race, consisting of 1,576 stairs, up the Empire State Building.

argument (8)

Argument (8) is a decent argument. The race up the Empire State Building is challenging, but not impossible, and, according to premise 2, Tom is not a couch potato. But the information in those two premises cannot support the conclusion as well as the premises in (7) support that argument's conclusion. Hence, anyone would be—or at least should be—less confident about the truth of the conclusion in argument (8). Argument (9), meanwhile, has the lowest degree of inductive strength of the three.

P1   George is sixty years old.

P2   George walks two miles twice a week.

C   Therefore, George will complete the race, consisting of 1,576 stairs, up the Empire State Building.

argument (9)

In (9), based on the information in the premises, there is a chance that the conclusion will be true, but that chance is not especially high.

Now, why is it that in some arguments the truth of the conclusion is guaranteed while in others it is only probable? Consider this deductively valid argument again:

P1   Mary is either in the library or in the cafeteria.

P2   She is not in the library.

C   Therefore, she is in the cafeteria.

argument (5)

The reason the conclusion is certain in (5) is because all of the information in the conclusion is contained in the premises. The information in the premises is simply moved around in order to get a particular conclusion. Moving this information around has to follow certain rules, but as long as these rules are followed, the conclusion is guaranteed to be true (if the premises are true).

Inductively strong arguments are different in a fundamental way. In these arguments, the conclusion goes beyond the information that is found in the premises. Instead of drawing out some information that is already contained in the premises, arguments that are inductively strong use the premises as grounds for a guess about some new information. Of course, this should not be a wild guess; but it is a guess in the sense that the conclusion is not information that is present in the premises.

Consider the difference between arguments (10) and (11), the first of which is deductively valid, the second inductively strong.

P1   The sun rose yesterday, the day before yesterday, the day before the day before yesterday, and the 1,000,000 days before that.

C   The sun rose the day before yesterday.

argument (10)

P1   The sun rose yesterday, the day before yesterday, the day before the day before yesterday, and the 1,000,000 days before that.

C   The sun will rise tomorrow.

argument (11)

Since argument (10) is deductively valid, the information in the conclusion has to be in the premise, and it is.

With respect to argument (11), it hardly seems like a guess that the sun will rise tomorrow, but that information is not contained in the premise. Moreover, if the premise contains only information about what has been observed in the past, then since tomorrow has not yet been observed, information about tomorrow cannot be in the premise. Of course, there does not seem to be any reason to think, at least with respect to the sun rising, that tomorrow will be different than the last 1,000,003 days. Thus, there is a very high probability that the sun will rise tomorrow. But it is still not a conclusion that can be drawn with absolute certainty.

These two ways of evaluating arguments are typically treated as separate branches of philosophy. *Deductive logic* is the system of rules that, if followed, will uphold the deductively valid standard. This system is also studied in mathematics and is essential for, among other things, computer science. *Inductive logic* is the system of rules and guidelines developed for the inductively strong standard. Inductive reasoning, which is the application of inductive logic, is—in one manner or another—the kind of reasoning that people most often use in their day-to-day lives. It is also used in most of the sciences. When people reason inductively, they cannot be completely certain about the conclusions that they draw. But the alternative, deductively valid reasoning, is simply not applicable to most of the problems encountered in everyday life.

1.3 Soundness and Reliability

The two standards for evaluating arguments we have been discussing, deductively valid and inductively strong, address the relationship between the premises and the conclusion. These two standards always use the notion: *if the premises are true*, then how certain is the conclusion? Hence, it is possible to determine if an argument is deductively valid or inductively strong without actually knowing if the premises are true or false. And even when the premises are false, it is still possible for an argument to be deductively valid or inductively strong.

At times, however, it is desirable to know if an argument has premises that are actually true. If an argument is deductively valid, and the premises are true, then the conclusion has to be a true statement. This is somewhat of an improvement over just being able to say that *if* the premises are true, then the conclusion will be true. Likewise for inductively strong arguments; if an argument is inductively strong and has true premises, then it is very likely that the conclusion is a true statement. That said, in philosophy the main focus is generally on the form of arguments and how premises support a conclusion. Philosophers usually leave it to others—scientists, journalists, Nancy Drew—to determine if premises are actually true.[2]

---

2. It is worth emphasizing that *truth* and *falsity* are terms that apply only to certain kinds of sentences: statements (i.e., declarative sentences). Arguments cannot be true or false. The notion of an argument being true or false does not even really make sense. Instead, the concepts that we have discussed in this chapter are used to describe arguments: deductively valid, deductively invalid, inductively strong, medium, or weak, sound or not sound, and reliable or not reliable.

The third and fourth standards for evaluating arguments are soundness and reliability.

An argument is ***sound*** when it is deductively valid and has all true premises.

An argument is ***reliable*** when it is inductively strong and has all true premises.

Notice that being sound or reliable depends on the premises being true, not the conclusion being true. There is no need to figure out whether the conclusion is true if the argument is deductively valid or inductively strong; rather, the conclusion has to be true (or is likely to be true) if the premises are. Moreover, if it is possible to just go out and check whether the conclusion is true or not, then there is really no need for the argument in the first place.

Arguments (12) and (13) are both deductively valid, but (12) is not sound, while (13) is sound.

P1 New York City is in Maryland.

P2 Claire is in New York City.

  C Therefore, Claire is in Maryland.

argument (12)

P1 George H. W. Bush's oldest son was the forty-third president of the United States.

P2 George H. W. Bush's oldest son is George W. Bush.

  C Therefore, George W. Bush was the forty-third president of the United States.

argument (13)

Argument (14) is reliable because it is inductively strong and has all true premises.

P1 The People's Republic of China has 1.34 billion citizens and is the world's largest country by population.

P2 The Republic of India has 1.2 billion citizens and is the world's second-largest country by population.

P3 The United States of America has 315 million citizens and is the world's third-largest country by population.

  C Therefore, in ten years, either China or India will be the largest country in the world by population.

argument (14)

Remember that it must be established that an argument is either deductively valid or inductively strong before worrying about whether the premises are true. Soundness and reliability are higher standards than deductively valid or inductively strong, and they require that one of these other two standards has already been attained. An argument that has true premises but is neither deductively valid nor inductively strong is not sound or reliable. For example, argument (3) has true premises (and a true conclusion), but it is not sound or reliable.

1.4   Some Argument Forms

Many arguments take a precise form or structure. For such arguments, the form stays the same, or basically the same, no matter what the argument is about. This section introduces six common argument forms. The purpose of this section is, first, to introduce the idea of an argument's form, and, second, to begin explaining how specific types of arguments work—and how it is that arguments with the same form, but with different content, still work the same way.

The first two types of arguments introduced in this section are called *modus ponens* and *modus tollens*. Any argument that has one of these two forms is deductively valid. The other four are the *inductive generalization, proportional syllogism, induction by confirmation,* and *analogical argument.* These, with one occasional exception, can never be deductively valid. They can, however, be used to construct inductively strong arguments, although the strength of any particular argument depends on its specific content.

1.4.1   Modus Ponens

The name *modus ponens* is the shortened version of *modus ponendo ponens,* which means (although it does not exactly translate as) the method that, by an affirming statement, an affirming conclusion.

Modus ponens consists of two premises and a conclusion. One of those premises must be a conditional statement. A conditional statement has the form: *if A, then B.* In a conditional statement, the first clause (the *A* clause in *if A, then B*) is called the antecedent. The second clause (the *B* clause in *if A, then B*) is called the consequent. In *If today is Thursday, then Sam is in court,* the antecedent is *today is Thursday*; the consequent is *Sam is in court.*

The other premise in this type of argument is the antecedent by itself, and then the conclusion is the consequent. For instance:

P1 If today is Thursday, then Sam is in court.

P2 Today is Thursday.

C Therefore, Sam is in court.

argument (15)

To understand this type of argument and why it is always deductively valid, it is useful to consider what *if A, then B* means. One way to think about a conditional statement is as a rule that does not get broken. As such, it is a rule stating that if the antecedent happens, then the consequent has to happen. Take the previous example: If today is Thursday, then Sam is in court. Since this statement is a rule, if today is Thursday, then it has to be the case that Sam is in court—if it were otherwise, the rule would be broken. Hence, modus ponens is simply (1) a statement of the rule, (2) a statement that the antecedent happened (or is happening), and (3) the conclusion that the consequence happened or is happening. In other words, it has this form:

P1 If A, then B.

P2 A.

C Therefore, B.

argument (16)

Note, however, that the conditional statement will also be true (and the rule still in force) when that antecedent does not happen, but the consequent does. For instance, today might not be Thursday, but Sam still ends up spending the day in court (maybe he is a very busy lawyer or a very bad criminal). The rule *If today is Thursday, then Sam is in court* isn't being broken; this is just a situation where the rule doesn't apply. This possibility is important to grasp because it is why any argument that has the same form as argument (17) is invalid—that is, the premises can be true when the conclusion is false.

P1 If today is Thursday, then Sam is in court.

P2 Sam is in court.

C Therefore, today is Thursday.

argument (17)

If, say, today is Friday and Sam is in court, then both premises are true, but the conclusion is false. Thus, the argument is not valid.

1.4.2 Modus Tollens

Modus tollens is the shortened version of *modus tollendo tollens*—the method that, by a denying statement, a denying conclusion. Like modus ponens, modus tollens is always deductively valid. It also has a premise containing a conditional statement, and it exploits the same simple feature of conditional statements, namely, if the antecedent happens, then the consequent has to happen. For modus tollens, however, the second premise is a denial of the consequent. For instance, Sam is *not* in court. And when the consequent has not happened, it can safely be concluded that the antecedent has not happened either: today is *not* Thursday.

> **P1** If today is Thursday, then Sam is in court.
>
> **P2** Sam is not in court.
>
> **C** Therefore, today is not Thursday.

argument (18)

Remember, if the antecedent happens, then the consequent has to happen. Hence, if the consequent didn't happen, then the antecedent couldn't have either. The form of modus tollens, then, is this:

> **P1** If A, then B.
>
> **P2** not B.
>
> **C** Therefore, not A.

argument (19)

1.4.3 Inductive Generalization

In an inductive generalization, the premises refer to a certain number of things that have been observed. Then, based on those observations, the conclusion is about all things of that type—most of which have not been observed. For example, let's say that someone has seen forty crows and all of them have been black. Based on that information, the person draws this conclusion: all crows are black.

> **P1** Forty crows have been observed.
>
> **P2** All of these crows were black.
>
> **C** Therefore, it is likely that all crows are black.

argument (20)

Clearly, this is invalid. Whether an inductive generalization is strong, medium, or weak, though, depends on several factors. One is the number of observations that have been made. The greater the number of observations, the more support the conclusion receives. To that end, (20) is not a particularly strong argument because the conclusion is based on a relatively small number of observations of crows.

Here is another example of an inductive generalization:

P1 Five hundred likely voters were asked about the upcoming election.

P2 Sixty percent of these individuals said that they would vote for Sarah.

  C It is likely that about 60 percent of all voters will vote for Sarah.

argument (21)

In this case, the instances that were observed were not uniform (some people said that they would vote for Sarah and some said that they would not), and the conclusion reflects that. Only part—about 60 percent—of the whole population is likely to vote for Sarah.

In argument (21), the inference is based on a larger sample of the population—five hundred people—which makes it a better argument than (20). But in addition to a large sample, it is important that the sample is diversified and representative of the entire population. If the people who are questioned are not randomly selected, then the conclusion is less well supported than it otherwise would be.

The inductive generalization has this structure:

P1 x number of Es have been observed.

P2 z percent of observed Es are F.

  C Therefore, it is probable that about z percent of all Es are F.

argument (22)

E is the entity that has been observed, and F is a property or feature of that entity. In arguments (20) and (21), E is *crows* and *voters*, and F is *black* and *will vote for Sarah*.

One final caveat about the inductive generalization is in order. The inductive generalization has just been explained in terms of populations—a part of a population is described in the premises, and the conclusion is about the whole population. An inductive generalization does not always have to focus on a population, though. Here is a famous example of an inductive generalization that the British philosopher David Hume (1711–1776) used in his *An Enquiry Concerning Human Understanding*:

> I have found, in all past instances, such sensible qualities conjoined with such secret powers: And [so] ... similar sensible qualities will always be conjoined with similar secret powers.[3]

The "secret powers" to which Hume is referring are the ability to provide nourishment, and the "sensible qualities" are the observable qualities of bread (i.e., what it looks like, tastes like, and so on). Otherwise written, this is the argument:

P1   Every time in the past, I have found that bread (i.e., what looks, tastes, and smells like bread) provides nourishment.

C   Therefore, bread will always (everywhere and at all times in the future) provide nourishment.

argument (23)

Maybe, in some sense, *every time that bread is eaten* constitutes a population, but it's not a population in the normal sense of the word. Nonetheless, (23) is still an inductive generalization because, based on the instances that have been observed, an inference is made about all instances of that sort.

1.4.4   Proportional Syllogism

In the proportional syllogism, the premises contain information about an entire population. Then, based on this information, a conclusion is drawn about some specific member or members of the population. For example:

P1   Ninety-four percent of all adolescents in Ohio have received the measles, mumps, and rubella vaccine.

P2   Maureen is an adolescent who lives in Ohio.

C   Therefore, there is a 94 percent chance that Maureen has received the measles, mumps, and rubella vaccine.

argument (24)

Argument (24) begins with a statement about the percentage of adolescents living in Ohio who have received the measles, mumps, and rubella

---

3. David Hume, *Enquiries Concerning Human Understanding and Concerning the Principles of Morals* (New York: Oxford University Press, 1777/1975), 37.

vaccine. The second premise states that Maureen is a member of this population. If the only available information about Maureen is that she is an adolescent living in Ohio, then the conclusion about her has to be based on what is known about this population. Thus, the best conclusion is *There is a 94 percent chance that Maureen has received the measles, mumps, and rubella vaccine* (or some variation of this, such as *It is very likely that Maureen has received the measles, mumps, and rubella vaccine*, which has a less precise although similar meaning).

The structure of the proportional syllogism is

P1 z percent of all Es are F.

P2 x is an E.

 C   Therefore, there is a z percent probability that x is F.

argument (25)

Argument (24) is deductively invalid—it is not certain, only probable that Maureen has received the measles, mumps, and rubella vaccine. But since that probability is high, 94 percent, the argument is inductively strong. Notice, however, that if the population is uniform (all of its members have some particular property or none of its members have some particular property), then the conclusion is certain, not probable, which means that the argument is deductively valid.[4]

1.4.5   Induction by Confirmation

The induction by confirmation is a type of argument that is used to provide justification for a hypothesis. It is quite common to want to understand an

---

4. Both of these arguments are deductively valid:

P1	All men are mortal.		**P1**	No gods are mortal.
P2	Socrates is a man.		**P2**	Athena is a god.
C	Therefore, Socrates is mortal.		**C**	Therefore, Athena is not mortal.

In the argument on the left, the first premise is equivalent to *100 percent of men are mortal*, and, on the right, *no gods are mortal* means that 0 percent of gods are mortal. Similarly, the conclusions could be changed to match the exact form of argument (25).

When this type of argument is deductively valid, it is called a *categorical syllogism* rather than a proportional syllogism. There are many different forms of the categorical syllogism—the categorical syllogism is a super-category of sorts. See appendix A for further explanation.

event or thing that cannot be observed directly. For example, we might want to understand (i) an event that happened in the past that no one witnessed, or at least no one who is available today; (ii) something that is too small to see, such as a quark or a neutrino; (iii) something that is too far away to directly inspect such as a planet in another galaxy; or (iv) a process such as evolution by natural selection that is too broad in its scope to be observed at any one point in time. In these cases, a *hypothesis* must be constructed. The hypothesis is a proposed explanation of the phenomenon (the event, thing, or process that cannot be observed). Constructing a hypothesis is a good starting point, but just offering an explanation often doesn't give anyone much reason to think that it is correct. The induction by confirmation is a type of argument that is used to generate support for hypotheses.

Here is a simple example. Bill is lying dead on his couch, the victim of a horrible murder. The police are called, and they construct this explanation of what happened: while they were watching television, Joe and Bill got into a heated argument; then Joe shot Bill. Based on this hypothesis, the police can formulate one or more *predictions* about what they expect to find if their hypothesis is correct. One predication is this: there will be a recently fired gun in Joe's possession. The next step is to check whether or not the prediction is correct. If the police find what they are expecting to find, then they have generated some support for their explanation of how Bill ended up dead. The police check Joe's car and find a recently fired gun. Thus, the hypothesis *Joe shot Bill* has received some confirmation (not total confirmation, but some degree of confirmation).

The structure of the induction by confirmation is shown in (26), and (27) is the argument just discussed.

P1 If the hypothesis is true, then *x* should be observed.

P2 *x* is observed.

C Therefore, it is likely that the hypothesis is true.

argument (26)

P1 If Joe shot Bill, then there should be a recently fired gun in Joe's possession.

P2 There is a recently fired gun in Joe's possession.

C Therefore, it is likely that Joe shot Bill.

argument (27)

Not just any prediction about what will be found can be used to confirm a hypothesis. The best predictions are ones that are likely to be correct only if the hypothesis is true. But even when a very good prediction is correct, there is still the possibility—however small—that the hypothesis is wrong.

1.4.6 Analogical Argument

The analogical argument is a variation of the inductive generalization. But since it is a commonly used type of argument, and it has some features that differ from those of the typical inductive generalization, it is worth examining separately. Here is an example:

P1   Moles and gophers are both small mammals that burrow and live underground.

P2   Moles have very poor eyesight.

C   Therefore, gophers probably have very poor eyesight.

argument (28)

The analogical argument is used to understand one thing by drawing an analogy with something else that is better understood. The thing that is better understood is the *analogue case*, and the other is the *subject case*. In argument (28), the analogue case is *moles* and the subject case is *gophers*. The basis of the analogical argument is the idea that the analogue case and the subject case are similar to each other. But in addition to some similarities, there is the *target feature* that only the analogue case is known to have. The conclusion of an analogical argument states that the subject case also has the target feature. In argument (28) the target feature is *very poor eyesight*.

This type of argument works best when the similarities between the analogue case and the subject case are relevant to the target feature. In other words, the analogue case and the subject case should be similar enough— and similar in the right kind of way—to make it likely that, because the analogue case has the target feature, the subject case will also have it. The similarities between moles and gophers that are stated in the premises of (28) are that they "are both small mammals that burrow and live underground." Being a small mammal, burrowing, and living underground are relevant, it seems, to an animal's visual abilities, and so it is reasonable to infer that, since moles have poor eyesight, gophers do as well. Thus, (28) is an inductively strong argument. But again, there is no guarantee that, just because the premises are true, the conclusion will be true.

The analogical argument has this structure:

P1 *A* and *S* are similar.

P2 *A* has feature *T*.

  C Therefore, *S* probably has feature *T*.

argument (29)

Now, why is the analogical argument a variation of the inductive generalization? Typically, the analogical argument will contain just the two cases—the analogue case and the subject case. The inductive generalization, meanwhile, has information in its premises about many things, maybe hundreds or even thousands, and usually a conclusion about the entire population of those things. But an inductive generalization can also have a conclusion like the one in this argument:

P1 I have observed hundreds of crows in my life.

P2 All of the crows that I have observed have been black.

  C Therefore, the next crow that I see will probably be black.

argument (30)

The conclusion could be *therefore, all crows are probably black*. But if all crows are probably black, then the next one that is encountered will probably be black. Thus, (30) is still an inductive generalization.

With that mind and speaking very generally, the inductive generalization and the analogical argument both make this inference: what has been observed has such-and-such feature; therefore, the next one of this kind that is observed will have the same feature. Table 1.2 describes how the two types of arguments are similar in a little more detail.

One unique feature of the analogical argument is that the similarities between the analogue case and the subject case must be—or at least should be—specified. In the inductive generalization, this isn't needed. The observed and the unobserved cases are all members of a population, and identifying that population is all that is required. For instance, in argument (30) the population is *all crows*; in argument (21) it is *all voters in that election*. Since they are all members of the same population, the observed and the unobserved cases must have some similarities.

Table 1.2
The inductive generalization and analogical argument

	Inductive Generalization	Analogical Argument
information in the premises	the cases that have been observed	the analogue case (and to a lesser extent the subject case)
what the conclusion is about	the entire population, or the next member of the population that will be encountered	the subject case (which is a member of the same population as the analogue case)
the target feature	the feature that the observed cases have and the entire population probably has (the feature may occur among only a portion of each); that's *F* in argument 22	the feature that the analogue case has and the subject case probably has as well

The second thing that is somewhat unique about the analogical argument is that the subject case itself has usually been examined, to some extent. But this is not even always true. Consider this analogical argument:

P1 The last novel that Nicole read by Thomas Pynchon, *Mason & Dixon*, was complex, but very interesting.

P2 The next novel by Pynchon that Nicole is going to read, *Inherent Vice*, is similar to *Mason & Dixon* insofar as it is also a fictional narrative written by the same author.

C Therefore, *Inherent Vice* will probably be complex, but very interesting.

argument (31)

Beyond being identified as a novel by Pynchon, the subject case in this argument, *Inherent Vice*, did not have to be examined in any sort of detail in order to complete premise 2. And at any rate, the subject case in any analogical argument is never examined with respect to whether it has the target feature. Notice as well that, although it isn't stated, *Mason & Dixon* and *Inherent Vice* belong to the same population: novels by Thomas Pynchon. But like all analogical arguments, the conclusion is just about one particular case—the subject case, not the entire population.

But it is not just the structure of the inductive generalization and the analogical argument that are similar. The justification for the conclusion is the same in both types of arguments. Because the examined case (or cases) are similar in some respects to the unexamined one (or ones), it is inferred that, like the examined, the unexamined will probably have the target feature.

1.5   A Note about Reading Arguments

It is easy to see that this argument is invalid:

P1   Eighty-five percent of the employees of Fitch, Smith & Peters have a graduate degree.

P2   Mary works for Fitch, Smith & Peters.

  C   Therefore, Mary has a graduate degree.

argument (32)

But it is sometimes thought that this one is valid:

P1   Eighty-five percent of the employees of Fitch, Smith & Peters have a graduate degree.

P2   Mary works for Fitch, Smith & Peters.

  C   Therefore, Mary *probably* has a graduate degree.

argument (33)

The thought is that, if the two premises are true, then it is guaranteed that Mary *probably* has a graduate degree. To a certain extent this makes sense, but it is not the correct way to interpret the argument or its conclusion. If something is probable, then it is not certain to happen, and that makes the argument invalid. As an illustration of this, notice that if someone says "I am certain that I will probably be there," the "I am certain" isn't adding anything to the statement. The person will probably be there, and that's all there is to it.

Furthermore, an argument that has these two premises:

P1   Eighty-five percent of the employees of Fitch, Smith & Peters have a graduate degree.

P2   Mary works for Fitch, Smith & Peters.

can have any of these conclusions, and the argument will have the same meaning:

C1   Therefore, Mary has a graduate degree.

C2   Therefore, Mary probably has a graduate degree.

C3   Therefore, there is an 85 percent chance that Mary has a graduate degree.

argument (34)

The third conclusion is more precise, but the detail included in C3 is implicit in the other two conclusions. Anyone reading the argument that has, say, the first conclusion just has to figure out for him- or herself that the conclusion is only probable (albeit pretty probable—there's an 85 percent chance).

Now that arguments have been introduced, the focus of this book turns fully to inductive logic. There is more material on deductive logic in appendix A. Three of the arguments that were introduced in this chapter— the induction by confirmation, the proportional syllogism, and the inductive generalization—are examined in more detail in chapters 2, 6, and 7. New types of inductive inferences are discussed in chapters 3, 4, and 8.

The next chapter covers the induction by confirmation. The induction by confirmation was, for a time, considered *the* scientific method. It is no longer solely recognized as such, but it is still an important type of inference for confirming an explanation. The induction by confirmation is also a good place to begin because this type of argument—especially in its longer form—requires the careful consideration of the role of each premise, but it does not rely on precise probabilities. Similarly, the inferences examined in chapters 3 and 4 do not need precise probabilities. Chapter 3 covers two variations of the induction by confirmation, the crucial experiment and the inference to the best explanation. Chapter 4 examines a class of inductive inferences that were first described by the philosopher John Stuart Mill in the 1800s and have since become known as *Mill's methods*.

Inductive logic is probabilistic, however, and exact probabilities are a part of many inductive inferences. Chapter 5 introduces some concepts and ideas we need to get started, and then the basic rules of probability are introduced at the beginning of chapter 6 (which is about the proportional syllogism). Probabilities are also used in chapters 7 and 8, which cover the inductive generalization and Bayes' rule.

1.6 Exercises

For exercises 1 through 6, determine whether the passage is an argument. If it is an argument, identify the premises and the conclusion.

1. Claire has seen hundreds of robins' eggs and all have been bluish-green, so the next robin's egg that she sees will be bluish-green.

2. All whales are mammals, and all mammals use their lungs to breathe air. Hence, all whales use their lungs to breathe air.

3. The largest currently living land animal is the African bush elephant. It is native to sub-Saharan Africa and, as an adult, typically weighs between 13,000 and 20,000 pounds.

4. In extremely heavy fighting during the last week of August, the Nationalists seized the bridgeheads—heavily fortified with barbed wire and machine guns—that guarded the approaches to Wuhan.[5]

5. The only way for Cixi to preserve her own power was to continue in her role as regent; accordingly she appointed her three-year-old nephew, Guangxu, as emperor, thus assuring herself of years more activity as the power behind the throne.[6]

6. Although old lands were being resettled and new ones constantly opened up in this period, the crude figures suggest that while the population tripled from the mid-Kangxi period to the late Qianlong, the acreage of arable land only doubled; the size of individual holdings therefore shrank.[7]

For exercises 7 through 25, determine if the argument is deductively valid or deductively invalid. If the argument is valid, determine if it is modus ponens or modus tollens. (It may be valid, but neither modus ponens nor modus tollens.) If the premises and the conclusion are not labeled, then write the argument as a list of premises and a conclusion.

7. **P1** The Magna Carta is older than the Declaration of Independence.
   P2 The Declaration of Independence is older than *The Adventures of Huckleberry Finn*.

---

5. Jonathan D. Spence, *The Search for Modern China* (New York: Norton, 1990), 347.

6. Spence, *The Search for Modern China*, 217.

7. Spence, *The Search for Modern China*, 94–95.

   C Therefore, the Magna Carta is older than *The Adventures of Huckleberry Finn*.

8. **P1** *The Adventures of Huckleberry Finn* is older than the Declaration of Independence.

   P2 The Declaration of Independence is older than the Magna Carta.

   C Therefore, *The Adventures of Huckleberry Finn* is older than the Magna Carta.

9. **P1** If the shape is a square, then the shape has four sides.

   P2 The shape has four sides.

   C Therefore, the shape is a square.

10. **P1** If the shape is a square, then the shape has four sides.

   P2 The shape does not have four sides.

   C Therefore, the shape is not a square.

11. **P1** All men are mortal.

   P2 Herb is not a man.

   C Therefore, Herb is not mortal.[8]

12. **P1** Claire is tall, athletic, and smart.

   P2 Claire's twin sister Erika is also tall and athletic.

   C Therefore, Erika is smart.

13. If Susan gets a pay raise, then she will buy a new car. And if she buys a new car, she will give her old car to her younger brother. If she gives her old car to her younger brother, then he will get a job delivering pizzas. Thus, if Susan gets a pay raise, her younger brother will get a job delivering pizzas.

14. **P1** Tom and Phillip are both going to Boston.

   P2 If either Tom or Phillip goes to Boston, then Jon will play in the basketball game on Saturday.

   C Therefore, Jon will play in the basketball game on Saturday.

---

8. One way to figure out if an argument is valid or invalid is to try to imagine a scenario in which the premises are true while the conclusion is false. If there is such a scenario, then the argument is invalid. For this argument, it's not too difficult to imagine that the first premise is true (since it is true). For the second premise, imagine that Herb is a dog. If Herb is a dog, he's mortal, and so the conclusion is false.

15. **P1** If Mary went to the store, then she got milk.
    P2 Mary went to the store.
    C Therefore, Mary got milk.

16. **P1** If Mary went to the store, then she got milk.
    P2 Mary got milk.
    C Therefore, Mary went to the store.

17. **P1** If Mary went to the store, then she got milk.
    P2 Mary did not go to the store.
    C Therefore, Mary did not get milk.

18. **P1** If Mary went to the store, then she got milk.
    P2 Mary did not get milk.
    C Therefore, Mary did not go to the store.

19. **P1** If Erika doesn't get a new muffler for her car, then her neighbor will file a complaint with the board of their condominium about her noisy car.
    P2 If her neighbor files a complaint with the board of their condominium about her noisy car, then Erika's free membership at the gym will be revoked.
    P3 If Erika's free membership to the gym is revoked, then she will stop working out.
    P4 Erika stopped working out.
    C Therefore, Erika didn't get a new muffler for her car.

20. **P1** All whales are mammals.
    P2 No mammal has gills.
    C Therefore, no whales have gills.

21. **P1** If Smith applied for the job and Jones did not, then Smith will get the job.
    P2 Smith applied for the job and Jones did not.
    C Therefore, Smith will get the job.

22. **P1** If the theory of spontaneous generation is true—that is, if living organisms can be produced by nonliving matter—then flies should appear on meat when the meat is in a sealed jar.
    P2 Meat was placed in a sealed jar, and flies did not appear on the meat.
    C Therefore, the theory of spontaneous generation is not true.

23. All swans are white. I know this because every swan that I have ever seen has been white. Plus, all the swans seen by other people whom I know have been white.

24. **P1** UCLA's main campus is in Moscow.
    C Therefore, UCLA's main campus is in Moscow or pigs can fly.

25. **P1** If Margaret's passport is in the drawer, then Margaret is not in Argentina.
    P2 Margaret is in Argentina.
    C Therefore, Margaret's passport is not in the drawer.

For exercises 26 through 30, determine if the argument is sound, reliable, or neither. For each, explain your answer.

26. **P1** The moon is larger than the earth.
    P2 The earth is larger than the sun.
    C Therefore, the moon is larger than the sun.

27. **P1** The capital of Pennsylvania was located in Philadelphia until 1799.
    P2 From 1799 until 1812, the capital of Pennsylvania was located in Lancaster.
    P3 From 1812 until today, the capital of Pennsylvania has been located in Harrisburg.
    C In ten years, the capital of Pennsylvania will be located in Harrisburg.

28. **P1** If the world is flat, then pigs can fly.
    P2 The world is flat.
    C Therefore, pigs can fly.

29. **P1** In every US presidential election since 1852, either the Democratic candidate or the Republican candidate has won.
    C The Democratic candidate or the Republican candidate will win the next US presidential election.

30. **P1** Barack Obama is a man.
    P2 All men are warm blooded.
    C Barack Obama is warm blooded.

For exercises 31 through 42, determine if the argument is an inductive generalization, proportional syllogism, induction by confirmation, or analogical argument. If the premises and the conclusion are not labeled, then write the argument as a list of premises and a conclusion.

If the argument is an inductive generalization or proportional syllogism, identify (i) the population and (ii) the subset of the population in the argument. If the argument is an induction by confirmation, identify the hypothesis and the prediction. If the argument is an analogical argument, identify the analogue case, the subject case, and the target feature.

31. **P1** Eighty-six percent of the students at Central City College grew up in Central City.

 P2 Fred is a student at Central City College.

 C Therefore, there is an 86 percent chance that Fred grew up in Central City.

32. **P1** Claire is tall, athletic, and smart.

 P2 Claire's twin sister Erika is also tall and athletic.

 C Therefore, Erika is smart.

33. Fifteen percent of the squirrels that I have observed have been vicious. Therefore, it is likely that 15 percent of all squirrels are vicious.

34. **P1** If the general theory of relativity is true, then light will curve as it passes near the sun.

 P2 During a solar eclipse in 1919, scientists found that light passing near the sun curved, instead of traveling in a straight line.

 C Therefore, the general theory of relativity is probably true.

35. The student government at State University conducted a survey of students to see how much support there was for an increase to the student fee to help pay for new undergraduate teaching laboratories. Four hundred students were briefly interviewed as they entered the main dining hall on campus. The results indicate that about 72 percent of the student body support the fee increase.[9]

36. At Central City College, 90 percent of the third-year students have completed at least two foreign language courses. Since Claire and Erika are third-year students, it is likely that both of them have completed at least two foreign language courses.

---

9. This is either an inductive generalization or a proportional syllogism. Do the premise(s) contain information about the entire population or part of the population? Is the conclusion about the entire population or about part of the population?

37. **P1** Hockey and soccer are similar. In both sports, an object is moved around the playing surface and the players try to put the object in the opposing team's goal.

    P2 Hockey is played on ice.

    C Therefore, soccer is played on ice.

38. If the theory of spontaneous generation is true—that is, if living organisms can be produced by nonliving matter—then mice should appear several days after some rags and old cheese are placed in an open barrel. Many people did this in the sixteenth and seventeenth centuries, either intentionally or inadvertently, and mice always appeared. Thus, the theory of spontaneous generation is probably true.

39. Almost all doctors have very messy handwriting. Mary is a doctor, so she probably has messy handwriting.

40. Every doctor I have met has had very messy handwriting. Therefore, all doctors have messy handwriting.

41. **P1** If it is true that my roommate wore my dark green T-shirt to the gym, then the T-shirt will be smelly and in his laundry basket.

    P2 The T-shirt is in his laundry basket, and it smells.

    C Therefore, my roommate probably wore my dark green T-shirt to the gym.

42. Ninety-four percent of the marbles in the jar are red; therefore, a randomly selected marble from the jar is likely to be red.

1.7 Answers

1. This is an argument.

   P1 Claire has seen hundreds of robins' eggs.

   P2 All of the hundreds of robins' eggs that she has seen have been bluish-green.

   C Therefore, the next robin's egg that Claire sees will be bluish-green.

2. This is an argument.

   P1 All whales are mammals.

   P2 All mammals use their lungs to breathe air.

   C Hence, all whales use their lungs to breathe air.

3. This is not an argument.

4. This is not an argument.

5. This is an argument.

   P1 The only way for Cixi to preserve her own power was to continue in her role as regent.

   P2 She appointed her three-year-old nephew, Guangxu, as emperor.

   C Thus, she assured herself of years more activity as the power behind the throne.

6. This is an argument.

   P1 From the mid-Kangxi period to the late Qianlong period, the population tripled.

   P2 From the mid-Kangxi period to the late Qianlong period, the acreage of arable land doubled.

   C Therefore, during this period, the amount of arable land held by each individual (on average) shrank.

7. This argument is valid. It has this form, which always makes a valid argument: A is older than B; B is older than C; therefore, A is older than C.

8. This argument is valid.

9. This argument is invalid. Compare it to argument (17) in section 1.4.1.

10. This argument is valid, and it is modus tollens.

11. This argument is invalid. Herb could be any other mortal creature.

12. This argument is invalid.

13. This argument is valid.

    P1 If Susan gets a pay raise, then she will buy a new car.

    P2 If she buys a new car, she will give her old car to her younger brother.

    P3 If she gives her old car to her younger brother, then he will get a job delivering pizzas.

    C Thus, if Susan gets a pay raise, her younger brother will get a job delivering pizzas.

14. This argument is valid.

15. This argument is valid, and it is modus ponens.

16. This argument is invalid.

17. This argument is invalid.

18. This argument is valid, and it is modus tollens.

19. This argument is invalid.

20. This argument is valid.

21. This argument is valid, and it's modus ponens. Recall that modus ponens has this form:

    P1 If A, then B.

    P2 A.

    C Therefore, B.

    In this argument, A is *Smith applied for the job and Jones did not*, and B is *Smith will get the job*.

22. This argument is valid, and it's modus tollens, although that's a little hard to spot. If it is simplified a bit, this is the argument:

    P1 If the theory of spontaneous generation is true, then flies should appear *(under these conditions)*.

    P2 Flies did not appear *(under those conditions)*.

    C Therefore, the theory of spontaneous generation is not true.

23. This argument is invalid. It can also be written this way:

    P1 Every swan that I have seen has been white.

    P2 All the swans seen by other people whom I know have been white.

    C Therefore, all swans are white.

24. This argument is valid. Remember, the definition of deductively valid begins with "if the premises are true." It doesn't matter that the premise—UCLA's main campus is in Moscow—is, in actuality, false. If it is true, is the conclusion guaranteed to be true? That depends on the meaning of *or*. For a statement that has the form *A or B*, all that is needed for the full statement to be true is one of A or B to be true. Hence, if A is true, then any wacky false clause can be tacked on with an *or* and the whole thing will still be true.

    In this case, if *UCLA's main campus is in Moscow* is true, then *UCLA's main campus is in Moscow* or *pigs can fly* has to be true. Thus, the argument is valid.

25. This argument is valid, and it is modus tollens. Recall that modus tollens has this form:

    P1 If A, then B.

    P2 not B.

      C Therefore, A.

    In this argument, B is *Margaret is not in Argentina*. The denial of that statement, not B, is *Margaret is in Argentina*—or, less elegantly, *It is not the case that Margaret is not in Argentina*.

26. This argument is not sound. It is valid, but the premises are false.

27. This argument is reliable. It is inductively strong and has all true premises.

28. This argument is not sound. It is valid, but premise two is false. (Because it is a conditional statement and both the antecedent and the consequent are false, premise one is actually true.)

29. This argument is reliable. It is inductively strong, and the premise is true.

30. This argument is sound. It is valid and has all true premises.

31. This is a proportional syllogism. The population is *students at Central City College*, and the subset of the population is *Fred*.

32. This is an analogical argument. The analogue case is *Claire*, and the subject case is *Erika*. The target feature is *smart*.

33. This is an inductive generalization. The subset of the population is *the squirrels that I have observed*, and the population is *all squirrels*.

34. This is an induction by confirmation. The hypothesis is *the general theory of relativity* and the prediction is "light will curve as it passes near the sun."

35. This is an inductive generalization. The subset of the population is *the students who were interviewed*. The population is *the entire student body*.

    P1 Four hundred students were interviewed.

    P2 Seventy-two percent of those students support an increase to the student fee to help pay for new undergraduate teaching laboratories.

      C Therefore, about 72 percent of the student body at State University support an increase to the student fee to help pay for new laboratories.

36. This is a proportional syllogism. The population is *third-year students at Central City College*. The subset of the population is *Claire and Erika*.

    P1 Ninety percent of the third-year students at Central City College have completed at least two foreign language courses.

    P2 Claire and Erika are third-year students at Central City College.

    C Therefore, probably, both of them have completed at least two foreign language courses.

37. This is an analogical argument. The analogue case is *hockey* and the subject case is *soccer*. The target feature is *played on ice*.

38. This is an induction by confirmation.

    P1 If the theory of spontaneous generation is true—that is, if living organisms can be produced by nonliving matter—then mice should appear several days after some rags and old cheese are placed in an open barrel.

    P2 Many times in the sixteenth and seventeenth centuries, some rags and old cheese were placed in an open barrel, and several days later mice always appeared.

    C Thus, the theory of spontaneous generation is probably true.

    The hypothesis is "the theory of spontaneous generation, which states that living organisms can be produced by nonliving matter." The prediction is "mice should appear several days after some rags and old cheese are placed in an open barrel."

39. This is a proportional syllogism.

    P1 Almost all doctors have very messy handwriting.

    P2 Mary is a doctor.

    C Therefore, Mary very likely has messy handwriting.

    The population here is *all doctors*, and the subset of this population is *Mary*. Note that, instead of an exact probability, "almost all" is used to describe the population. Then, that high probability, whatever it is, is represented in the conclusion as "very likely."

40. This is an inductive generalization.

    P1 Every doctor I have met has had very messy handwriting.

    C Therefore, all doctors probably have messy handwriting.

The population is *all doctors*, and the subset of this population is *every doctor I have met*.

41. This is an induction by confirmation. The hypothesis is "my roommate wore my dark green T-shirt to the gym," and the prediction is "the T-shirt will be smelly and in his laundry basket."

42. This is a proportional syllogism.

   P1 Ninety-four percent of the marbles in the jar are red.

   P2 One marble is about to be randomly selected from this jar.

   C Therefore, this marble is likely to be red (or "there is a 94 percent chance that this marble will be red").

The population is *the marbles in the jar*, and the subset of this population is *the one marble taken from the jar*.

2 The Induction by Confirmation

In the previous chapter, we introduced a simple version of the induction by confirmation. In this chapter, we examine the induction by confirmation more closely and explore its use in more complex cases. The following passage about Edmond Halley and his investigations into the orbits of comets contains an induction by confirmation. Halley was confronted with a problem that he could not examine directly. As a consequence, he was forced to propose a hypothesis that had to be confirmed indirectly. He got his confirmation—although, unfortunately, not until after his death.

2.1 Halley's Comet

The German mathematician and astronomer Johannes Kepler (1571–1630) believed that comets travel in straight lines. They appear once, and then are never seen again. By the late 1600s, the more common view was that comets follow parabolic orbits—that is, U-shaped paths around the sun. But still, once the comets make their U-turn and are gone, they are never seen again. Or so it was thought.

The English astronomer Edmond Halley (1656–1742) became interested in calculating the orbit of comets after witnessing one in 1680 while traveling to Paris. He had little success, however, until Newton's great work *Philosophiæ Naturalis Principia Mathematica* was published in 1687. Based on Newton's law of universal gravitation and laws of motion, plus information about comets that had been sighted in the past, Halley proposed that comets travel in ellipses, just like the planets.

This meant that a comet that Halley saw in 1682 could be the same one that was seen by Kepler in 1607, by the German astronomer Peter Apian in 1531, and by the Italian mathematician Paolo Toscanelli in 1456. All of these were bright comets that had taken the same path across the sky, and, as Halley noticed, the interval between each one of these four sightings was very similar: 75 or 76 years. If comets orbit the sun but their exact paths are influenced by the gravitational affects of the planets, then that would explain why this comet passed by Earth on a slightly irregular schedule.

Halley realized that if he was correct, the comet that he had seen in 1682 would return. He predicted, "It is probable that its return will not be until after the period of 76 years or more, about the end of the year 1758, or the beginning of the next."[1]

After Halley's death, two other astronomers, Alexis Clairaut and Jérôme Lalande, made some slight modifications to Halley's prediction. They refined Halley's calculations of the gravitational affects that Jupiter would have on the comet, and added the predicted affect of Saturn, which Halley had not included. Their more specific prediction was that the comet would hit its perihelion, the edge of the ellipse when the comet makes its turn, in March or April of 1759. It would, however, be seen from Earth before then.

On December 25, 1758, Johann Palitzsch, a German farmer and an amateur astronomer, became the first person to spot the comet, and on March 13, 1759, the comet made its turn around the sun. Soon after, the comet became "known throughout Europe by the name of Dr. Halley's comet."[2]

2.2 The Hypothesis, Prediction, and Data

2.2.1 The Hypothesis
As stated in chapter 1, the induction by confirmation is used when trying to understand something that cannot be inspected directly. The *hypothesis* is a proposed description or explanation of the phenomenon that cannot be inspected.

Halley suggested that comets travel in elliptical orbits around the sun and reappear at regular intervals. That, very briefly stated, was his hypothesis.

---

1. D. W. Hughes, "The History of Halley's Comet," *Philosophical Transactions of the Royal Society of London, Series A, Mathematical and Physical Sciences* 323 (1987): 360.

2. Charles Burney, *An Essay towards a History of the Principal Comets That Have Appeared since the Year 1742* (London: Printed for T. Becket and P. A. De Hondt, 1769), ii.

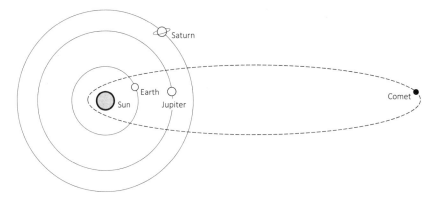

Figure 2.1
A diagram representing Halley's hypothesis.

Notice that this is just a proposal. If it was possible to look and see the route that comets take, then the hypothesis would not be needed. But since it is impossible to watch a comet travel through its entire orbit (and it could be seen only for a very tiny portion of its orbit in Halley's day), a hypothesis had to be formulated.

Hypotheses are needed in other situations, as well. In addition to activities in distant parts of the solar system, there are events that happened in the past when no one was around to witness them or events for which a reliable record no longer exists. There are also many activities studied in biology, chemistry, and physics that are too small to see, even with the aid of powerful magnification. For all of these types of cases, hypotheses have to be created.

A good hypothesis is based on data, and sometimes other guidelines. Halley's hypothesis is based on Newton's law of universal gravitation and laws of motion, as well as a historical record of comet sightings. But a hypothesis also goes beyond the data. If it just restated the data, then it would immediately be known that it was correct and the induction by confirmation would not be needed.

2.2.2 The Prediction
The next part of the induction by confirmation is the prediction. The prediction is a claim, based on the hypothesis, about what will be found. This notion of "based on" is very important. The move from the hypothesis

to the prediction is itself an inference. If it is laid out as its own argument, the full hypothesis plus, perhaps, some other background information are the premises and the prediction is the conclusion. And this inference is, in principle anyway, deductively valid, which means that if the hypothesis is true, then the prediction has to be true. This aspect of the induction by confirmation is so significant that another name for this argument is the *hypothetico-deductive model*—even though, as we have seen, the full argument is not deductively valid.

Halley's hypothesis was that *comets travel in elliptical orbits around the sun*. He also knew that a bright comet had passed by Earth in 1456, 1531, 1607, and 1682. From his hypothesis and the assumption that it was the same comet each of those times, plus Newton's laws and a suitable definition of *elliptical orbit*, it follows with certainty that the comet would reappear at the end of 1758 or beginning of 1759. Specifying all of the needed premises would take some work, but the point is, if completed, this is a deductively valid argument:

P1   Comets travel in elliptical orbits around the sun.

P2   A bright comet passed by Earth in 1456, 1531, 1607, and 1682.
$$\vdots$$

C   A bright comet will appear at the end of 1758 or beginning of 1759.

One caveat, however, is that although Halley believed that the comet he was making a prediction about was the same one that he had seen in 1682, Kepler saw in 1607, Apian in 1531, and Toscanelli in 1456, his prediction was not that *this same comet will return at the end of 1758 or beginning of 1759*. The prediction has to be a statement that can actually be checked, and there would be no way to check that a comet, if it did appear, was the same as one that had appeared centuries earlier. Hence, the prediction, in this case, is just that a bright comet will appear at the end of 1758 or beginning of 1759.

Another important feature of the relationship between the prediction and the hypothesis is that the prediction should be a claim that is only likely to be true if the hypothesis is true (which is different from the previous assertion that if the hypothesis is true, then the prediction has to be true). Halley could have predicted that *at least one comet will be seen in the eighteenth century*. But this would not have been a very useful prediction because, even if his hypothesis was wrong, this prediction would still, most likely, have turned out to be true just because several comets usually show up each century.

2.2.3   The Data

Data (singular: datum) are a type of information. Of all the information that exists, some of it is data and some is not. To be data, information must be gathered by interacting with and observing some part of the world (or universe). By way of example, consider these two pieces of information:

(1) Mount Everest is 29,017 feet high.

(2) There is no largest prime number.

Both of these are information, but only the first was generated by interacting with the world. In 2005, a team of Chinese mountaineers and researchers organized by the Chinese Academy of Sciences climbed Mount Everest and made the relevant measurements.[3] Meanwhile, the second piece of information was not found by going out and examining anything in the world. Rather, Euclid just had to think about it and devise the appropriate proof, which can be found in his *Elements* (Book IX, proposition 20). Thus, (1) is a datum, (2) is not.

Interacting with a part of the world does not only mean doing something as extreme as climbing a mountain and measuring it. Experiments that are performed in a laboratory count as interacting with a part of the world as long as real material from the world is manipulated in the experiment. Even just watching an event occur—for example, counting the number of commuters who enter a train station during rush hour—is a way of collecting data.

But, on the other hand, running a computer simulation of a process is not interacting with a part of the world. Take, for instance, this series of events.

> On Tuesday, August 23, 2005, an Air Force reconnaissance plane picked up signs of a disturbance over the Bahamas. There were "several small vortices," it reported, spirals of wind rotating in a counterclockwise motion from east to west—away from the expanse of the Atlantic and toward the United States. This disruption in wind patterns was hard to detect from clouds or from satellite data, but cargo ships were beginning to recognize it. The National Hurricane

---

3. Agençe France-Presse, "Everest Not as Tall as Thought," ABC Science, October 10, 2005, http://www.abc.net.au/science.

Center thought there was enough evidence to characterize the disturbance as a tropical cyclone, labeling it Tropical Depression Twelve. It was a "tricky" storm that might develop into something more serious or might just as easily dissipate; about half of all tropical depressions in the Atlantic Basin eventually become hurricanes.

The depression strengthened quickly, however, and by Wednesday afternoon one of the Hurricane Center's computer models was already predicting a double landfall in the United States—a first one over southern Florida and a second that might "[take] the cyclone to New Orleans." The storm had gathered enough strength to become a hurricane and it was given a name, Katrina.[4]

There are data here: the reports of small vortices, for one. Data from satellites and cloud observations are also mentioned, as are data about the strength of this tropical depression, although it isn't specified. The output of the Hurricane Center's computer model is different, however. That's a simulation of the way the world might be, not information about the way the world is, so it's not data.

In the induction by confirmation, data are compared to the prediction. If the data indicate that the prediction is correct, then that becomes the basis for concluding that the hypothesis is probably true. Conversely, if the data do not match the prediction, then that suggests that the hypothesis is false.

In Halley's case, all of the observations of comets are data. But these data should be separated into two categories. In the first category are the data that were used to formulate the hypothesis. Halley relied on historical records of comet sightings, plus the comets that he saw himself, to construct his hypothesis. The sighting of a comet in 1758 belongs to the second category. This datum was used to confirm the prediction that had been made earlier. In general, it is useful to keep these two categories separate—(1) the data that are used to create the hypothesis and (2) the data that are used to check the prediction—because they have different roles in the induction by confirmation.

With respect to collecting data, the paradigmatic way for events to unfold is as follows. First, some initial data are collected. Next, based on that data, a hypothesis is constructed. Once the hypothesis is set, a prediction is formulated. Finally, the prediction is checked, which entails collecting new

---

4. Nate Silver, *The Signal and the Noise* (New York: Penguin Press, 2012), 108–109.

Table 2.1
The data in the upper left corner are used to create the hypothesis—the hypothesis should, after all, be based on some data. The data in the lower right are the data that are compared to the prediction. The arrow in the center of the diagram represents the idea that the prediction is based on the hypothesis.

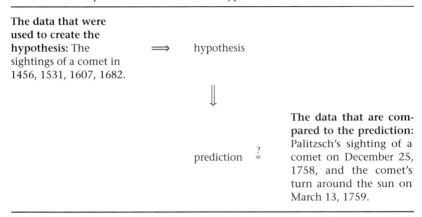

data (i.e., category 2 data). Things don't always unfold in this order, however. Sometimes a prediction can be checked using data that were collected even before the hypothesis was created. That's okay, as long as the data that are compared to the prediction were not used to construct the hypothesis. This is important. The prediction will always agree with the data that were used to construct the hypothesis. Comparing these data (category 1 data) to the prediction is basically cheating when it comes to testing the hypothesis and does not provide a good indication of whether the hypothesis is correct or not.

2.3   The Induction by Confirmation

2.3.1   The Structure of the Argument
In an argument, the order of the premises does not matter. For the induction by confirmation, however, it will be useful to keep the premises in the order shown here. There are important details to keep straight and each premise has a very specific role in the argument. Using the order explained in this section makes setting up the argument much easier.

Premise 1: State the hypothesis and explain its important features.

Premise 2: State the prediction. (Use this form: "If this hypothesis is true, then ... *the prediction*.")

Premise 3: Describe the data that are used to check the prediction.

Premise 4: State whether or not the data match the prediction.

Every induction by confirmation should begin with these four premises. Label the first three with the titles *hypothesis*, *prediction*, and *data*. After these four, the argument can be completed in a few different ways.

(1) If the data do not match the prediction—that is, if the data are not what was predicted—then the argument is completed this way:

> **Premise 4** The data do not match the prediction.
>
> **Conclusion** Therefore, the hypothesis is probably false.

(2) If the data do match the prediction, then we need a fifth premise. This premise states whether there is another reasonable explanation for the data. Since the prediction matched the data, the hypothesis described in the first premise is one explanation for the data. But before we draw a conclusion, we must determine if there are any other reasonable explanations for the data in premise 3.

(2a)

> **Premise 4** The data match the prediction.
>
> **Premise 5** The hypothesis is the best explanation for the data... (*explain*).
>
> **Conclusion** Therefore, the hypothesis is probably true.

(2b)

> **Premise 4** The data match the prediction.
>
> **Premise 5** There is another reasonable explanation for the data... (*explain*).
>
> **Conclusion** Therefore, the hypothesis is indeterminate.

We will discuss premise 5 more thoroughly, but first, the next section reviews the argument for Halley's hypothesis.

2.3.2 Halley's Argument

This is the argument that occurs in the passage at the beginning of this chapter.

Premise 1, hypothesis   Comets obey Newton's law of universal gravitation and laws of motion, they travel in elliptical orbits around the sun, and they reappear at regular intervals.

Premise 2, prediction   If this hypothesis is true, then a bright comet will be seen at the end of 1758 or beginning of 1759. (This prediction was later modified to: the comet will make its turn around the sun in March or April of 1759.)

Premise 3, data   On December 25, 1758, Johann Palitzsch spotted a bright comet. This comet made its turn around the sun on March 13, 1759.

Premise 4   The data match the prediction.

Premise 5   There are other explanations for the data. The comet that was sighted on December 25, 1758, might have been a new comet that was passing by Earth for the first time, not the comet that Halley saw and had been seen earlier by Kepler, Apian, and Toscanelli. This is unlikely, though. A comet passing by Earth is a relatively rare event, and since Halley and then Clairaut and Lalande indicated with a high degree of accuracy when the comet would appear, Halley's hypothesis seems to be the most reasonable explanation for why Palitzsch spotted a bright comet when he did.

Conclusion   Therefore, Halley's hypothesis is probably correct. Comets probably do travel in elliptical orbits around the sun.

argument (1)

As long as the data match the prediction, the hypothesis in the first premise is always going to provide an explanation for the data in premise 3. In this argument, Halley's hypothesis can explain why Johann Palitzsch saw a comet on December 25, 1758: this comet continuously follows a regular elliptical orbit, and it was then (in 1758) passing by Earth again. But in addition to the hypothesis that is in the first premise, there will always be other explanations for the data. One such explanation, which is relatively plausible, is mentioned in premise 5. But as long as the hypothesis seems to be the most reasonable explanation for the data, then we can conclude that this hypothesis is probably correct.

In the next passage, there is more than one reasonable explanation for the data. While reading the passage, try to identify the hypothesis, the prediction, and the data. Then try to think of other explanations (besides the hypothesis) for the data.

2.4 Other Conclusions

2.4.1 Why Do Humans Reason?

Two cognitive scientists, Hugo Mercier and Dan Sperber, have a unique theory about why humans developed the ability to reason. Traditionally, it has been thought that humans acquired this ability because it allows us to make predictions about the future, understand novel stimuli, and solve complex problems. Contrary to the standard view, Mercier and Sperber suggest that the primary purpose of reasoning is to persuade others by winning arguments. We use our ability to reason to put together compelling arguments and to critically evaluate other people's arguments. Individuals with stronger reasoning skills do this better, and, hence, their views triumph—and whether those views are accurate or not is besides the point.[5]

Although this may not typically be thought of as a (or *the*) purpose of reasoning, one need not look too far to see it in action. *Business Insider* reports that in meetings at Google,

> one of the two co-founders would provoke an argument over a business or product decision. Then they would both sit back, and watch and listen as their new lieutenants verbally cut each other down. As soon as any argument started to go circular, Page would call a winner and start a new fight. ... Google's managers judged themselves by who most often walked out of Brin and Page's debate-oriented meetings a winner. Slowly, those who won the most arguments got the biggest management jobs at Google—and with those jobs, control over huge territories such as search, YouTube, mobile, or social.[6]

A bit more conventionally, the adversarial style of the US judicial system—where prosecutors and defense lawyers go at it, letting the jury or the judge call the winner—is based on the notion that the party in the right is the one whose lawyer makes the most convincing argument.

One consequence of this model, according to Mercier and Sperber, is that people should reason better when they are in groups than when they are

---

5. Hugo Mercier and Dan Sperber, "Why Do Humans Reason? Arguments for an Argumentative Theory," *Behavioral and Brain Sciences* 34 (2011): 57–111.

6. Nicholas Carlson, "Sex and Politics at Google: It's a Game of Thrones in Mountain View," *Business Insider*, September 18, 2013, http://www3.businessinsider.com/sex-and-politics-at-google-its-a-game-of-thrones-in-mountain-view-2013-9.

working alone. Working on complex problems with others allows individuals to use their reasoning ability for its primary purpose. Hence, the group environment should facilitate the best reasoning as people try to make their own views triumph. There is some evidence for this. In a study at the University of Nebraska, psychologists gave the Wason selection task to 143 college undergraduates who had to either work alone or in groups of five or six. The Wason selection task is a short test designed to test people's grasp of conditional statements. The researchers found that 75 percent of the groups completed the task successfully while only 9 percent of the individuals working alone were successful.[7]

2.4.2   An Indeterminate Hypothesis

Here are the first four premises for the argument in the passage above.

P1, hypothesis   People developed the ability to reason in order to win arguments. As such, the ability is designed to persuade others and critique people's arguments.

P2, prediction   If the hypothesis is correct, then there should be evidence that people reason better in groups than they do alone. (This is because, in groups, people can use the ability to reason as it was designed to be used. When they are alone, they cannot.)

P3, data   Researchers have found that, when working on the Wason selection task, groups performed better than individuals working alone. In one experiment, 75 percent of the groups working on the task solved it, while only 9 percent of the people working alone were successful.

P4   The data match the prediction.

The hypothesis is one explanation for the data. Are there any other explanations for why people working in groups do better than individuals working alone? Well, sure. People working together are likely to have more ideas and strategies than a single person working by him- or herself. People working in a group might also be more relaxed because they are helping each other and there is less pressure on each one of them.

7. David Moshman and Molly Geil, "Collaborative Reasoning: Evidence for Collective Rationality," *Thinking and Reasoning* 4 (1998): 231–248.

These alternative explanations for the data do not mean that Mercier and Sperber's hypothesis is wrong. But at the same time, because there are these other good explanations for the data, we cannot conclude that their hypothesis is probably correct. Since there is at least one good alternative explanation for the data, there also has to be another reasonable hypothesis that can explain why humans have the ability to reason (although, for the purpose of this argument, what exactly that hypothesis might be does not have to be determined).

What Mercier and Sperber's hypothesis really needs is another prediction and more data. But in the meantime, the argument is completed this way:

P5   There are other reasonable explanations for the data. People working in groups may do better because they have more ideas and strategies. They may also find working in groups less stressful, which helps them do better.

C   Therefore, the hypothesis is indeterminate.

argument (2)

It is not too satisfying to have an argument with this conclusion, but, until a different prediction is offered, we have no alternative.

2.4.3   Premise 5

There are two different ways to think about premise 5. On the one hand, it is a bit redundant. If the prediction in premise 2 is a very good prediction, and if it matches the data, then it will be exceedingly unlikely that the hypothesis is not true. (A weak prediction is one that will match the data even if the hypothesis is false.) Hence, if a good prediction is formulated and then matches the data, there will not be any competing explanations for the data. But predictions are not always perfect. In many cases, it is difficult to come up with a really good prediction that can be easily compared to the data. Even in Halley's case, it took fifty-three years for the data to show up.

On the other hand, since predictions are not always perfect, a lot can be done in premise 5 to make the argument stronger. When the data match the prediction, the induction by confirmation is always invalid. At best, the argument can be inductively strong. What premise 5 does is make it stronger. Consider the argument for Halley's hypothesis. The data matched the prediction, so everything is on the right track. By stating the next most likely explanation for the data (that it was some other comet) and then explaining why this is not a better explanation than Halley's hypothesis, the conclusion gets more support than it would if premise 5 had just been skipped. Premise 5 is basically an opportunity to add a little bit more support for the conclusion—and, consequently, it gives anyone reading the argument more reason to accept the conclusion.

Premise 5 is even more important in the argument for Mercier and Sperber's hypothesis about why humans have the ability to reason. If premise 5 was not included in that argument, then the conclusion would have been different. Just based on the data matching the prediction (and without premise 5) the conclusion would be: "Therefore, the hypothesis probably is correct." The "wrong" conclusion would have been drawn, which is to say a conclusion that is not as well supported by the premises.

Here are some guidelines for constructing premise 5 when faced with a passage like the ones in this chapter. If the passage gives any indication that there are other reasonable explanations for the data, then start there. This is especially useful if the passage refers to experts who have doubts or disagree about the best interpretation of the data. Otherwise, common sense is the only guide. Generally, if a passage is not exceptionally technical, then, after some pondering, it will be possible to come up with other explanations— reasonable or not—for the data.

2.4.4 A Failed Hypothesis: Spontaneous Generation

When someone is trying to demonstrate that a hypothesis is correct, sometimes things just do not go as hoped and it turns out that the hypothesis is probably incorrect. Other times, someone is doubtful about a hypothesis and believes that, by testing it, the hypothesis will be shown to be wrong. As long as generating a prediction and collecting the data are done honestly, the intentions of the person who is testing the hypothesis do not matter.

Here is a case where someone did have doubts about the hypothesis. The prediction in this passage does not match the data, and so the conclusion is that the hypothesis is wrong.

The Italian physician Francesco Redi (1626–1697) was skeptical about what was, at the time, a widely accepted theory: spontaneous generation. A number of Ancient Greek philosophers including Aristotle argued that under the right conditions living plants and animals could arise from nonliving matter, and this belief was still widely accepted in Redi's day. For example, it was thought that wheat or bread wrapped in rags generated mice, mud generated frogs, and flies came from decaying meat. In 1668, Redi published a book, *Experiments on the Generation of Insects*, that described a series of his experiments testing the theory of spontaneous generation.[8]

In the most well-known of these experiments, Redi put a slice of veal, and the remains of a snake, a fish, and some eels into four separate jars. He sealed these jars tightly with paper covers. He put the same remains in four other jars, but left these jars open. Shortly thereafter, he found flies and maggots (the larvae of flies) on the meat in the open jars; after about a week the maggots turned into flies. Nothing appeared on the meat in the covered jars.

Redi also considered the possibility that the spontaneous generation theory would predict that flies would be generated from decaying meat only when fresh air was available. To test this prediction, he put meat and fish in a large jar and covered the jar with a fine cloth that allowed air to enter. He then placed this jar within a frame covered with the same cloth. Again, nothing appeared on the meat, although flies appeared around the cage and maggots were found on the outer surface of the cage's cloth.

Here are the premises and the conclusion for this argument.

P1, hypothesis   Under certain conditions, plants and animals are spontaneously generated from nonliving matter.

P2, prediction   If this hypothesis is true, then maggots and flies should appear in any environment where there is decaying meat. If meat is placed in jars that are (1) left uncovered, (2) tightly sealed, and (3) covered with a fine cloth, maggots and flies should appear on the meat in all of the jars. Or, if fresh air is needed for spontaneous generation, then the maggots and flies should appear on the meat in the open jars and on the meat in the jars covered with a cloth that allows air into the jar.

P3, data   Redi placed meat in three sets of jars. The first four jars he left open, the next four he completely sealed with paper, and one jar he covered with a fine cloth and then placed inside a frame covered with

8. Francesco Redi, *Esperienze Intorno alla Generazione degl' Insetti* (*Experiments on the Generation of Insects*), translated by Mab Bigelow (Chicago: Open Court, 1909).

the same cloth. After a few days, the meat in the open jars was covered with maggots, which turned into flies after about a week. The jar covered with the cloth had flies around the frame that contained the jar and maggots were on the surface of the cloth, but no maggots or flies were on the meat. There were no maggots or flies around the sealed jars at all.

P4   The data do not match the prediction.

  C   Therefore, the hypothesis is probably false.

argument (3)

Remember, if the prediction does not match the data, then that (the not matching) immediately provides all the support that is needed for this conclusion, and premise 5 is not needed. There certainly are other explanations for the data, but stating them will not provide any further support for the conclusion that the hypothesis is false.

2.5   The Inference

2.5.1   An Indirect Inference

The induction by confirmation is an interesting type of argument because it achieves a tricky goal. On the one hand, we have a hypothesis that seeks to explain some aspect of the world (or universe). But on the other hand, the hypothesis, by definition, cannot be checked directly. For instance, no one could just look up into the sky and see if Halley's suggestion that comets travel in elliptical orbits around the sun was correct. The solution to this problem is to use predictions that are based on the hypothesis, and which can be directly checked. Based on the fit between the data and the prediction, and on considerations about other explanations for the data, a claim is made about the hypothesis—it is probably correct, incorrect, or indeterminate.

So, while the hypothesis cannot be checked directly, the prediction can be. It is on the basis of the relationship between the prediction and data that a conclusion is drawn about the hypothesis.

2.5.2   Valid and Invalid Arguments

Consider two of the conclusions for the induction by confirmation: "The hypothesis is probably correct," and "The hypothesis is incorrect." Call the first one "the positive conclusion" and the second one "the negative conclusion."[9] The version of the induction by confirmation that was introduced in chapter 1 always had the positive conclusion.

P1 If the hypothesis is true, then x should be observed.

P2 x is observed.

C Therefore, the hypothesis is probably true.

argument (4)

With the positive conclusion, the induction by confirmation is a version of a type of argument called *affirming the consequent*, which has this form:

P1 If A, then B.

P2 B.

C Therefore, A.

argument (5)

In the induction by confirmation, the A statement is the hypothesis, and the B statement is the prediction.

Affirming the consequent is always a deductively invalid argument. In many cases, however, it can be inductively strong—but not in all cases, so it is important to evaluate each one carefully.[10] When the longer version of the induction by confirmation (the one with five premises) has a positive conclusion, it is still a version of affirming the consequent. The additional premises make it a little bit difficult to see this, but it is, and it is always deductively invalid.

---

9. The conclusion "The hypothesis is indeterminate" is a variant of the positive conclusion, where *indeterminate* means something like "maybe correct." Thus, such an argument has a medium to low degree of inductive strength.

10. Here's an example of affirming the consequent that is inductively strong:

P1 If Chris went to the bakery, then he got a birthday cake.

P2 Chris got a birthday cake.

C Therefore, Chris went to the bakery.

And here is an example of affirming the consequent that is inductively weak:

P1 If Chris is a physician, then he went to college.

P2 Chris went to college.

C Therefore, Chris is a physician.

The situation is different when the induction by confirmation has a negative conclusion. With the negative conclusion, the simplest form of the induction by confirmation looks like this:

P1 If the hypothesis is true, then x should be observed.

P2 x is not observed.

 C Therefore, the hypothesis is false.

argument (6)

Argument (6) is a type of argument called *modus tollens*, which was introduced in chapter 1. Modus tollens—shown in (7) in its most basic form—is always deductively valid.

P1 If A, then B.

P2 not B.

 C Therefore, not A.

argument (7)

Again, it is not so easy to see that the longer version of the induction by confirmation has the modus tollens form, but it's there.

There is a big difference between an induction by confirmation that has a positive conclusion ("Therefore, the hypothesis is probably true") and an induction by confirmation that has a negative conclusion ("Therefore, the hypothesis is false"). The latter is valid, while former is not. This means that— at least in principle—it is possible to say when a hypothesis is definitely false, but it can never be stated with absolute certainty that a hypothesis is true.

Philosophically, this is a very important point, especially in the philosophy of science and epistemology (the philosophical study of knowledge). The philosopher of science Karl Popper (1902–1994) went so far as to hold that the induction by confirmation with the negative conclusion is *the* way that science proceeds.[11] Scientists form hypotheses and then submit the predictions to empirical tests with the intention of drawing the conclusion "Therefore, the hypothesis is false," as Redi did with his test of spontaneous generation. If the data match the prediction, then the hypothesis lives on to repeat the process. But, Popper claimed, the conclusion "The hypothesis is probably true" is unwarranted. Any conclusion other than "The hypothesis is false" is less than certain, and so not the aim of science—according to Popper.

The notion that certainty is the desired goal of science is attractive, and good science does proceed by submitting hypotheses to rigorous testing—in essence, trying to determine if the hypothesis is false. But Popper doesn't allow any hypotheses to be accepted as correct, or even as probably correct. A hypothesis that has withstood many rigorous tests is just one that—according to Popper—has not yet been falsified. *Not yet falsified* is, perhaps, better than *falsified*, but *probably correct* seems to be a more appropriate assessment of a hypothesis that consistently produces predictions that match the data and is always the best explanation for the data.

So Popper's proposal is rejected. But the question that will end this chapter is, Should even the induction by confirmation that has the negative conclusion be treated as a deductively valid argument? If it turns out that a prediction does not match the data, should the conclusion be that the hypothesis is *definitely* false? Or should the conclusion be that the hypothesis is *probably* false?

Consider a new example. A detective begins with a little bit of data. $1.3 million is missing from the company where John works. John had access to the money, and John has broken the law in the past. Based on these data, the detective forms this hypothesis: John stole the $1.3 million from his company. The detective now needs to confirm this hypothesis. As it stands, the hypothesis should not be accepted as true, and no court is going to convict John. The detective formulates many predictions: John will have an unusually large sum of money in his bank account; John will have a secret bank account; John's relatives will have suddenly gotten richer; John will have recently purchased expensive real estate; there will be copies of the company's financial records in John's home. But none of the data that the detective uncovers match these predictions. In the end, John is not charged with the crime. That's as is should be, but is the hypothesis definitely false or only probably false? It seems reasonable to use "The hypothesis is probably false" as the conclusion. After all, there is always a chance that John took the money and, being especially clever, erased all evidence that would implicate him.

---

11. Karl R. Popper, *The Logic of Scientific Discovery* (London: Hutchinson, 1959). Originally published as *Logik der Forschung* (Vienna: Julius Springer Verlag, 1935).

The root of the problem here is that it is often surprisingly difficult to formulate a good prediction. It's not only hard to come up with a prediction that will be true only when the hypothesis is true; it's sometimes hard to even know if a prediction is really based on the hypothesis or not. For example,

P2, prediction   If John stole the money, then the detective should find evidence on John's computer of a secret bank account.

The detective finds no evidence on John's computer of a secret bank account. Is that because John didn't steal the money or is it because *The detective should find evidence on John's computer of a secret bank account* is a bad prediction? There is an answer to this question, but it's not always possible to know for sure what that answer is. Thus, it is safer to draw the conclusion that the hypothesis is *probably* false. This issue—and a possible solution—is discussed in chapter 8. Stating it briefly, the solution is that, perhaps, the prediction should be treated as a probabilistic claim rather than as a definite one.

2.6   Exercises

Each of these passages contains an induction by confirmation. Read the passage carefully and write out the premises and the conclusion. Order the premises as shown in the chapter. The conclusion will be one of the following: the hypothesis is probably true, the hypothesis is probably false, or the hypothesis is indeterminate.

1. *The car that wouldn't start*   Early Saturday morning, Matt left his apartment and got into his car. Unfortunately, the car would not start, and so Matt called his father to get some advice about what to do. Matt's mother answered the phone and when Matt explained the problem to her, she yelled to her husband, "Matt's car won't start."

   Matt's father figured that the battery was the problem because having a battery that is not functioning properly is a very common reason for cars not to start. Plus he knew that the battery in Matt's car had not been replaced for a very long time. He yelled to his wife, "Tell him to turn on the lights. If they don't go on, then the problem is the battery." Matt's mother told this to Matt, and Matt turned the switch for the headlights. They didn't come on. After more shouting, this information was relayed to Matt's father who punched the air in satisfaction.

2. ***The case of the missing pop-tarts*** Just before leaving for class, Steve goes to the kitchen to get a pop-tart. When he looks in the cupboard, he finds that his last box of pop-tarts is gone. Steve presumes that one of his three roommates has taken them, and it seems most likely that it was Fred. Steve knows that Fred was up late last night watching television; he knows that Fred likes to snack while watching late-night television; and he knows that, in the past, Fred has taken other people's food without asking for permission.

    Steve figures that if Fred opened the box of pop-tarts and started eating them while he was watching television, he didn't finish them and took the remaining pop-tarts to his bedroom to save for later. Steve hurries up to Fred's bedroom, bursts in without knocking, and looks around the room. Although he finds Fred snoring away in bed, Steve does not find any pop-tarts. Annoyed, he leaves for class, buys a pretzel on the way, and is late for his 9:00 a.m. Race, Crime & Justice.

3. ***A house in Amityville*** The events that occurred at 112 Ocean Avenue in Amityville, New York, make it the most famous haunted house in America. In June of 1965, the DeFeo family moved into the house. Nine years later, the oldest child, twenty-three year-old Ronald "Butch" Defeo Jr., killed his parents and all four of his siblings with a .35 caliber rifle while they were sleeping. The gruesome murders received national news coverage, but it was the experiences of the next family that made the house at 112 Ocean Avenue infamous. Even though they knew about the murders, in December 1975, George and Kathy Lutz purchased the house and moved in with their three children. Twenty-eight days later the Lutzes fled, leaving their belongings and ultimately selling the house to the bank for a loss.

    According to George, shortly after they moved in they became concerned by a series of unusual events. On their first day in the house, their dog tried to escape, nearly killing itself in the process. All of the Lutzes heard inexplicable loud noises such as scrapes and creaking. And objects were moved and even removed from the house, including a substantial amount of money that disappeared just as it was about to be used to help pay for a wedding. These events made George suspect that the house might be haunted by the family that had been murdered there only a little over a year earlier, but Kathy wasn't sure. George knew, though, that if the house was haunted, then there would been even more terrifying supernatural events as the murdered family attempted to drive them away.

Soon Kathy had to agree that the house was haunted. George began to wake up regularly at 3:15 a.m. feeling uneasy—and 3:15 a.m. was the time when the DeFeos had been killed. Red welts mysteriously appeared on Kathy's chest, which the Lutzes believed were from an unseen force stomping on her. A small room with red walls was discovered in the basement, and the Lutzes' dog would cower and become skittish whenever it went near the room. And finally, the Lutzes' five-year-old daughter began speaking to a friend only she could see: a demonic pig-like creature with glowing red eyes named Jodie.

Now that the Lutzes were certain, they left, never to return.

4. *A Pynchon mystery*   Last Tuesday, long-suffering fans of the reclusive writer Thomas Pynchon received a double gift. Pynchon's latest book, *Inherent Vice*, a stoned-out detective story set in early-'70s L.A., was released by Penguin Press. And to promote it, the publisher put out a cool video trailer featuring a narrator whose slow, lazy cadence sounds suspiciously like that of Pynchon's, as evidenced by a guest appearance on *The Simpsons* and [a] clip from what appears to be a German TV spot. Inquiries by [the blogger] GalleyCat and others as to whether Pynchon is the guy channeling the novel's main character, beach bum private eye Doc Sportello, have been met with "no comment" from Penguin Press and the video's producers, Meerkat Media. And, of course, the man himself is mum (Would Pynchon fans expect anything else?).

In an effort to solve the mystery, [*The Wall Street Journal* blog] Speakeasy did a little sleuthing and called Ed Primeau, a Michigan-based sound engineer and voice identification expert. Like handwriting analysis, voice identification is an inexact science, often used by law enforcement to rule out a suspect rather than to provide a 100 percent clear-cut ID. Still, people have unique vocal timbres and deliveries, especially Pynchon, who sounds like actor John Astin (i.e., Gomez Addams from the old TV show), mixed with a Midwest corn farmer, with a dollop of aging stoner.

So, is it possible to rule out the the man in the "Inherent Vice" trailer as being the same guy in the Simpsons episode and German TV clip?

Not at all, according to Primeau. In fact, he says, based on a preliminary analysis the speech pattern and inflection is "virtually identical" in all three clips. "It's a very unique style of delivery," Primeau says. "It's very up-and-down. He'll hit these accented spots every few words. You know the TV show "Dragnet," how Joe Friday talked? It's the opposite of that." . . . Primeau's conclusion: "Beyond a reasonable degree of professional certainty, I believe these voices were delivered by the same person."

5. ***New England's Dark Day***   At noon, it was black as night. It was May 19, 1780 and some people in New England thought judgment day was at hand. Accounts of that day, which became known as "New England's Dark Day," include mentions of midday meals by candlelight, night birds coming out to sing, flowers folding their petals, and strange behavior from animals. The mystery of this day has been solved by researchers at the University of Missouri who say evidence from tree rings reveals massive wildfires as the likely cause.

"The patterns in tree rings tell a story," said Erin McMurry, research assistant in the MU College of Agriculture, Food and Natural Resources Tree Ring Laboratory. "We think of tree rings as ecological artifacts. We know how to date the rings and create a chronology, so we can tell when there has been a fire or a drought occurred and unlock the history the tree has been holding for years."

Limited ability for long-distance communication prevented colonists from knowing the cause of the darkness. It was dark in Maine and along the southern coast of New England with the greatest intensity occurring in northeast Massachusetts, southern New Hampshire, and southwest Maine. In the midst of the Revolutionary War, Gen. George Washington noted the dark day in his diary while he was in New Jersey.

Nearly 230 years later, MU researchers combined written accounts and fire scar evidence to determine that the dark day was caused by massive wildfires burning in Canada.

"A fire comes along and heat goes through the bark, killing the living tissue. A couple of years later, the bark falls off revealing the wood and an injury to the tree. When looking at the rings [years later], you see charcoal formation on the outside and a resin formation on the top that creates a dark spot," said Richard Guyette, director of the Tree Ring Lab and research associate professor of forestry in the MU School of Natural Resources.

The researchers studied tree rings from the Algonquin Highlands of southern Ontario and many other locations. They found that a major fire had burned in 1780 affecting atmospheric conditions hundreds of miles away. Large smoke columns were created and carried into the upper atmosphere.

"This study was a unique opportunity to take historical accounts and combine them with modern technology and the physical historical evidence from the tree rings and solve a mystery with science," McMurry said.

6. ***Ether: The backdrop of existence***   By the early 1800s physicists knew that light behaved as a wave. And waves, scientists knew. From a ripple in a pond to a sound moving through the air, all waves seemed to share a few essential features. Like sculptures, waves always require a medium—some physical substrate that the waves must travel through. Because light is a wave, the thinking went, it must also require a medium, an invisible substance that permeated the universe. Scientists called this hidden medium the ether.

In 1887, Albert Michelson and Edward Morley designed an experiment that would search for this ether. They set up an interferometer—a device with two arms in the shape of an L that was optimized to measure change. A single source of light would [split,] travel the length of both arms, bounce off mirrors at the ends, then recombine. [See figure 2.2.] ... If the length of time it took the light to travel down either arm changed by even a faction of a microsecond, the recombined light would glow darker.

Michelson and Morley set up their interferometer and monitored the light for months as the earth moved around the sun. Depending on which way the earth was traveling, the stationary ether should have altered the time it took for the light to bounce down the perpendicular arms. Measure this change, and you have found the ether.

Of course, the experiment found no such thing, thus beginning the destruction of a cosmology hundreds of years old.

7. ***Pasteur and spontaneous generation***   Even after Francesco Redi's experiments in the senventeenth century, many people clung to the theory of spontaneous generation. The discovery of microorganisms not long after Redi's book was published seemed to reveal a whole new realm where spontaneous generation could occur. It was not until 1859 that the French chemist Louis Pasteur was able to satisfactorily put the issue to rest.

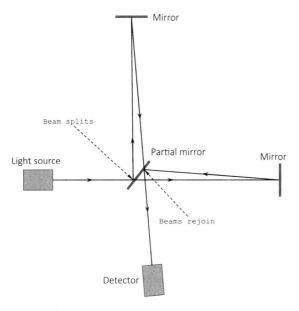

Figure 2.2
The design of an interferometer. The earth traveling through the stationary ether would create a wind-like effect, not unlike sticking one's arm out the window of a moving car. In the interferometer, after the light splits, the light traveling up and down one length would be traveling into and then with the "wind," while the light traveling up and down the other length would always have the "wind" hitting it from the side. The light traveling into and then with the "ether wind" would be slowed down more than the other.

Russell Levine and Chris Evers relate the event:

The French Academy of Sciences sponsored a contest for the best experiment either proving or disproving spontaneous generation. Pasteur's winning experiment was a variation of [two earlier experiments]. He boiled meat broth in a flask, heated the neck of the flask in a flame until it became pliable, and bent it into the shape of an S. [See figure 2.3.] Air could enter the flask, but airborne microorganisms could not—they would settle by gravity in the neck. As Pasteur had expected, no microorganisms grew. When Pasteur tilted the flask so that the broth reached the lowest point in the neck, where any airborne particles would have settled, the broth rapidly became cloudy with life. Pasteur had both refuted the theory of spontaneous generation and convincingly demonstrated that microorganisms are everywhere—even in the air.[12]

Figure 2.3
Louis Pasteur examining a flask with an S-shaped neck. Robert Thom, *Pasteur: The Chemist Who Transformed Medicine*. Used by permission of the University of Michigan Museum of Art, Collection of the University of Michigan Health System, Gift of Pfizer Inc. UMHS.32.

8. ***Was Napoleon poisoned?*** For decades, scholars and scientists have argued that the exiled dictator, who died in 1821 on the remote island of St. Helena in the South Atlantic, was the victim of arsenic, whether by accident or design.

   The murder theory held that his British captors poisoned him; the accident theory said that colored wallpaper in his bedroom contained an arsenic-based dye that mold transformed into poisonous fumes.

   The evidence behind both theories was that scientists had found arsenic in hairs from Napoleon's head.... "There is nothing improbable about the hypothesis of arsenic poisoning," wrote Frank McLynn in *Napoleon: A Biography.* "Science gives it rather more than warranted assertibility."

---

12. Russell Levine and Chris Evers, "The Slow Death of Spontaneous Generation (1668–1859)" (Washington, DC: National Health Museum, 1999).

But now, a team of scientists at Italy's National Institute of Nuclear Physics in Milan-Bicocca and Pavia has uncovered strong evidence to the contrary. They conducted a detailed analysis of hairs taken from Napoleon's head at four times in his life—as a boy in Corsica, during his exile on the island of Elba, the day he died on St. Helena at age 51, and the day afterward—and discovered that the arsenic levels underwent no significant rises.

Casting a wide net, the scientists also studied hairs from his son, Napoleon II, and his wife, Empress Josephine. Here, too, they found that the arsenic levels were similar and uniformly high.

The big surprise was that the old levels were roughly 100 times the readings that the scientists obtained for comparison from the hairs of living people.

"The concentrations of arsenic in the hair taken from Napoleon after his death were much higher," the scientists wrote. But the levels were "quite comparable with that found not only in the hair of the emperor in other periods of his life, but also in those of his son and first wife."

The results, they added, "undoubtedly reveal a chronic exposure that we believe can be simply attributed to environmental factors, unfortunately no longer easily identifiable, or habits involving food and therapeutics."

A team of 10 scientists reported their results in a recent issue of the Italian journal *Il Nuovo Saggiatore* (*The New Experimenter*). The hair samples of Napoleon and his family came from the Glauco-Lombardi Museum in Parma, Italy, the Malmaison Museum in Paris and the Napoleonic Museum in Rome.

The scientists measured the arsenic levels with great precision by inserting the hairs into a nuclear reactor in Pavia, near Milan. The resulting activation let the team identify trace elements but did not harm the hairs, some more than two centuries old.

Note: There are actually two specific hypotheses here: the intentional poisoning hypothesis and the accidental poisoning hypothesis. The argument in the passage, however, is for the more general "victim of arsenic" hypothesis.

Sources

Steven Kurutz, "Yup, It's Him: A Pynchon Mystery Solved," *Wall Street Journal*, August 11, 2009.

University of Missouri New Bureau. "Mystery of Infamous 'New England Dark Day' Solved by Tree Rings." June 9, 2008.

Michael Moyer, "Is Space Digital?" *Scientific American*, February 2012, 30–37.

William J. Broad, "Hair Analysis Deflates Napoleon Poisoning Theories." *New York Times*, June 10, 2008.

2.7   Answers

1. *The car that wouldn't start*

   P1, hypothesis   The battery in Matt's car is dead.

   P2, prediction   If this hypothesis is correct, then the headlights will not come on when the switch is turned to "on."

   P3, data   Matt tried turning on the car's headlights, but they did not work.
   ("The battery in Matt's car is old" and "A malfunctioning battery is a very common reason for a car not to start" are data, but they do not go in premise 3 because they were used to create the hypothesis, not test the prediction.)

   P4   The data match the prediction.

   P5   There are other explanations for the data. The headlights might not have come on because the bulbs are no longer functioning, or there could have been a wiring problem somewhere between the switch for the lights and the lights themselves. The hypothesis is, however, a better explanation for the data than either of these two explanations. Although lightbulbs do stop working after a period of time, it is unlikely that the bulbs in both of the car's headlights would stop working at the same time that the car itself won't start. And not only are wiring problems relatively rare in most cars, it is, again, unlikely that a wiring problem affecting the headlights would occur at the same time that the car itself will not start.

   C   Therefore, the hypothesis is probably correct.

2. *The case of the missing pop-tarts*

   P1, hypothesis   Fred took Steve's pop-tarts and ate some of them while he was watching television late at night.

P2, prediction   If this hypothesis is true, then the remaining pop-tarts will be found in Fred's bedroom.

P3, data   Steve looked around Fred's bedroom, but he did find any pop-tarts.

(Note that these are also data: (a) Fred was up late last night watching television, (b) Fred likes to snack while watching late night television, and (c) in the past, Fred has taken other people's food without asking for permission. They do not belong in premise 3, however, because they are data that were used to construct the hypothesis.)

P4   The data do not match the prediction.

 C   Therefore, the hypothesis is probably false.

3. *A house in Amityville*

P1, hypothesis   The house at 112 Ocean Avenue in Amityville, NY, is haunted. The haunting is related to the killing of the DeFeo family, which occurred there in 1974.

P2, prediction   If this hypothesis is correct, then odd, supernatural events will occur in the house. These events could be, for example, strange coincidences relating to the murders, and maybe strange behavior by the present occupants of the house, especially children or animals.

P3, data   The passage reports that the following events occurred in the house:

- George Lutz often woke up at 3:15 a.m., the time of the DeFeo murders.
- Red welts appeared on Kathy Lutz's chest.
- A small room with red walls was discovered in the basement, and the Lutz's dog seemed to dislike going near the room.
- The Lutz's five-year-old daughter developed an imaginary friend named Jodie. Jodie was a demonic pig-like creature with glowing red eyes.

(The incidents that caused George Lutz to form his hypothesis—their dog trying to run away, inexplicable loud noises, objects being moved about the house, and probably the murders themselves—are data, but they do not belong in this premise because they are the data that were used to create the hypothesis.)

P4   The data match the prediction.

P5   There are other reasonable explanations for the data besides the house being haunted. Waking up regularly at 3:15 a.m. could have many causes. The most reasonable explanation is that George Lutz just got in the habit of waking up at this time. That the murders occurred around 3:15 a.m. could just be a coincidence. Kathy Lutz's welts could also have any number of causes—for example, a rash or an allergic reaction. An unseen force causing them seems the least likely of all the possibilities. That the dog was skittish around a small room in the basement could be because the dog didn't want to go into a small room. Or the dog simply might not have liked being in the basement. And finally, a child developing an imaginary friend is not unusual; it is something that many children do. And that Jodie was the product of the five-year-old's imagination is a more reasonable explanation than that she was a supernatural creature that only the child could see.

C   Therefore, the hypothesis is indeterminate.

4. *A Pynchon mystery*

P1, hypothesis   Thomas Pynchon, the author of *Inherent Vice*, is narrating the video trailer that is being used to promote his book.

P2, prediction   If the hypothesis is true, then the professional voice analysis will find that the vocal qualities (e.g., speech pattern, vocal timber, and inflection) of the narrator in the promotional video for *Inherent Vice* will be similar to the two known recordings of Pynchon's voice, one from an episode of *The Simpsons* and the other from a German TV advertisement.

P3, data   A voice analysis of the three audio files by a professional sound engineer and voice identification expert, Ed Primeau, indicated that the "speech pattern and inflection" of the voices on all three clips are "virtually identical."

P4   The data match the prediction.

P5   There are other explanations for why the voices in the three audio clips are the same. As the passage says, voice analysis isn't that exact; and different people can have similar voices. Nonetheless, the uniqueness of the voice in each of the clips and the confidence of the voice analyst suggest that these other explanations are not correct—or at least not better explanations than the hypothesis.

C   Therefore, the hypothesis is probably true.

5. *New England's Dark Day*

P1, hypothesis   The unusual darkness in New England was caused by large wildfires in Canada. The smoke given off by these fires reached the upper atmosphere and completely blocked the sun over parts of New England on May 19, 1780.

P2, prediction   If the hypothesis is true, when tree rings are examined in forests near New England, there should be dark spots among the rings indicating fire damage that occurred in 1780.

P3, data   University of Missouri researchers found charcoal and resin formations among the rings of trees in Southern Ontario and other (presumably nearby) locations. These formations are the type expected when a fire has damaged a tree, and their location among the rings indicates that the damage occurred in 1780.

P4   The data match the prediction.

P5   There are other explanations for the charcoal and resin that were found in the tree rings. They could have been caused by some smaller fire that damaged the trees, or they could have been caused by a large wildfire that occurred some other time during 1780—after all, the tree rings don't indicate an exact date. However, since the trees that were affected were found in many different locations, a large wildfire that could have caused the sun to be temporarily blocked seems to be the best explanation for what the researchers found. And if there was such a large wildfire in 1780, it is reasonable to assume that it was the cause of this unusual dark day that happened nearby in that same year.

  C   Therefore, the hypothesis is probably true.

6. *Ether: The backdrop of existence*

P1, hypothesis   Ether is an "invisible substance that permeates the universe." This is the substance through which light waves travel.

P2, prediction   If the hypothesis is correct, then the light traveling down each arm in an interferometer should arrive at the detector at slightly different times. (They would arrive at different times because the ether would be hitting one light beam from the side while the other beam was traveling into and then with the "ether wind.") That the light arrived at slightly different times would be evident because the light would "glow darker" at the detector than at the source.

P3, data   Michelson and Morley performed the experiment in 1887. They found that there was no difference in the speed that light traveled down either arm of the interferometer; the intensity of the light was the same at the detector and at the source.

P4   The data do not match the prediction.

C   Therefore, the hypothesis is probably false.

7. *Pasteur and spontaneous generation*

P1, hypothesis   Plants and animals can be spontaneously generated from nonliving matter.

P2, prediction   If the hypothesis is correct, then living organisms will appear in a substance such as meat broth when it is prepared under the following conditions. First, it is boiled so that it starts free of any living microorganisms. Next, precautions are taken to make sure that no organisms are able to access the broth through the air, but the broth is still exposed to fresh air.

P3, data   Pasteur boiled meat broth in a flask. At the same time, he heated and then bent the neck of the flask into an S-shape so that air could enter the flask, but microorganisms could not. No microorganisms appeared in the broth after it cooled.

P4   The data do not match the prediction.

C   Therefore, the hypothesis is probably false.

Note: In the argument above, the hypothesis states that spontaneous generation occurs. The hypothesis could have been that spontaneous generation is *not* possible. In that case, this would be the prediction:

P2, prediction   If the hypothesis is correct, then nothing living will appear in a substance such as meat broth when it is prepared under the following conditions. First, it is boiled so that it starts free of any living microorganisms. Next, precautions are taken to make sure that no organisms are able to access the broth through the air, but the broth is still exposed to fresh air.

And this would be premise 5 and the conclusion:

P5   This is a very straightforward experiment, and there do not seem to be any other explanations for the data besides the hypothesis. The possibility that there was something wrong with the broth that prevented microorganisms from appearing is ruled out because microorganisms did appear in the broth once it was moved into the neck of the flask (to the point that it could be reached by microorganisms).

C   Therefore, the hypothesis is probably correct.

8. *Was Napoleon poisoned?*

P1, hypothesis   Napoleon died from arsenic poisoning. The arsenic was either administered intentionally by the British, who were imprisoning Napoleon when he died, or Napoleon inhaled fumes created by mold on the wallpaper in his bedroom, which was colored with an arsenic-based dye.

P2, prediction   If this hypothesis is correct, there should be higher levels of arsenic in the hair taken from Napoleon the day after he died (and possible on the day that he died) than in hairs of his from earlier in his life. The hairs from the time of his death should also contain higher levels of arsenic than hairs taken from his wife and son.

P3, data   Researchers measured the levels of arsenic in hairs taken from Napoleon at four different times: when he was a boy, when he was exiled on Elba (in 1814–15), the day that he died, and the day after he died (in 1821). They also measured the amount of arsenic in hairs taken from Napoleon's son and wife. They found that the levels of arsenic were high, but they were the same for all of the hair samples.

P4   The data do not match the prediction.

C   Therefore, the hypothesis is probably false.

3 More on the Induction by Confirmation

The previous chapter covered the induction by confirmation, the type of argument used to evaluate a hypothesis. This chapter is about two types of inferences that are related to the induction by confirmation: the *crucial experiment* and the *inference to the best explanation*. The crucial experiment is a variation of the argument discussed in the previous chapter and is still, properly speaking, a type of induction by confirmation. The inference to the best explanation is a separate type of argument, although it is sometimes confused with the induction by confirmation because it shares some of its features. It has the initial set of data and a hypothesis, but it does not include the prediction or the subsequent confirmation (or disconfirmation) of the hypothesis.

3.1 The Crucial Experiment

Sometimes a situation arises where two hypotheses compete to explain the same phenomenon. Such a situation might be resolved in different ways, but the method that has particularly interested philosophers and historians of science is called *experimentum crucis*—in English, *the crucial experiment*.

The basic idea is this: with two hypotheses in mind, a single experiment is designed and two predictions are made about the outcome of the experiment—one prediction based on each hypotheses. The experiment has to be one that will yield a different prediction from each hypothesis, which is often what makes designing a crucial experiment tricky. The experiment is performed, and if all goes well, one of the predictions will match the data and the other one will not. Of course, it is possible that neither prediction will match the data, but in the ideal situation, one of them will.

A successful crucial experiment is useful for practical reasons—it determines which of the two hypotheses is probably correct—but it is also admired because of its elegance. With just one set of data, one hypothesis is ruled out and another hypothesis is ruled in.

The following passage contains a crucial experiment. One hypothesis is Isaac Newton's and the other is Albert Einstein's. The passage describes the experiment that indicated which one of them was correct.

Isaac Newton's three laws of motion and his law of universal gravitation—laid out in his *Philosophiæ Naturalis Principia Mathematica* (1687)—dominated scientific practice for over 200 years. But in 1905, the young Albert Einstein wrote five papers that would completely change physics. One of them, "Zur Elektrodynamik bewegter Körper" ("On the Electrodynamics of Moving Bodies"), described his special theory of relativity. The theory combines space (the three dimensions: height, depth, and width) and time into a single four-dimensional continuum: *spacetime*. Unfortunately, special relativity cannot account for gravity. The laws of special relativity only apply in the absence of a gravitational force.

It took until 1915 for Einstein to incorporate gravity into the now general theory of relativity. In essence, Einstein proposed that what we think of as gravity is the effect of curvatures in spacetime. Imagine that spacetime is a smooth sheet. Massive objects like the sun distort the sheet, and these distortions determine the path of other objects—for instance, Earth's orbit around the sun.

Even before the general theory of relativity was finished, Einstein noticed that it could be tested by measuring how much the light from a star shifts as it passes by the sun. Because the sun warps spacetime, light passing by it should curve. Or, in other words, the sun's gravity should bend the beam of light. Newton's universal law of gravitation, which states that objects are attracted to each other in proportion to their size and the distance between them, also predicts that light will bend as it passes by a massive object like the sun. But Newton's theory predicts a smaller shift than does Einstein's.

Of course, under normal conditions, the sun's brightness makes it impossible to see the light from the stars that are behind it. When the sun is blocked during a total solar eclipse, however, those stars are visible. An eclipse that could decide between Einstein's and Newton's theories was expected on May 29, 1919. This eclipse would occur just as the sun was passing in front of the Hyades star cluster. The general theory of relativity predicted that the light from those stars would bend a tiny amount as it passed by the sun: four-thousands of one degree. According to Newton's gravitational law, the light would bend by even less: only half as much as Einstein's theory predicted.

To perform the test, the English astronomer Arthur Eddington first measured the location of the stars in this cluster on clear nights in January and
February 1919 when no large bodies were interfering with their light as it
traveled to Earth. Then, because a total eclipse is visible from only a few places
on Earth, Eddington and his team traveled to Príncipe, a small island off the
west coast of Africa.

The morning of May 29 was raining and overcast. For a while, it appeared
that Eddington would not be able to see the eclipse or the light from the stars at
all. But at half past one the sky cleared. Less than an hour later, during the six
minutes of the total eclipse, Eddington and his team took sixteen photographs
of the position of the stars. Once finished, they returned to London to study
the data. On November 6, 1919, Eddington reported his findings, and on
November 7 the *Times* of London announced, "Revolution in Science, New
Theory of the Universe, Newtonian Ideas Overthrown."

The same basic format that was introduced in the previous chapter is
used for the crucial experiment with some minor modifications. The two
hypotheses are stated in premise one this way:

P1a, hypothesis   Space and time are part of a four-dimensional continuum called "spacetime." Gravity is the effect that large bodies have on
spacetime.

P1b, hypothesis   The objects in the universe follow Newton's law of
universal gravitation: "Objects are attracted to each other in proportion
to their size and the distance between them."

The predictions are set up similarly. The prediction from the first hypothesis
(the one in *premise 1a*) is in *premise 2a*, and the prediction from the second
hypothesis is in *premise 2b*.

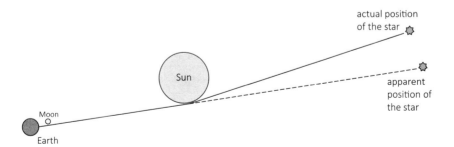

Figure 3.1
Light bending as it passes by the sun. Because the light bends, a viewer on Earth
perceives the star in a different location.

P2a, prediction   If Einstein's hypothesis is correct, when light from stars in the Hyades star cluster pass by the sun, the light will curve, not travel in a straight line. It will curve by four-thousands of one degree. Thus, the location of the stars will appear to have shifted.

P2b, prediction   Similarly, if Newton's hypothesis is correct, when light from stars in the Hyades star cluster pass by the sun, the light will curve, not travel in a straight line. But this hypothesis predicts that the light will curve by less, only about two-thousands of one degree. So, while the location of the stars will appear to have shifted, the shift will be by a smaller amount than is predicted by Einstein's theory.

Premise 3 is the same as in the regular induction by confirmation.

P3, data   Sir Arthur Eddington measured the position of stars in the Hyades star cluster twice, once when the light from these stars was not passing through the sun's—or any large object's—gravitational field, and again, during a solar eclipse, when the light from these stars was passing through the sun's gravitational field. Eddington found that the apparent position of the stars was shifted during the solar eclipse by the amount expected if their light curved by four-thousands of a degree as it passed by the sun.

Premise 4 reports the relationship between the data and both predictions.

P4   The data match the prediction from Einstein's hypothesis, the prediction in premise 2a. The data do not match the prediction based on Newton's hypothesis, the prediction in premise 2b.

Premise 5 is also the same as in the regular induction by confirmation. And, although every argument is different, if a good competing alternative—like Newton's hypothesis—cannot explain the data, that may suggest that there are not any other reasonable explanations for the data in premise 4. But, again, every argument is different, and even in a crucial experiment, it is possible that there will be another reasonable explanation for the data besides the hypothesis that has survived so far. In this case, however,

P5   The match between the data and Einstein's very specific prediction suggests that his hypothesis is the best explanation for the data. The best alternative theory, Newton's, is not able to explain the data, and the only other obvious explanation is that the data are the result of measurement errors. This is possible given the nature of the experiment, but the acceptance of the data by the scientific community weighs against measurement error.

Finally, the conclusion about each hypothesis:

C   Therefore, Einstein's general theory of relativity is probably correct, and Newton's universal law of gravitation is probably incorrect.

In all, the argument requires only a few modifications to the basic induction by confirmation. The first two premises are both split into an *(a)* part and a *(b)* part. Premise 4 and the conclusion are a little bit longer because they must report something about both predictions or both hypotheses. Premises 3 and 5 are the same as they are in the regular version of the induction by confirmation.

3.2   The Inference to the Best Explanation

The inference to the best explanation is a type of inductive argument that is similar to, and easily confused with, the induction by confirmation. The following passage contains Jared Diamond's argument that cannibalism occurred among the Anasazi, a large society that occupied what is now the southwestern United States from 600 CE until about 1200.

> The signs of warfare-related cannibalism among the Anasazi are an interesting story in themselves. While everyone acknowledges that cannibalism may be practiced in emergencies by desperate people, such as the Donner Party trapped by snow at Donner Pass en route to California in the winter of 1846–47, or by starving Russians during the siege of Leningrad during World War II, the existence of non-emergency cannibalism is controversial. ... Many or most European and American anthropologists, brought up to regard cannibalism with horror in their own societies, are also horrified at the thought of it being practiced by peoples that they admire and study, and so they deny its occurrence and consider claims of it as racist slander. They dismiss all the descriptions of cannibalism by non-European peoples themselves or by early European explorers as unreliable hearsay, and they would evidently be convinced only by a videotape taken by a government official or, most convincing of all, by an anthropologist. ...
>
> Such objections have created controversy around the many reports of human remains, with evidence consistent with cannibalism, found at Anasazi sites. The strongest evidence comes from an Anasazi site at which a house and its contents had been smashed, and the scattered bones of seven people were left inside the house, consistent with their having been killed in a war

raid rather than properly buried. Some of the bones had been cracked in the same way that bones of animals consumed for food were cracked to extract the marrow. Other bones showed smooth ends, a hallmark of animal bones boiled in pots, but not of ones not boiled in pots. Broken pots themselves from that Anasazi site had residues of the human muscle protein myoglobin on the pots' inside, consistent with human flesh having been cooked in the pots. But skeptics might still object that boiling human meat in pots, and cracking open human bones, does not prove that other humans actually consumed the meat of the former owners of those bones (though why else would they go to all that trouble of boiling and cracking bones to be left scattered on the floor?). The most direct sign of cannibalism at the site is that dried human feces, found in the house's hearth and still well preserved after nearly a thousand years in that dry climate, proved to contain human muscle protein, which is absent from normal human feces, even from the feces of people with injured and bleeding intestines. This makes it probable that whoever attacked that site, killed the inhabitants, cracked open their bones, boiled their flesh in pots, scattered the bones, and relieved himself or herself by depositing feces in that hearth had actually consumed the flesh of his or her victims.[1]

There is an issue here that needs an explanation: what was done to the bodies of these individuals, members of the Anasazi society, after they died? Moreover, as Diamond points out, there is no way to simply check what happened to these bodies, nor are there any reliable records available. Consequently, we need a hypothesis. And that's what Diamond provides. His hypothesis is that the Anasazi engaged in cannibalism.

To form this hypothesis, as with any good hypothesis, Diamond relies on available data:

1. Some of the human bones found at the site had been cracked, presumably to extract the marrow. (They were cracked in the same way that animal bones are cracked to extract marrow.)
2. Other human bones found at the site had smooth ends, which is a characteristic of bones that have been boiled in pots (and it's not found on bones that have not been boiled).
3. Broken pots found at that site had the residue of the human muscle protein myoglobin on the inside, which suggests that human flesh was cooked in the pots.
4. Dried human feces, found in the house's hearth, contain human muscle protein.

1. Jared Diamond, *Collapse: How Societies Choose to Fail or Succeed* (New York: Penguin, 2005), 151–152.

But generating the hypothesis is as far as this goes. Diamond doesn't make a prediction based on this hypothesis, and it wouldn't be that easy for him to do so. Rather, he is just proposing that his hypothesis is the best explanation for the data. Hence, this is called *inference to the best explanation*—or sometimes *abduction* to set it apart from other types of inductive inferences.

Another example and one commonly used to introduce the inference to the best explanation is this:

> One morning you walk out your front door and see that the grass in your front lawn is wet. From this you conclude that it rained last night. It is, of course, possible that during the night a neighbor watered your lawn or firefighters sprayed your (unburned) house with water and drenched the lawn. But these hypotheses appear unlikely compared with it having rained last night.

Here the datum is the wet grass, and the explanation—that is, the hypothesis—is that it rained last night.

In this short example, it is easy to see that an inference to the best explanation is just the preliminary stage of the induction by confirmation: based on some data, a hypothesis is formed. In this particular case, it would be possible to form a prediction—for instance, if it rained, then the street and other people's lawns will also be wet. That prediction could then be checked, and the hypothesis would be confirmed or disconfirmed. But even when those steps aren't taken, it seems pretty likely that the correct explanation has been identified. On the other hand, in Diamond's cannibalism argument, there are no other data to gather, and so, even if a prediction was made, it couldn't then be checked.

Whatever the reason might be for not making a prediction and then collecting additional data, without those things, the argument is an inference to the best explanation, not an induction by confirmation. Recall table 2.1 from chapter 2, which shows how the data, hypothesis, and prediction are related in the induction by confirmation. In the inference to the best explanation, everything happens on just the top row. There is the data that are used to create the hypothesis and the hypothesis, and that's it.

3.2.1 The Best Hypothesis

The simplest way to write out the premises and the conclusion for an inference to the best explanation is to put the data in the premises and make the explanation for the data—that is, the best hypothesis—the conclusion. In this form, the wet grass example is simply:

    P1 The grass in the front lawn is wet.

     C Therefore, it rained last night.

argument (1)

And this is Diamond's argument:

    P1 Some of the human bones found at the site had been cracked, presumably to extract the marrow. (They were cracked in the same way that animal bones are cracked to extract marrow.)

    P2 Other human bones found at the site had smooth ends, which is a characteristic of bones that have been boiled in pots (and it's not found on bones that have not been boiled).

    P3 Broken pots found at that site had the residue of the human muscle protein myoglobin on the inside, which suggests that human flesh was cooked in the pots.

    P4 Dried human feces, found in the house's hearth, contain human muscle protein.

     C Therefore, the Anasazi engaged in cannibalism.

argument (2)

It is also useful, however, to list not only the data but also the set of hypotheses that could possibly explain the data. The complete argument, then, takes this format:

Given the data, $d_1, d_2, \cdots d_n$, and hypotheses $h_1, h_2, \cdots h_n$, infer the hypothesis that best explains the set of data.

For Diamond's argument, let h_1 be *the Anasazi engaged in cannibalism.* In the passage about the Anasazi, there are two other hypotheses in addition to h_1. In the middle of second paragraph, Diamond considers this hypothesis:

    h_2 Human meat was boiled in the pots that were found at the site, and human bones were cracked open, but no human flesh was consumed.

And toward the end of that paragraph, he mentions and immediately eliminates this hypothesis:

    h_3 People with injured and bleeding intestines made the human feces that contain human muscle protein.

The failure of h_3 is made clear in the passage. This hypothesis cannot correctly explain why human muscle protein was found in the human feces. Plus, it doesn't explain the other data either. Hence, h_3 is simply insufficient. The second hypothesis, h_2, can explain why some bones were cracked, other bones appeared to have been boiled, and myoglobin residue was found on the inside of the pots. The explanation is that all of this was done, but no meat was eaten. But while h_2 can explain that data, it's not as straightforward as h_1. After people go through the process of cooking and preparing food, they plan to eat it (or someone else does). They don't discard what they've just prepared. Additionally, h_2 can't explain why the human feces contain human muscle protein.

Another reasonable hypothesis is this:

h_4 The Anasazi were only the victims of cannibalism, not the practitioners of it; some separate group ate the remains of the Anasazi who were killed at this site.

Although there is nothing in the passage to rule out this hypothesis, other claims by Diamond make it appear unlikely. First, the Anasazi society was large, with many geographically disperse settlements that were interconnected by trade, politics, and religion. Thus, this was a situation where different groups, all of whom were Anasazi, might have violent interactions. And second, Diamond simply states—and it is reasonable to believe him, at least provisionally—that "while the Anasazi did indeed attack each other as their population grew and as the climate deteriorated, the civilizations of the U.S. Southwest were too distant from other populous societies to have been seriously threatened by any external enemies."[2] Hence, h_4—others, not the Anasazi, practiced cannibalism—also fails as a satisfactory explanation for the data. The best explanation is h_1 because it is the only hypothesis that is able to correctly explain all of the data in a straightforward way.

In the wet grass example, there are at least three hypotheses, all of which can explain the data.

h_1 It rained last night.

h_2 A neighbor watered your lawn during the night.

h_3 Firefighters sprayed your house and lawn with water during the night.

Hypotheses h_2 and h_3 cannot be ruled out by the available datum, which is only that the grass in the front lawn is wet, but they fail in relatively

---

2. Diamond, *Collapse*, 156.

obvious ways. While the first hypothesis is a straightforward explanation for wet grass, these other two seem contrived.

A hypothesis that is "straightforward" in its explanation of the data and not "contrived" is a starting point for thinking about what makes one hypothesis better than others, but typically philosophers prefer concepts that can stand up a bit more strongly to close analysis. (For instance, someone might ask what makes one hypothesis more straightforward than another, and it won't do to simply state that one hypothesis is obviously more straightforward.) Instead, appeals are typically made to, among other things, *coherence*, *simplicity*, and *generality*. Briefly, these are the basic ideas.

> **Coherence** means the hypothesis, the data, and any other available facts all cohere or hold (or fit) together. In the cannibalism example, hypothesis 2—the hypothesis that the meat was prepared but not eaten—does not cohere very well with the reasons that people usually have for cooking meat or with the data in premise 4.

> **Simplicity** means, as it appears to, that one hypothesis is less complex than another. Although it is not always the case that the simpler explanation is the correct one, preferring a simpler explanation to a more complex one is often a good guideline when evaluating hypotheses. For instance, that it rained is a much simpler explanation for the wet grass than the fire department believed your house was on fire, arrived and hosed it down, realized their mistake and left, and did all of this without waking you.

> **Generality** is the idea that a hypothesis is able to correctly explain a wide range of data. If one hypothesis is able to explain a wider range of data than another, then it is presumed to be a better explanation. For example, each datum in the cannibalism example could have been given a different explanation (i.e., a separate hypothesis for each), but the one hypothesis that can explain all of the data is preferable.

3.2.2   The IBE and IC

The obvious and significant difference between the inference to the best explanation and the induction by confirmation is that the hypothesis is not tested in the inference to the best explanation—that is, a prediction based on the hypothesis is not compared to new data. Another subtle difference occurs in the step from the initial set of data to the hypothesis (a step made by both the inference to the best explanation and the induction by confirmation). For the induction by confirmation, someone can come up with any hypothesis he or she likes as long as it is consistent with that initial set of data. The prediction, the data in premise 4, and premise 5 will sort out the merits of that hypothesis. In the inference to the best explanation, the hypothesis that is selected is the one that is better—or seems to be better—than all of the competing hypotheses. Of course, the hypothesis in the induction by confirmation can also be the one that seems to be better than all of the competing hypotheses, but it need not be.

This means that the inference to the best explanation will always provide a conventional explanation for the phenomenon. That's usually fine, but Einstein's theory of general relativity and Halley's description of comets were unconventional explanations, and Redi's skepticism about spontaneous generation challenged a commonly held view. It is by virtue of premises 2 through 5 in the induction by confirmation that Einstein's and Halley's hypotheses were accepted and spontaneous generation was rejected. Moreover, when there are two seemingly very good hypotheses, it is much preferable to sort them out with a crucial experiment than to use coherence, simplicity, and generality to judge between them.

A second difference is that the form of the inference to the best explanation is less precise than that of the induction by confirmation or the other types of arguments discussed in section 4 of chapter 1. In the inference to the best explanation, the premises contain the available data and the explanation for the data is the conclusion—or the other possible hypotheses might be included among the premises as well. Compare the example of an inference to the best explanation to a proportional syllogism.

P1 The grass in the front lawn is wet.

C Therefore, it rained last night.

argument (1)

P1 Eighty percent of the students at Central City College grew up in Central City.

P2 Morgan is a student at Central City College.

C Therefore, there is an 80 percent chance that Morgan grew up in Central City.

argument (3)

If the conclusion were missing from argument (3), anyone, as long as he or she was familiar with the form of the proportional syllogism, could easily complete the argument, and everyone who did so would get the same conclusion. That contrasts with the inference to the best explanation. Given the premise in argument (1), everyone should get the conclusion "Therefore, it rained last night," but there is no hard-and-fast rule ensuring that they will. This holds even if all of the contending hypotheses are included.

P1, d_1 The grass in the front lawn is wet.

P2, h_1 It rained last night.

P3, h_2 A neighbor watered your lawn during the night.

P4, h_3 Firefighters sprayed your house and lawn with water during the night.

C   Therefore, it rained last night.

argument (4)

Assuming that there are no auxiliary facts that make hypothesis 2 or 3 likely, hopefully everyone would see that the first hypothesis is the best explanation for the wet grass. But, again, nothing about the structure of the argument indicates that the first hypothesis should be the conclusion.

Every inductive inference does not need to have a structure that is as well specified as the proportional syllogism—or the induction by confirmation, inductive generalization, and analogical argument. But the form of the inference to the best explanation makes it harder to set down guidelines for determining when such an argument is inductively strong instead of weak. In the end, we just have coherence, simplicity, and generality for justifying the inference from the data to one of the hypotheses.

That said, the inference to the best explanation is constantly used in everyday life, in science, in medicine, and, as Diamond's example demonstrates, in historical investigations.

3.3   Exercises

For 1–4, each passages contains a crucial experiment. Read the passage carefully and write out the premises and the conclusion. Order the premises as shown in the chapter.

1. ***Watching the earth rotate***   Watching the path that the sun takes
   across the sky, every observer has the impression that the earth remains
   stationary while the sun rotates around it. And although the view
   that the earth is stationary was held for millennia, by the late 1600s
   most astronomers accepted the theory that the earth rotates on its
   axis and around the sun. Still, gathering definitive evidence for the
   rotation hypothesis was difficult. In 1679, Isaac Newton predicted that
   if an object was dropped from a sufficient height, because of the earth's
   rotation, it would land slightly to the east of where it was released.
   Newton's contemporary Robert Hooke then made a small correction to
   the prediction: the object should land to the southeast. But, in any case,
   this was tried and the results were not convincing.

   It was not until 1851 that the French physicist Léon Foucault devised
   an ingenious experiment that would provide clear evidence confirming
   the rotation hypothesis—or, perhaps, the long since dismissed alternative. The experiment used a pendulum that was hung so that it could
   swing in any direction. For the experiment to work, the weight at the
   end of the pendulum had be perfectly symmetrical and the pendulum
   had to be put into motion very gently so that it would swing in a plane
   without any sideways motion. Foucault solved the latter problem by
   starting with the weight tied back with a thin cord. He then held a
   match below the cord until the flame burned through it, releasing the
   weight in a perfectly straight plane.

   Setting up such a pendulum—first in his cellar and then from the
   ceiling of the dome in the Panthéon in Paris—Foucault found that
   its motion, that is, the plane in which it swings, appears to rotate. In
   Paris, the path of Foucault's pendulum shifted 11.25 degrees an hour.
   If the pendulum stayed in motion long enough, an observer watching
   Foucault's demonstration in the Panthéon would see the pendulum
   swinging north to south at one time and then eight hours later swinging
   east to west.

   Or, at least, the path of the pendulum appears to change. As long as
   nothing interferes with it, the pendulum swings in the same plane. It's
   the earth that is rotating slowly beneath it.[3]

---

3. It is, perhaps, easier to understand how this works by imagining a pendulum
placed at the North Pole with the earth spinning quickly beneath it. Someone releases

2. *Cholera in a slum in London*   The British physician John Snow (1813–
1858) was the first to understand how cholera is transmitted and
affects its victims. According to the theory that he sought to replace,
the agent that causes cholera is a vapor given off by people who are
infected. Once airborne, the vapor is inhaled by new potential victims.
Snow, in contrast, suggested that, in patients infected with cholera,
"the morbid poison [is] thrown off in the evacuations"—that is, the
agent is discharged in the victim's diarrhea.[4] It can then be spread
on the hands of caretakers who prepare food without washing their
hands or, if the waste contaminates a water supply, by drinking that
water.

In support of his theory, Snow compiled a great deal of evidence
including an experiment that occurred naturally in Horsleydown, a
London neighborhood, in 1849. In what was basically a slum, two rows
of houses each faced a courtyard with a back alley between them. (See
the map in figure 3.2.) The northern row of houses faced Trusscott's
Court, and the southern row was called the Surrey Buildings. Between
them were the outhouses for each dwelling. The outhouses shared a
drain, which emptied into an open sewer.

The first case of cholera in these residences occurred on July 20 in one
of the Surrey Buildings. From that point, the outbreak lasted twenty-one
days. Snow afterward reported that "in Surrey Buildings the cholera
committed fearful devastation, whilst in the adjoining court [i.e., the
homes on Trusscott's Court] there was but one fatal case, and another
case that ended in recovery."[5] There had been fifteen to twenty cases
of cholera in the Surrey Buildings, eleven of which resulted in deaths.
Those deaths occurred in seven of the fourteen houses in the Surrey
Buildings row.

---

the pendulum, and it swings back and forth in one plane. With each swing away
from the person, it will point to a different spot as the earth rotates—toward North
America, then Asia, then Europe, North America again, and so forth.

4. John Snow, *On the Mode of Communication of Cholera*, 2nd ed. (London: John
Churchill, 1855), 16.

5. Snow, *On the Mode of Communication of Cholera*, 1855, 23.

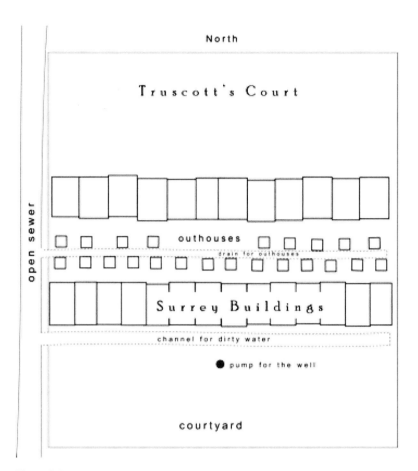

Figure 3.2
A map of the two courts in Horsleydown.

The only significant difference between the two rows of homes was a drain for dirty water that ran in front of the Surrey Buildings. Snow reports,

> In the former court [i.e., the Surrey Buildings courtyard], the slops of dirty water, poured down by the inhabitants into a channel in front of the houses, got into the well from which they obtained their water; this being the only difference that Mr. Grant, the Assistant for the Commissioners of Sewers, could find between the circumstances of the two courts, as he stated in a report that he made to the Commissioners. ... Owing to something being out of order, the water had for some time occasionally

burst out at the top of the well, and overflowed into the gutter or channel, afterwards flowing back again mixed with the impurities; and crevices were left in the ground or pavement, allowing part of the contents of the gutter to flow at all times into the well; and when it was afterwards emptied, a large quantity of black and highly offensive deposit was found.[6]

3. **Pink flowers**   Even before Gregor Mendel's famous experiments with pea plants in the middle of the nineteenth century, it was known that hereditary information is passed from parents to offspring. But how that information is passed remained unclear. Prior to Mendel—and, for a time, even after his experiments—the mechanism was believed to be some sort of mixing. The philosopher Kwame Anthony Appiah explains it this way:

> Most biologists of [Mendel's] day believed that plants and animals inherited their characteristics from their parents by a blending of genetic material, rather like the mixing of fluids. It was supposed, for example, that when the pollen from a white-flowering pea fertilized a red-flowering pea, the seeds would usually produce peas with pink flowers, because the material that made the flowers white in one plant blended with the material that made the other flowers red to produce this intermediate coloring.[7]

Mendel, in contrast, proposed that genetic information is carried in discrete units, what are now called *genes*. Genes occur in pairs and control the expression of observable traits. The different forms that a gene can take are called *alleles*. When an organism has matching alleles for a given gene, the organism is *homozygous* (with respect to that gene). When an organism has different alleles for a particular gene, the organism is *heterozygous* (with respect to that gene). During reproduction, each parent contributes one allele from each pair to each offspring.

Appiah proposes an experiment.

> Let's see how Mendel's theory would work out for the genetics of the flower color of peas, assuming a much-simplified version of his theory of inheritance. Suppose peas with red flowers have two red-making alleles for petal color, and peas with white flowers have two white-making alleles. We'll call the red-making alleles **R** and the white-making ones **W**. So when these red- and white-flowering peas are crossed, each of their offspring will

6. Snow, *On the Mode of Communication of Cholera*, 1855, 23–24.

7. Kwame Anthony Appiah, *Thinking It Through: An Introduction to Contemporary Philosophy* (New York: Oxford University Press, 2003), 131.

get one **R** and one **W** allele. Let's suppose that this is what makes them have pink flowers.[8]

What would happen when a pink-flowered plant is "mated"—or crossed, as biologists say— with one of the red-flowered plants?

> If the blending theory had been correct, then crossing one of the heterozygous pink-flowering peas with a red-flowering pea should have produced offspring all of the same color. The pink-making genetic material would have blended with an equal quantity of the red-making material to produce a pea that was, say, a deeper, redder shade of pink.[9]

Mendel's theory, meanwhile, predicts that some of the offspring will be red-flowered and some will have pink flowers. This is because all of the pink flowered plants have one **W** allele and one **R** allele, while all of the red flowered plants had two **R** alleles. If, as Mendel's theory says, one allele from each parent is passed onto each offspring, then the plants in the next generation will have pairs containing either (i) two **R** alleles or (ii) one **W** allele and one **R** allele. That means, according to his theory, that the plants with two **R** alleles will have red flowers and the plants with one **W** allele and one **R** allele will have pink flowers.

And that, as every high school student would guess, is what happens.

4. ***Drunken ultimatums***   The so-called ultimatum game contains a world of psychological and economic mysteries. In a laboratory setting, one person is given an allotment of money (say, $100) and instructed to offer a second person a portion. If the second player says yes to the offer, both keep the cash. If the second player says no, both walk away with nothing.

The rational move in any single game is for the second person to take whatever is offered. (It's more than he came in with.) But in fact, most people reject offers of less than 30 percent of the total, punishing offers they perceive as unfair. Why?

The academic debate boils down to two competing explanations. On one hand, players might be strategically suppressing their self-interest, turning down cash now in the hope that if there are future games, the

---

8. Appiah, *Thinking It Through*, 131.

9. Appiah, *Thinking It Through*, 131–132.

"proposer" will make better offers. On the other hand, players might simply be lashing out in anger.

The researchers Carey Morewedge and Tamar Krishnamurti, of Carnegie Mellon University, and Dan Ariely, of Duke, recently tested the competing explanations—by exploring how drunken people played the game. As described in a working paper now under peer review, Morewedge and Krishnamurti took a "data truck" to a strip of bars on the South Side of Pittsburgh (where participants were "often at a level of intoxication that is greater than is ethical to induce") and also did controlled testing, in labs, of people randomly selected to get drunk.

The scholars were interested in drunkenness because intoxication, as other social-science experiments have shown, doesn't fuzz up judgment so much as cause the drinker to overly focus on the most prominent cue in his or her environment. If the long-term-strategy hypothesis were true, drunken players would be more inclined to accept any amount of cash. (Money on the table generates more visceral responses than long-term goals do.) If the anger/revenge theory were true, however, drunken players would become less likely to accept low offers: raw anger would trump money-lust.

In both setups, drunken players were less likely than their sober peers to accept offers of less than 50 percent of the total. The finding suggests, the authors said, that the principal impulse driving subjects was a wish for revenge.

Exercises 5–10 are about the inference to the best explanation. For exercises 5 and 6, write out the argument using the same format as argument (4) at the end of the chapter. Include the datum or data that need to be explained, the best hypothesis, and at least one other hypothesis. (In these cases, the best explanation is the simplest one, but also identify one or two other possible explanations.)

5. Michael has a one-room apartment in Florida. In the room, there is a table with a vase on it, one chair, a couch, a coffee table, Michael's bed, and his cat, Tigger. When he leaves in the morning, he locks the door. When he returns, everything is as he left it, but the vase is on the floor and broken. How did the vase break?

6. Jack is driving through Wyoming in his 1998 Honda Civic, which runs well, but has a broken fuel gauge. Outside of Laramie, he fills up the

gas tank. Four hours and 285 miles later, he is in Pinedale. He considers getting gas again, but decides to keep moving. Forty-five minutes later, the engine sputters and then stops. Jack coasts over to the shoulder of the road and gets out. Why did his car stop running?

7. On Wednesday afternoon, Sam tried out for his high school's junior varsity basketball team. He had several mishaps during the tryout. First, he bounced the ball off his foot during the dribbling drill. The coach gave him another basketball, and he completed the drill, at which point the coach told him that he had traveled. Sam wasn't sure what that meant, but it sounded good, and so he thanked the coach. Next, during the free-throw drill, he hit the rim four times and missed the rim on his other six shots. During the defensive drill, Sam wasn't sure what to do, and so he grabbed the player with the ball by the arm and kicked the ball out of bounds.

The next day, Sam's name wasn't on the list of players who made the team.

That evening, he told his mother that he had not made the team. First, she said, "It must be that the coach doesn't like you." Sam thought about it, but he didn't think so. Then his mother said, "You're probably too good to be playing on that team." Again, Sam was skeptical. Sam thought that, probably, he hadn't made the team because his basketball skills and knowledge of the game were insufficient.

(a) What data are described in the above passage?

(b) What hypotheses are offered in the passage?

(c) Which explanation is the best and why?

8. In Arthur Conan Doyle's short story "The Red-headed League," Holmes's client, Mr. Jabez Wilson, begins relating his case with this:

> "I have a small pawnbroker's business at Coburg Square, near the City. It's not a very large affair, and of late years it has not done more than just give me a living. I used to be able to keep two assistants, but now I only keep one; and I would have a job to pay him but that he is willing to come for half wages so as to learn the business."
>
> "What is the name of this obliging youth?" asked Sherlock Holmes.
>
> "His name is Vincent Spaulding, and he's not such a youth, either. It's hard to say his age. I should not wish a smarter assistant, Mr. Holmes; and I know very well that he could better himself and earn twice what I am

able to give him. But, after all, if he is satisfied, why should I put ideas in his head?"

Jabez Wilson's business is run from his home, and he lives there with this Vincent Spaulding and a servant, "a girl of fourteen, who does a bit of simple cooking and keeps the place clean."

Later, after Spaulding, whose real name is John Clay, is caught while trying to steal thirty thousand French gold coins from the City and Suburban Bank, Holmes explains the inference to his friend Dr. Watson.

> "From the time that I heard of the assistant having come for half wages, it was obvious to me that he had some strong motive for securing the situation."
>
> "But how could you guess what the motive was?"
>
> "Had there been women in the house, I should have suspected a mere vulgar intrigue. That, however, was out of the question. The man's business was a small one, and there was nothing in his house which could account for such elaborate preparations, and such an expenditure as they were at. It must, then, be something out of the house."

The datum in need of an explanation is this: Jabez Wilson's assistant, although smart and capable, is working for half of the normal wage of someone in that position.

(a) What are the hypotheses?

(b) Which hypothesis does Holmes conclude is the best explanation, and why is that hypothesis better than the others?

9.   Snow's detective work into cholera began when he noticed a telling detail in the published accounts of the 1848 epidemic. Asiatic cholera had been absent from Britain for several years, but it had recently broken out on the Continent, including the city of Hamburg. In September of that year, the German steamer *Elbe* docked in London, having left port at Hamburg a few days earlier. A crewman named John Harnold checked into a lodging house in Horsleydown. On September 22, he came down with cholera and died within a matter of hours. A few days later, a man named Blenkinsopp took over the room; he was seized by the disease on September 30. . . .

Snow recognized immediately that this sequence of events posed a severe challenge to the opponents of the contagion model. The coincidence was simply too much for the miasma theory to bear. Two cases of cholera in a single room in the space of a week might be compatible with the miasma model, if one believed that the room itself contained some kind of noxious agent that poisoned its inhabitants. But it was stretching matters beyond belief to suggest that the room should suddenly become prone to those poisonous vapors the very day it was occupied by a sailor traveling from a city besieged by the disease. As Snow would later write: "Who can doubt that the case of John Harnold, the seaman from Hamburgh, mentioned above, was the true cause of the malady in Blenkinsopp, who came, and lodged, and slept, in the only room in all London in which there had been a case of true Asiatic cholera for a number of years?"[10]

John Snow's theory about how cholera spreads was discussed in exercise 2. In that passage, the two competing hypotheses were (i) *Snow's*: the agent that causes cholera leaves the body of someone infected via his or her diarrhea and spreads to others by contaminating a drinking water supply or when someone comes in contact with the waste and then does not wash his or her hands, and (ii) *the vapor theory*: the agent that causes cholera is a vapor given off by someone infected with cholera; it is then inhaled by others. In the passage above, which is from Steven Johnson's book *The Ghost Map*, those are, together, referred to as the *contagion model*—both propose that the disease is contagious and so passes from the infected to the uninfected. The other theory in this passage is the *miasma theory*. This is, in Snow's words, "the hypothesis of a cholera poison generally diffused in the air, and not emanating from the sick"—that is, it's in the air, but it is not, as the vapor theory says, given off by those who are infected.[11]

(a) According to this passage, what needs to be explained?

(b) What are the relevant data?

(c) Which theory, according to the passage, is the better explanation and why?

10. A gigantic object the size of a planet has appeared on astronomers' screens lurking near Mercury, with UFO hunters around the world wondering whether it's an alien ship. The object appears from nowhere in a sequence of images of a coronal ejection from the Sun, taken by a

10. John Snow, *On the Mode of Communication of Cholera*, (London: John Churchill, 1849), 29–30.

11. Snow, *On the Mode of Communication of Cholera*, 1849, 6.

NASA telescope [*def.* coronal ejection: a burst of plasma from the sun's outer atmosphere (i.e., its corona)]. As the flare races past Mercury, a huge round object appears next to it—but NASA scientists insist that the object is merely a result of the way the images are processed.

Over 100,000 YouTube users have watched the sequence taken by the Heliospheric Imager-1 telescope. It was uploaded by user siniXster and he says in his commentary: "It's cylindrical on either side and has a shape in the middle. It definitely looks like a ship to me, and very obviously, it's cloaked."

However, experts say that there is no alien race hiding away in our solar system. The image from the telescope was analyzed by the United States Naval Research Laboratory, with engineer Nathan Rich explaining that the "object" is actually the image of Mercury from the previous day. To make sure that the solar flare stood out, researchers compared the image with one taken the day before and subtracted anything that appeared twice—because that would mean it's interfering background light.[12] In this process stars are easily eliminated, but moving objects, like planets, are more difficult to remove. Rich told Space.com: "When [this averaging process] is done between the previous day and the current day and there is a feature like a planet, this introduces dark artifacts in the background where the planet was on the previous day, which then show up as bright areas in the enhanced image."

Astronomer Dr. Heather Couper also agrees that it's not a huge Death Star. She told MailOnline: "The scientists have not managed to subtract the image of Mercury. The technical guys are saying the problem is that when you try to subtract something that's moving the pixels blend into each other. It's imaging processing that they haven't got their heads around. No way could it be an alien spaceship the size of Mercury because Mercury is the size of our moon and we would know about it."

(a) What phenomenon needs an explanation?

(b) What are the two hypotheses?

(c) Which is the better explanation and why?

---

12. As a simpler example of this process, imagine someone taking a picture, in a brightly lit room, of the beam of light from a flashlight. In the resulting image, the beam barely stands out. As a fix, a second picture is taken of the room, lit the same way, but without the flashlight. All of the light that is in this second image is then subtracted from the first image, leaving the beam from the flashlight clearly visible.

Sources

Christopher Shea, "Drunken Ultimatums," *New York Times*, December 13, 2009.

Steven Johnson, *The Ghost Map: The Story of London's Most Terrifying Epidemic—and How It Changed Science, Cities, and the Modern World*, New York: Riverhead, 2006, 69–70.

Ted Thornhill, "Is This an Alien Spacecraft Parked Next to Mercury? Giant Object the Size of a Planet Has Astronomers Baffled," *Daily Mail*, December 8, 2011.

3.4 Answers

1. *Watching the earth rotate*

   P1a, hypothesis   The earth is stationary. It does not rotate on its axis, and it does not rotate around the sun.

   P1b, hypothesis   The earth rotates on its axis, and it rotates around the sun.

   P2a, prediction   If the stationary earth hypothesis is true, then the path of the pendulum in Foucault's experiment will not appear to rotate.

   P2b, prediction   If the rotating earth hypothesis is true, then the path of the pendulum in Foucault's experiment will seem to rotate very slowly as it swings.

   P3, data   Foucault did the experiment with a pendulum in 1851. The plane in which the pendulum swung appeared to rotate 11.25 degrees an hour.

   P4   The data match the prediction from the rotating earth hypothesis, the prediction in premise 2b. The data do not match the prediction from the stationary earth hypothesis, the prediction in premise 2a.

   P5   Since there are only two possible hypotheses here, either the earth rotates or it is stationary, and only one, the rotating earth hypothesis, can explain the data, that hypothesis appears to be the best explanation for the data. The only other explanation would be experimental error, but even that is a little hard to envision. If there was any problem with the experiment—for instance, if Foucault's pendulum were unable to swing in any direction (that is, if it was like the pendulum in a grandfather clock)—then Foucault would not have gotten the result that he did.

C   Therefore, the rotating earth hypothesis is probably true, and the stationary earth hypothesis is probably false.

2. *Cholera in a slum in London*

P1a, hypothesis   The agent that causes cholera is a vapor given off by someone infected with cholera. It is then inhaled by others.

P1b, hypothesis   The agent that causes cholera leaves the body of someone infected via his or her diarrhea and spreads to others either by contaminating a drinking water supply or getting on the hands of a caretaker who later prepares food.

P2a, prediction   If the airborne hypothesis is correct, then once a case of cholera occurs in the Surrey Buildings, it will spread relatively evenly among the inhabitants of the Trusscott's Court houses and the Surrey Buildings because the agent that causes cholera is in the air and can be inhaled just as easily by the inhabitants of either set of buildings.

P2b, prediction   If Snow's hypothesis is correct, then once a case of cholera occurs in one of the Surrey Buildings, it will primarily spread to other individuals living in the Surrey Buildings—either by the actions of each victim's caretakers or by taking water from the well that is contaminated by the waste water drain. At the same time, cholera will not spread at all, or will spread barely at all, to individuals living in the buildings facing Trusscott's Court who do not have convenient access to water from the well in front of the Surrey Buildings.

P3, data   There were fifteen to twenty cases of cholera in the Surrey Buildings and eleven deaths, while in the Trusscott's Court houses there were two cases and only one death. (The placement of the waste water drain and the defective well in front of Surrey Buildings—as well as the outhouses and the open sewer—are data, but not data that go in premise 3. These are data that, given the hypotheses, were used to form the predictions.)

P4   The data match the prediction from Snow's hypothesis, the prediction in premise 2b. The data do not match the prediction made by the airborne hypothesis, the prediction in premise 2a.

P5   Even without knowing exactly how the people in the two sets of buildings were moving around and interacting during the outbreak,

Snow's hypothesis is a very good explanation for the distribution of cases—fifteen to twenty on one side, two on the other. The are the two cases that occurred in the Trusscott's Court side, which, although they do not fit quite the same account as given for the Surrey Building cases, can still be explained by Snow's hypothesis and (a) the proximity of all the outhouses, (b) the open sewer along the edge of both courtyards, or (c) someone from one of the Trusscott's Court houses using the Surrey Buildings' well.

On the other hand, the alternative hypothesis can also provide an after-the-fact explanation: the agent was airborne and it just happened to spread east and west (among the Surrey Buildings) much more prevalently than it spread from the Surrey Buildings up to the buildings in Trusscott's Court. That is possible, but Snow's hypothesis does a much better job of explaining why the data turned out as they did (and, at any rate, the airborne hypothesis produced a prediction that did not match the data). It is also possible that there is some other mechanism by which cholera spreads, for instance, only by direct contact. This can't be ruled out, but, again, given the dirty water drain (which would be contaminated when the water used to wash bedding or clothing worn by infected individuals was disposed there) and the well, Snow's hypothesis can better explain how the cholera spread from house to house among the Surrey Buildings.

C   Therefore, Snow's hypothesis is probably correct, and the airborne hypothesis is probably incorrect.

3. *Pink flowers*

P1a, hypothesis   According to the blending theory, the genetic material that is contributed by each parent blends when it is passed onto the offspring "rather like the mixing of fluids."

P1b, hypothesis   Mendel's theory states that genetic material is carried by units that occur in pairs. Each parent contributes one allele from each of its gene pairs to each offspring. The composition of the pair determines the trait. For instance, in the example in the passage, having two **R** alleles causes the plant to have red flowers; having two **W** alleles causes the plant to have white flowers; and having one **R** allele and one **W** allele gives the plant pink flowers.

P2a, prediction   If the blending theory is correct, when a plant with pink flowers is crossed with one with red flowers, the color of the offspring's petals will be a darker shade of pink—a color intermediate between the color of the parents' flowers.

P2b, prediction   If Mendel's theory is correct, when a plant with pink flowers is crossed with one with red flowers, some of the offspring will have red flowers and some will have pink flowers that are the same shade as are found on the pink-flowered parent.

P3, data   According to the passage, when this experiment is performed, some of the offspring have red flowers and some have pink flowers, and the pink flowers are the same shade of pink as is found on the pink-flowered parent.

P4   The data match the prediction from Mendel's hypothesis, the prediction in premise 2b. The data do not match the prediction from the blending hypothesis, the prediction in premise 2a.

P5   Mendel's theory seems to be the best explanation for the data in premise 3. It's a simple explanation that explains what is observed, while the blending theory fails to do that. Further, although we now know that the biochemistry of genetics is much more complex than Mendel's theory, even a more complex theory wouldn't be able to explain these data any better than Mendel's does. (We might want to see how well Mendel's theory can explain hereditary information passed from parents to offspring for other traits and in other species, but that issue doesn't concern being able to explain these data.)

C   Therefore, Mendel's theory is probably correct, and the blending theory is probably incorrect.

4. *Drunken ultimatums*

P1a, hypothesis   The second player in the ultimatum game turns down low offers because he or she is engaged in a long-term strategy whereby punishing unfair offers now will, hopefully, yield better offers in the future.

P1b, hypothesis   The second player in the ultimatum game turns down low offers because he or she is angry at the unfair offer and wants to punish the first player by denying that player any money.

P2a, prediction   If the long-term strategy hypothesis is true, then when the second player is drunk—and so only focusing on the most salient cue in his or her environment—that player will accept unfair offers (i.e., when the most salient cue is the money, the drunken player should take whatever money is offered).

P2b, prediction   If the anger hypothesis is true, then when the second player is drunk—and so only focusing on the most salient cue in his or her environment—that player will reject unfair offers. That is, if the most salient cue is anger, the drunken player should act on that anger and reject offers perceived as unfair.

P3, data   Researchers found that, when drunk, the second player tended to reject any offer below 50 percent of the total.

P4   The data match the prediction from the anger hypothesis (the prediction in premise 2b) and do not match the prediction from the long-term strategy hypothesis (the prediction in premise 2a).

P5   The anger hypothesis seems to be the best explanation for the data. It is possible that, because the players were drunk, they did not fully understand the game. But turning down the money rather than taking it, which seems to indicate some amount of cognition, suggests that the players understood the task.

C   Therefore, the anger hypothesis is probably correct, and the long-term strategy hypothesis is probably false.

5. The argument is

P1, d_1   The vase is on the floor and broken.

P2, h_1   The cat knocked the vase off the table.

P3, h_2   There was an earthquake (in Florida) and it shook the building knocking the vase off the table.

P4, h_3   Someone broke into Michael's apartment, didn't take anything, but knocked over the vase.

C   Therefore, the cat knocked the vase off the table.

6. The argument is

P1, d_1   Jack's car stopped running.

P2, h_1   The car ran out of gas.

P3, h_2 Something else has gone wrong with the car—for instance, the fuel pump is broken, the fuel filter is clogged, or one of the car's sensors malfunctioned.

P4, h_3 Jack's car is equipped with OnStar, and, for some reason, that service thought that the car had been stolen and remotely stopped it.

C Therefore, the car ran out of gas.

7. (a) The data are, first, Sam tried out for the team and didn't make it; second, during the tryout, he bounced the ball off his foot during the dribbling drill, he traveled during the dribbling drill, he missed all ten of his free throws (six of which didn't even hit the basket), and, while playing defense, he grabbed the player with the ball by the arm and kicked the ball out of bounds.

   (b) Three hypotheses are given in the passage. The first two were proposed by Sam's mother and the third by Sam.

   h_1 Sam did not make the team because the coach does not like him.

   h_2 Sam did not make the team because he is too good to be on the junior varsity team.

   h_3 Sam did not make the team because his basketball skills and knowledge of the game are insufficient.

   (c) The third hypothesis, Sam didn't make the team because his basketball skills and knowledge of the game are insufficient, is the best explanation. This explanation fits (i.e., coheres) with all of the data. Incidentally, *insufficient skills and knowledge of the game* also explains why most people don't make sports teams, and so it has generality. The first two hypotheses can explain this datum: he tried out for the team and didn't make it. But that's it, and it appears that Sam's mother may not even be aware of the other data. Hence, the first and second hypotheses do not fit that well with the events that happened at the practice; in fact, the second hypothesis—he is too good to be on the junior varsity team—conflicts with those data.

8. (a) There are four hypotheses.

   h_1 John Clay wants to learn the pawnbroker business.

   h_2 John Clay has aims on a woman in Wilson's house.

h₃ John Clay wants to steal from Wilson's business or from his home.

h₄ John Clay wants to be in Wilson's house so that he can access something outside of the house.

(b) The best explanation of the datum, according to Holmes, is h_4; Clay wants to be in Wilson's house so that he can access something outside of the house. The second hypothesis is eliminated because there is no woman in the house. The third is ruled out by Wilson having only a small business and a modest home. The first is not quite so easily ruled out, although Holmes apparently never takes it seriously. There are auxiliary facts, however, that fail to cohere with h_1. People have a tendency to seek the highest wage that they can get, or, when they don't do that, it's because they find a particular job valuable in other ways—rewarding, enjoyable, or likely to have a much greater payoff in the future. But Clay, who is smart and capable, hasn't taken the highest wage that he can get, and his job does not appear rewarding, enjoyable, or likely to have a much greater payoff in the future. Meanwhile, if it is possible that Clay is devious (which it turns out that he is), then h_4 fits quite well with a smart and capable man taking a position as a pawnbroker's assistant for half the normal wage.

Coherence is the primary concept applied here, although between h_1 and h_4, it could also be argued that h_4 is simpler.

So, what did Clay want outside of this house? He needed access to Jabez Wilson's house so that he could tunnel from the cellar of that building to the nearby bank.

9. (a) What needs to be explained is how cholera spreads and, in particular, how Harnold and Blenkinsopp contracted it.

(b) The relevant data are:

d₁ In 1848, there had not been any cases of cholera in Great Britain for many years, but there was an outbreak in Hamburg, Germany.

d₂ John Harnold traveled from Hamburg to London, got a room in a lodging house in Horsleydown, came down with cholera, and died.

d₃ A few days after Harnold died, Blenkinsopp moved into Harnold's room. He contracted cholera.

(c) The two hypotheses are, first, the contagion model (which can be either Snow's or the vapor hypothesis) and, second, the miasma model—the poisonous vapor is sometimes in the air, but not given off by individuals suffering from cholera. In the second paragraph of the passage, it is argued that the miasma theory is an unsatisfactory explanation for the data.

If it is granted that the poisonous vapor suddenly appeared in the room, then the miasma theory can explain both men contracting cholera. That leaves unexplained why the poison appeared in that room, though, and it becomes a remarkable coincidence that Harnold, who had been in Hamburg where there was an outbreak of cholera, was the first person in Great Britain to be exposed to this poison and contract cholera.

According to Snow's theory, it is not a coincidence that Harnold was the first case of cholera in Great Britain. Harnold contracted cholera in Hamburg, came to London, and started displaying signs of cholera once in the room in Horsleydown. Blenkinsopp then became infected because some remnant of diarrhea (which Harnold would have been discharging at a severe rate before he died) remained in the room; Blenkinsopp inadvertently touched it, then touched some food and ingested the infectious agent.

10. (a) An explanation is needed for the object that appears next to Mercury in the images taken by the Heliospheric Imager-1.

   (b) The first hypothesis mentioned in the passage is that the object next to Mercury is a giant spaceship. The second hypothesis is that what appears to be an object is "the image of Mercury from the previous day" and it is in the images because of the way in which the images were processed.

   (c) The second hypothesis is the better explanation for the "object" in the image. The spaceship hypothesis is an explanation for the object itself, but this hypothesis does not fit well with the other relevant data. The images were processed before they were put online the passage reports, and the spaceship hypothesis conflicts with what is known about how the image processing works. (The artifact in the image is an expected result of manipulating the image so that the coronal ejection stands out.) The spaceship hypothesis also conflicts with the claim, made by Dr. Couper, that if the object was a spaceship, then, because of its size and relative proximity to Earth, it would have been noticed by scientists.

The second hypothesis is the simpler hypothesis insofar as it doesn't require the presence of a massive but hidden spaceship in our solar system. And it, of course, fits with the image having been processed.

Defenders of the spaceship hypothesis can claim, as the YouTube user siniXster does, that the spaceship is "cloaked" and that is why it has not been detected despite being so large and in our solar system. This only makes the hypothesis more complex, however. *Cloaked* must be explained, and the explanation has to include not just how the ship avoids being detected visually, but also how it avoids being detected by any other means—for instance, why it doesn't seem to be emitting any electromagnetic radiation and why its gravity is not affecting other objects. Perhaps such explanations can be given, but the result is going to be much less simple than the other hypothesis and it is still going to conflict with the fact that the image was processed so that the coronal ejection would be easily visible.

4 Mill's Methods

On April 6, 1907, the civil engineer and epidemiologist George Soper read a paper to the Biological Society of Washington, DC. It began:

> In the winter of 1906 I was called on to investigate a household epidemic of typhoid fever which had broken out in the latter part of August at Oyster Bay, N.Y. The epidemic had been studied carefully immediately after it took place, but its cause had not been ascertained with as much certainty as seemed desirable to the owner of the property.[1]

In a case like this, there is an event—for Soper, it was an outbreak of typhoid fever. That event has some cause, but that cause is, at the moment, unknown. This chapter focuses on several different methods that are used to infer the probable cause of such an event.

These methods were described and analyzed by the British philosopher John Stuart Mill (1806–1873) in his book *A System of Logic: Ratiocinative and Inductive*, first published in 1843. Since then, philosophers have noted various problems with Mill's analysis of these methods. But nonetheless, they are frequently used to determine the likely causes of various phenomena.

When considering causes and their effects, there are, broadly speaking, two types of investigations that can be undertaken. Sometimes a circumstance exists (i.e., a potential cause) and the task is to determine what effect or effects that circumstance has had. For example, if a block of radioactive uranium is left in the basement of an elementary school, it is reasonable to assume that the uranium is the cause of some specific set of effects. The task, then, is to identify those effects. This chapter focuses on the opposite sort of investigation: identifying the likely cause when the effect is already known, which was Soper's task when he investigated the typhoid fever outbreak in Oyster Bay.

---

1. George A. Soper, "The Work of a Chronic Typhoid Germ Distributor," *Journal of the American Medical Association* 48 (1907): 2019.

4.1   Necessary and Sufficient Conditions

Before looking at Mill's methods, we need to examine two concepts that Mill was not fully aware of, but which are useful for thinking about causes: the *necessary condition* and the *sufficient condition*. These terms are used in everyday discourse, and their colloquial meaning is pretty close the technical definitions given below. Before examining the definitions, though, consider two everyday uses of the terms.

Mary tells Jeff that going to every class is necessary to get an A in Introduction to Sociology. Mary probably means that, to get an A, Jeff has to go to every class, but Jeff will not get an A just by going to every class and doing nothing else. Going to every class is necessary, but other things—doing the reading, completing the assignments, studying—are necessary as well.

Next, Mary tells Claire that doing a good job on the final paper is sufficient to get an A in European History. In this case, Mary probably means that *just* doing a good job on the final paper will get Claire an A. Claire can make other efforts in this class, but she doesn't need to in order to get an A. Doing a good job on the final paper will suffice.

These two examples capture the basic idea of necessary and sufficient conditions. Going to every Introduction to Sociology class is a *necessary condition*, which means that going to every class has to occur in order to get the result (an A). But because it is only a necessary condition, going to every class cannot, on its own, bring about the result. In the second example, doing a good job on the final paper is a *sufficient condition*, which means that doing a good job on the final paper will, by itself, bring about the result (an A). Those are the basic ideas, but the concepts need precise definitions. Here is the definition of a necessary condition.

> C is a **necessary condition** for E when it is the case that if C does not occur, then E will not occur, and whenever E occurs, C has also occurred. (But C can occur when E does not.)

And these are some examples of necessary conditions:

- Having four sides is a necessary condition for being a square.
- Being at least thirty-five years old is a necessary condition for being President of the United States.
- The presence of oxygen is a necessary condition for combustion.

This is the definition for a sufficient condition:

C is a **sufficient condition** for E when it is the case that if C occurs, then E has to occur. (But E may occur when C does not.)

And these are some examples of sufficient conditions:

- Being divisible by ten is a sufficient condition for being an even number.
- Being human is a sufficient condition for being a mammal.
- Being guillotined is a sufficient condition for death.

Causes and effects can always be analyzed using necessary and sufficient conditions.[2] To bring about a particular effect, a sufficient condition must be present, and that sufficient condition can occur in one of three ways. (1) The sufficient condition can be sufficient, but not necessary. For example, drowning causes death; drowning is a sufficient condition, but not a necessary one for death. (2) The sufficient condition can be a necessary and sufficient condition. For example, being infected with the bacterium *Vibrio cholera* is a necessary condition and a sufficient condition for contracting cholera.

And (3), there can be a set of necessary conditions that are *jointly sufficient*. For instance, to create a (natural) rainbow,

(i) water droplets must be in the atmosphere,

(ii) sunlight must hit them at the correct angle, and

(iii) a viewer must be appropriately positioned.

Together, these necessary conditions are sufficient for creating a rainbow.

That being said, sometimes a condition that is necessary, but not by itself sufficient, is considered the cause of some event. For example, someone might say: "Having sex without using any form of birth control caused the pregnancy," even though having sex without using birth control is only a necessary condition for pregnancy.

More often, though, a necessary condition is considered simply a partial cause of an event. In the 1960 presidential election, John F. Kennedy won

---

2. It is also true, however, that necessary and sufficient conditions apply to cases where there is not a cause and an effect. For example, being a sister is a sufficient condition for being female, but being a sister does not cause a person to be female.

by receiving 303 Electoral College votes to Richard Nixon's 219. Hence, in that election, getting the most number of votes in New York State, and collecting that state's 45 Electoral College votes, was a necessary condition for winning the election—or, in other words, it was a partial cause.

4.1.1   Conditionals and Necessary and Sufficient Conditions

The conditional statement, which was introduced in chapter 1, can also be analyzed in terms of necessary and sufficient conditions. Recall that a conditional statement is one that has the form *If A, then B*. The *A* clause is the *antecedent*, and the *B* clause is the *consequent*. With respect to necessary and sufficient conditions:

> In a conditional statement, the antecedent is a sufficient condition for the consequent.

Consider these examples:

- If Kate went to her office, then she saw the letter.
- If Mary went to the store, then she got milk.
- If Marie was guillotined, then she is dead.

In a conditional statement, if the antecedent occurs, then the consequent has to occur. That's the same as saying that that the antecedent is a sufficient condition for the consequent. Thus,

- *Kate went to her office* is a sufficient condition for *Kate saw the letter.*
- *Mary went to the store* is a sufficient condition for *Mary got milk.*
- *Marie was guillotined* is a sufficient condition for *Marie is dead.*

Regarding the consequent,

> In a conditional statement, the consequent is a necessary condition for the antecedent.

This is also because when the antecedent occurs, then the consequent has to occur. Think about the general case: If *A*, then *B*. Every time that *A* occurs, *B* has to happen. And when *B* does not occur, then *A* cannot have occurred. That makes *B* a necessary condition for *A*.

Let's start with this example:

- If Jones is an aunt, then Jones is female.

Jones is female is a necessary condition for *Jones is an aunt*. If it is not the case that Jones is female, then it cannot be the case that Jones is an aunt.

And every time it is true that Jones is an aunt, it is also the case that Jones is a female.

- If Jones is an attorney, then Jones graduated from college.

In this example, *Jones graduated from college* is a necessary condition for *Jones is an attorney*, and the analysis is straightforward. If Jones did not graduate from college, then Jones cannot be an attorney. And for Jones to be an attorney, it must be that Jones graduated from college.

- If Amy won the election, then all of the sophomores voted for her.

Here, *all of the sophomores voted for Amy* is a necessary condition for *Amy won the election*. And the analysis of this example is the same as it was for the previous two.

The six examples used so far are designed to clearly illustrate that the antecedent is a sufficient condition and the consequent is a necessary condition. The same holds, however, no matter what the conditional statement is, although sometimes the analysis is a little bit less obvious. For instance:

- If Marie was guillotined, then she is dead.

Being guillotined is sufficient for death; that's obvious. But being dead (the consequent) is also a necessary condition for having been guillotined. (If, in the end, Marie doesn't end up dead, then she wasn't actually guillotined, even if someone tried. Other necessary conditions for being guillotined are (i) being beheaded and (ii) having that happen by the right kind of machine—i.e., a guillotine.)

And likewise for this example:

- If Jones is an aunt, then Jones is female.

It has already been explained that *Jones is female* is a necessary condition for *Jones is an aunt*. But also, *Jones is an aunt* is a sufficient condition for *Jones is female*—or it might be more natural to say: knowing that Jones is an aunt is a sufficient condition for knowing that Jones is female.

Relatedly, it's important to keep in mind that, in the end, for conditional statements what matters are the antecedent and the consequent, and that's it. In *if Jack is here, then Jill is here*, the antecedent, *Jack is here*, is a sufficient condition for *Jill is here*; the consequent, *Jill is here*, is a necessary condition for *Jack is here*; and the only way to figure that out is to note which is the antecedent and which is the consequent. If, instead, the sentence is *if Jill is here, then Jack is here,* then the reverse is true—*Jill is here* is a sufficient condition and *Jack is here* is a necessary condition.

4.2 Mill's First Three Methods

John Stuart Mill identified five different methods for finding the likely cause of an event. In this section, *the method of agreement, the method of difference,* and the *joint method of agreement and difference* are explained. With these three methods, the investigation begins with a set of possible causes, and, from that set, unlikely causes are eliminated and the probable cause is selected. Interestingly, no information about exactly how the cause operated is needed. We draw the conclusion simply by matching the presence or absence of the cause with the effect.

Using Mill's language, *antecedent circumstance* refers to a possible cause (antecedent because the cause has to precede the effect), and the *phenomenon* is the effect. For the set of antecedent circumstances, we include only the ones that seem to be relevant. In any situation, there are far too many possible causes to consider all of them, and so it has to be hoped that the real cause is among those in the selected set. But since that cannot be guaranteed, the conclusion is only probable, not certain.

4.2.1 The Method of Agreement
Mill states his first method, the method of agreement, this way:

> If two or more instances of the phenomenon under investigation have only one circumstance in common, the circumstance in which alone all the instances agree, is the cause ... of the given phenomenon.[3]

As an example of this method, consider the following situation. Jack, Jill, and Joan have lunch at a local diner. Afterward, all three have food poisoning. For lunch, they variously had (A) iced tea, (B) water, (C) chicken, (D) french fries, and (E) soup.

The method of agreement is used here because "two or more instances of the phenomenon under investigation have only one [antecedent] circumstance in common." As table 4.1 illustrates, the three cases of food

---

3. John Stuart Mill, *A System of Logic: Ratiocinative and Inductive,* 8th ed. (New York: Harper, 1882), 280.

Mill's Methods 105

Table 4.1
An example for the method of agreement

Cases	Antecedent Circumstances					Phenomenon
	A	B	C	D	E	
Jack	present	—	—	present	present	present
Jill	present	present	present	present	—	present
Joan	—	present	present	present	—	present

poisoning (the phenomenon) have only D—the french fries—in common. All of the other antecedent circumstances are, at times, absent when the phenomenon is present. For instance, Joan got food poisoning even though she didn't have the iced tea (A), and so having the iced tea is eliminated as a possible cause. Likewise for B, C, and E. Since the cause is, probably, the one antecedent circumstance that matches all occurrences of the phenomenon, D is identified as the likely cause.

The information provided in the table belongs in the premises of the argument, which are written this way:

P1 For Jack, antecedent circumstances A, D, and E are present, and the phenomenon is present.

P2 For Jill, antecedent circumstances A, B, C, and D are present, and the phenomenon is present.

P3 For Joan, antecedent circumstances B, C, and D are present, and the phenomenon is present.

And then this is the conclusion, drawn using the method of agreement:

C Therefore, circumstance D (the french fries) probably caused the phenomenon (the food poisoning).

argument (1)

4.2.2 The Method of Difference

If an instance in which the phenomenon under investigation occurs, and an instance in which it does not occur, have every circumstance in common save one, that one occurring only in the former; the circumstance in which alone the two instances differ is ... the cause ... of the phenomenon.[4]

---

4. Mill, *A System of Logic*, 280.

As Mill would have it, the method of difference is used when there are two
cases to examine, and, between the two cases, the antecedent circumstances
are the same in every way except one. For instance, as they are in table 4.2.
Jack and Jill are identical with respect to antecedent circumstances A, B,
D, and E. The first, A, is absent for both of them, and the other three—B,
D, and E—are present for both of them. They are not identical, however,
with respect to the phenomenon. Jack has it and Jill does not. And the one
antecedent circumstance that matches that pattern is C.

Thus, the conclusion is

  C   Therefore, circumstance C probably caused the phenomenon.

argument (2)

The method of difference can be broadened from what Mill intended,
however, by defining it this way:

> An antecedent condition is the cause when (i) there is one case in which that
> antecedent circumstance is present and the phenomenon is also present, and
> (ii) there are one or more cases in which the phenomenon *does not* occur and
> that antecedent circumstance also *does not* occur.

Now a scenario like the one in table 4.3 can be analyzed using the method
of difference. Here, A, C, D, and E are eliminated because they are present
when the phenomenon is absent. B, on the other hand, is present when

Table 4.2
Method of difference example

Cases	A	B	C	D	E	Phenomenon
Jack	—	present	present	present	present	present
Jill	—	present	—	present	present	—

Table 4.3
A second example of the method of difference

Cases	A	B	C	D	E	Phenomenon
Jack	—	—	present	—	present	—
Jill	present	present	present	—	—	present
Joan	present	—	—	present	present	—

the phenomenon is present and absent when it is absent. Listed as premises and a conclusion, this is the argument:

P1 For Jack, antecedent circumstances C and E are present, and the phenomenon is absent.

P2 For Jill, antecedent circumstances A, B, and C are present, and the phenomenon is present.

P3 For Joan, antecedent circumstances A, D, and E are present, and the phenomenon is absent.

C Therefore, circumstance B probably caused the phenomenon.

argument (3)

4.2.3 Necessary and Sufficient Conditions Again

The method of agreement and the method of difference are used to identify different types of causes. The method of agreement identifies a cause that is a necessary condition for the effect, and the method of difference identifies a cause that is a sufficient condition. It is worth being mindful, however, that, insofar as the phenomenon occurred, all of the necessary conditions and a sufficient condition were present—although all are, perhaps, not included in the set of antecedent circumstances being examined. What the method of agreement does is eliminate antecedent events that cannot be necessary conditions and identifies one that can be. The method of difference, meanwhile, eliminates antecedent events that cannot be sufficient conditions and identifies one that can be.

Recall that, for a necessary condition, the phenomenon is present only when the necessary condition is present. Consider the example in table 4.1. A, B, C, and E cannot be necessary conditions for the phenomenon because they are all absent at times when the phenomenon occurs. Since D is present, every time that the phenomenon occurs, D can be a necessary condition for the phenomenon.

But to be more certain that the cause is a necessary one, the situation must look something like the one in table 4.4. As Mill says in his definition, the method of agreement uses only those cases where the phenomenon (i.e., the effect) is present. If there are any cases where the phenomenon is absent, those cases are set aside. Thus, in table 4.4, it's not a problem that circumstance D, the likely cause, is present for Kate, but the phenomenon is not. Rather, this clearly illustrates that the method of agreement identifies a

Table 4.4
An example in which the method of agreement is used to identify the likely cause.

	Antecedent Circumstances					
Cases	A	B	C	D	E	Phenomenon
Tom	—	present	—	present	—	present
Phil	present	—	—	present	present	present
Mary	present	—	present	present	—	present
Kate	—	present	present	present	—	—

Table 4.5
In this example, the method of difference is used to identity two causes, both of which are sufficient conditions.

	Antecedent Circumstances					
Cases	A	B	C	D	E	Phenomenon
Tom	present	—	present	present	—	present
Phil	present	—	present	—	present	—
Mary	—	present	—	—	—	present
Kate	—	—	present	—	—	—

necessary condition. A necessary condition has to be present for the effect to occur, but it cannot, by itself, bring about the effect. It can, therefore, be present at times when the effect is not. Moreover, the presence of D when the effect is absent makes it clear that D cannot be a sufficient condition.

Now consider the example in table 4.3. For a sufficient condition, the phenomenon is always present when the sufficient condition is present, and the sufficient condition is never present when the phenomenon is not. None of A, C, D, or E can be a sufficient condition for the phenomenon because they are all present at times when the phenomenon is absent. B can be a sufficient condition because, when it is present, the phenomenon is always present. (Or stated differently: B is never present when the phenomenon is absent.) But, again, a slightly different scenario, like the one in table 4.5, illustrates unequivocally that the method of difference identifies a sufficient condition—or, actually, two sufficient conditions.

Here B and D are both probable causes of the phenomenon. Neither, however, can be a necessary condition because, at times, the phenomenon is present when each one is absent. But, when each one is present, the phenomenon is also present. Hence, they are both sufficient conditions.

Moreover, A cannot be a necessary condition for the phenomenon because it is absent when the phenomenon occurs (in the case of Mary), and it cannot be a sufficient condition because it is present, in the case of Phil, when the phenomenon is absent. And the same holds for C and E.

4.2.4   The Joint Method of Agreement and Difference

Mill's third method, the joint method of agreement and difference, in essence joins the method of agreement and the method of difference. In Mill's words:

> If two or more instances in which the phenomenon occurs have only one
> circumstance in common, while two or more instances in which it does not
> occur have nothing in common save the absence of that circumstance, the
> circumstance in which alone the two sets of instances differ, is ... the cause ...
> of the phenomenon.[5]

According to the joint method, the probable cause is the one antecedent circumstance that is always present when the phenomenon is present and always absent when the phenomenon is absent. For instance, in table 4.6, when the phenomenon occurs, only D is always present, and when the phenomenon is absent, only D is always absent. So, using the joint method of agreement and difference, this conclusion is drawn:

   C   Therefore, circumstance D is probably the cause of the phenomenon.

argument (4)

As might be guessed from the analysis in the previous section, the joint method identifies a cause that is both a necessary condition and a sufficient

Table 4.6
Example for the joint method of agreement and difference.

Cases	Antecedent Circumstances					Phenomenon
	A	B	C	D	E	
Jack	present	—	—	present	present	present
Jill	present	present	present	present	—	present
Joan	—	—	present	—	—	—
Erika	present	present	—	—	—	—
Ellen	—	present	present	present	present	present
Emma	—	—	—	—	present	—

5. Mill, *A System of Logic*, 284.

condition for the phenomenon. Notice that A, B, C, and E cannot be sufficient conditions for the phenomenon because they are all present at times when the phenomenon is absent. And A, B, C, and E cannot be necessary conditions because they are all absent at times when the phenomenon is present. D can be a necessary condition because the phenomenon occurs only when D is present; and D can be a sufficient condition because whenever D is present, the phenomenon occurs.

4.3 Typhoid Mary

Now back to Soper's investigation. The house in Oyster Bay had been rented for the summer of 1906 by a New York City banker. Between August 27 and September 3, six of the eleven individuals in the household contracted typhoid fever, a life-threatening disease marked by high fever, weakness, stomach pain, and sometimes a rash. Those six were infected even though typhoid fever was rare in Oyster Bay and no other cases occurred there that summer.

When Soper arrived, he first considered the possibility that the typhoid fever had been introduced by the milk or cream that the household had purchased. He found, however, that

> the milk supply of this house was the same as used by most of the other persons in the village, all of whom remained well. The cream also was from a source which supplied several other families in the vicinity.[6]

Next Soper tested the water supply. After that turned up no evidence of contamination:

> My suspicion for a time attached to clams. It was found that soft clams had frequently been obtained in the summer from an old Indian woman who lived in a tent on the beach not far from the house. It was impossible to find this woman, but I made inspections of the sources of soft clams at Oyster Bay, which showed that they were sometimes taken from places where they were polluted with sewage.[7]

Again, this led to a dead end. Soper reports:

> But if clams had been responsible for the outbreak it did not seem clear why the fever should have been confined to this house. Soft clams form a very common

---

6. Soper, "The Work of a Chronic Typhoid Germ Distributor," 2019.
7. Soper, "The Work of a Chronic Typhoid Germ Distributor," 2020.

article of diet among the native inhabitants of Oyster Bay. On inquiring closely into the question of the food eaten before the outbreak it was eventually found that no clams had been eaten subsequent to July 15. This removed the possibility that the epidemic had been caused by clams.[8]

The next two possibilities that Soper considered were equally unsuccessful.

The supplies of vegetables and fruit were next considered. It was found that the persons attacked had not eaten any raw fruit or vegetables which had not also been eaten by many persons who escaped the fever. ... Attention was now concentrated for a time on the first cases to determine whether the infection could have occurred during a temporary absence from Oyster Bay. It was found that those persons who were taken sick at the outset had not been on a visit, or picnic, or, in fact, away from Oyster Bay on any account for several weeks prior to the onset of the illness.[9]

Finally, Soper's attention turned to any changes that may have occurred to the household itself right before the first case of typhoid fever.

It was found that the family had changed cooks on August 4. This was about three weeks before the typhoid epidemic broke out. A cook who had been with the family several years had been discharged and a new one employed. Little was known about the new cook's history. She had been engaged at an employment bureau which gave her an excellent recommendation. She remained in the family only a short time, leaving about three weeks after the outbreak of typhoid occurred. Her present whereabouts were unknown. The cook was described as an Irish woman about 40 years of age, tall, heavy, single. She seemed to be in perfect health.[10]

Now Soper had an antecedent circumstance that all of the individuals who had contracted typhoid fever had in common—they ate food prepared by this cook. And this antecedent condition was not shared by anyone else in Oyster Bay, none of whom contracted typhoid fever. However, not everyone who ate the cook's food contracted typhoid fever. Of the eleven, there were five people in the household who, for reasons unknown, escaped the infection.

Examining table 4.7 reveals that neither the milk, nor the cream, nor the vegetables and fruit can be a sufficient condition for the typhoid fever.

8. Soper, "The Work of a Chronic Typhoid Germ Distributor," 2020.
9. Soper, "The Work of a Chronic Typhoid Germ Distributor," 2020.
10. Soper, "The Work of a Chronic Typhoid Germ Distributor," 2021.

Table 4.7
Possible causes of typhoid fever in Oyster Bay during the summer of 1906.

Cases				*Antecedent Circumstances*			
	milk	cream	clams	vegetables and fruit	absent from Oyster Bay	ate the cook's food	*typhoid fever*
daughter 1	yes	yes	no	yes	no	yes	yes
daughter 2	yes	yes	no	yes	no	yes	yes
wife	yes	yes	no	yes	no	yes	yes
maid 1	yes	yes	no	yes	no	yes	yes
maid 2	yes	yes	no	yes	no	yes	yes
gardener	yes	yes	no	yes	no	yes	yes
five others in the household	yes	yes	no	yes	no	yes	no
other people in Oyster Bay	yes	yes	yes	yes	probably	no	no

All were present in cases where the typhoid fever was not. Moreover, the clams and the absence from Oyster Bay cannot be anything—they do not match up at all with the typhoid fever. Eating the cook's food can be a necessary condition because, in every case where there was an incidence of typhoid fever, the person had eaten the cook's food. But based on the information in the table, it can only be a necessary condition. Eating the cook's food cannot be a sufficient condition because of the five individuals who (presumably) ate the cook's food but did not contract typhoid fever. The milk, the cream, and the vegetables and fruit have not been eliminated as necessary conditions either. Thus, any one of these conclusions is warranted:

C   Therefore, the milk probably caused this outbreak of typhoid fever.

C   Therefore, the cream probably caused this outbreak of typhoid fever.

C   Therefore, the vegetables and fruit probably caused this outbreak of typhoid fever.

C   Therefore, the cook probably caused this outbreak of typhoid fever.

But considering the evidence on its own merits suggests that the cook is much more likely to be a significant partial cause than any of the other antecedent circumstances. After all, even if some other necessary condition had to be present in addition to the milk, the cream, or the vegetables and fruit, there was ample chance that the condition would have been present for some other resident of Oyster Bay. Since there were no other outbreaks, it seems unlikely that any of these could have been, in any way, a partial cause. Thus, tentatively, this is the best conclusion:

C   Therefore, the cook probably caused this outbreak of typhoid fever.

argument (5)

Argument (5)—the conclusion about the cook plus the information in table 4.7—uses the method of agreement. The antecedent circumstance *the cook prepared the food* is always present when the effect, typhoid fever, is present. (Because *the cook prepared the food* is also present when the effect is absent, the joint method of agreement and difference is not the method used for this inference.)

With this conclusion about the cook in mind, Soper tracked her down in New York City. Unfortunately, she was uncooperative.

> She refused to speak to me or any one about herself or her history except on matters which she knew were already well known. It became necessary to work out the cook's history without her help. This effort has been only partially satisfactory. Her whereabouts for only a part of the time in the last ten years have been ascertained. About two years of time among the last five years remain unaccounted for. In the last ten years she has worked for eight families to my positive knowledge; in seven of these typhoid has followed her. She has always escaped in the epidemics with which she has been connected.[11]

This information is used to form a second argument. In this, the seven households that experienced typhoid fever have the antecedent circumstance *employed the cook* in common.

The seven affected households did have other circumstances in common as well. All were large wealthy families, and all employed five to seven servants. And, no doubt, there could have been other antecedent circumstances that they all shared. But the presence of the cook is a good candidate for the cause, and so this conclusion is warranted:

C   The cook is probably the cause of these outbreaks of typhoid fever.

argument (6)

This inference is, again, made using the method of agreement. In every case where typhoid fever occurred, the cook is present. This demonstrates that the cook is a necessary but not a sufficient condition for typhoid fever. (Probably, another necessary condition was that the victim consume

---

11. Soper, "The Work of a Chronic Typhoid Germ Distributor," 2021.

Table 4.8
The cook and typhoid fever.

	Antecedent Circumstances		
Cases	...	employed the cook	typhoid fever
Mamaroneck household (1900)		yes	yes
New York City household (1901)		yes	yes
Dark Harbor household (1902)		yes	yes
Sands Point household (1904)		yes	yes
Oyster Bay household (1906)		yes	yes
Tuxedo Park household (1906)		yes	yes
New York City household (1907)		yes	yes
"this family ... of two people of advanced age and one servant"		yes	no

Soper, "The Work of a Chronic Typhoid Germ Distributor," 2022.

something prepared by the cook and served raw.) Since the cause is a necessary condition, it does not matter that there was one household where the cook was employed, but there were no occurrences of typhoid fever.

The general medical officer of the New York City Department of Health accepted the conclusion of Soper's second argument. The cook was taken into custody and her blood, urine, and stool were tested for the bacterium that causes typhoid fever. The stool sample was positive. Although she was healthy, she was a carrier of *Salmonella typhi*. And the cook, Mary Mallon, has ever since been known as Typhoid Mary.

4.4   Mill's Fourth and Fifth Methods

Mill's final two methods, *the method of residues* and *the method of concomitant variations*, are a little bit different from the three methods so far discussed. These methods identify causes, but they track the relevant information in different ways.

4.4.1   The Method of Residues

Subduct [i.e., subtract] from any phenomenon such part as is known by previous inductions to be the effect of certain antecedents, and the residue of the phenomenon is the effect of the remaining antecedents.[12]

---

12. Mill, *A System of Logic*, 285.

For the method of residues to be used, first, different kinds of causes for a certain type of phenomenon must already be known. Second, some of the occurrences of the phenomenon must be attributable to some of those causes. Then, using this method, it is inferred that the remaining occurrences of the phenomenon resulted from the remaining cause. For example, HIV, the virus that causes AIDS, is transmitted by several different means:

(i)   having sex with someone who is infected;
(ii) receiving a blood transfusion or blood product that is contaminated with the virus;
(iii) sharing a needle with someone who is infected; or
(iv) for infants, receiving the virus from an infected mother during pregnancy or birth, or when breastfeeding.

Now, imagine that in some city 55 percent of new HIV infections are known to have been caused by individuals having sex with someone who has HIV, 15 percent are known to have been caused by sharing needles, and 10 percent are known to have been caused by contaminated blood supplies and blood products. That's 80 percent of the city's new HIV infections. It can then be concluded that 20 percent of new HIV infections were caused by mothers infecting their babies.

The basic format for an argument using the method of residues is shown in argument (7). The portions do not, however, have to be represented as percentages, and there can be as many different causes (and premises) as needed.

P1   A, B, C, and D can all cause phenomenon E.
P2   A caused w percent of the cases of E.
P3   B caused x percent of the cases of E.
P4   C caused y percent of the cases of E.
C   Therefore, D caused the remaining z percent of the cases of E.

argument (7)

One famous application of the method of residues is the discovery, by Marie Curie (1867–1934), of the elements polonium and radium in 1898. One year before the discovery, Curie had begun investigating radioactivity, a newly discovered property that was initially thought to belong only to uranium. Using a new procedure for measuring levels of radioactivity, she examined pitchblende, a mineral mostly composed of uranium. Curie found, however, that pitchblende was several times more radioactive than pure uranium. She concluded that pitchblende must contain a radioactive element besides the uranium. Written out, Curie's argument looks like this:

P1   Pitchblende, which contains uranium and other elements, produces x amount of radiation.

P2   Pure uranium produces y amount of radiation.

C   Therefore, another element in pitchblende must produce x minus y amount of radiation.

argument (8)

Further work by her and her husband, Pierre Curie, revealed two previously unknown elements: polonium (named for Marie Curie's native Poland) and radium.

4.4.2   The Method of Concomitant Variations

Whatever phenomenon varies in any manner whenever another phenomenon varies in some particular manner, is either a cause or an effect of that phenomenon, or is connected with it through some fact of causation.[13]

The method of concomitant variations is similar to the method of agreement except that, for this method, the agreement is quantitative. The cause and effect are not just always present together, they also vary together—typically, they rise and fall together. And while the cause and effect are, at different times, present at different levels, neither is ever entirely absent. Here is an argument that uses the method of concomitant variations and data compiled by the Centers for Disease Control and Prevention.[14]

P1   For the period from 1928 to 2007, suicide rates among 25- to 64-year-olds were highest in 1932, which was during the lowest period of the Great Depression.

P2   For the period from 1928 to 2007, suicide rates among 25- to 64-year-olds were high during the 1973–1975 oil crisis and the 1980–1982 recession.

---

13. Mill, *A System of Logic*, 287.

14. Centers for Disease Control and Prevention, "CDC Study Finds Suicide Rates Rise and Fall with Economy," April 14, 2011, http://www.cdc.gov/media/releases/2011/p0414_suiciderates.html; Feijun Luo et al., "Impact of Business Cycles on US Suicide Rates, 1928–2007," *American Journal of Public Health* 101 (2011): 1139–1146.

P3   For the period from 1928 to 2007, suicide rates among 25- to 64-year-olds were lowest in 2000, which was near the end of the dot-com boom.

P4   For the period from 1928 to 2007, suicide rates among 25- to 64-year-olds were low when the economy was growing during World War II and during 1991 to 2001.

C   Therefore, the state of the economy and the suicide rate are probably causally related.

argument (9.1)

The US economy is always present (as long as the United States is in existence). And likewise for suicides in the United States; they are always present at some level. So while neither can ever be suspended, both increase and decrease. The method of concomitant variations is used to make an inference based on those changes.

This method is used to infer that two events are causally related, but it is always possible that, although they vary together, there is no causal relationship between them. It could be that there is a third event that is, directly or indirectly, causing both of them, and so the two events occur at about the same time even though neither one is the cause of the other. Or it may be that varying together is just a coincidence. Furthermore, even if the two events are causally related, this method is not designed to indicate which one is the cause and which is the effect. With the other methods, the occurrence of the antecedent circumstance prior to the occurrence of the phenomenon indicates which one is the cause (since the cause has to come before the effect). When using the method of concomitant variations, however, it is often not possible to tell which event occurs first; both are just present at the time of measurement.

That being said, even if one event cannot be observed occurring before another, with some care it is sometimes possible to make a conjecture about which of two events is the cause and which is the effect. In the argument above, it seems reasonable to assume that the state of the economy is the cause and the suicide rates are the effect, which makes the conclusion of the argument:

C   Therefore, the state of the economy is a cause or partial cause of many suicides.

argument (9.2)

4.5 Exercises

For questions 1 through 13, complete the sentence with *necessary, sufficient,* or *necessary and sufficient.*

1. Igniting a mixture of nitroglycerin and sawdust is a _____ condition for creating an explosion.

2. A source of fuel is a _____ condition for an internal combustion engine to run.

3. Placing a block of ice in a bucket of warm water is a _____ condition for melting the ice.

4. Throwing a brick through a glass window pane is a _____ condition for breaking the glass.

5. Scoring the most number of points is a _____ condition for winning the basketball game.

6. Having two wheels is a _____ condition for being a bicycle.

7. Leaving aside the first few mammals, a _____ condition for being a mammal is that both parents are mammals.

8. Wearing a costume on October 31 is a _____ condition for celebrating Halloween. Explain your answer.

9. Use this statement: *If Mary went to the store, then she got milk* to complete this sentence:

    Mary went to the store is a _____ condition for Mary got milk.

10. Use this statement: *If someone is a doctor, then that person went to medical school* to complete this sentence:

    Having gone to medical school is a _____ condition for being a doctor.

11. Use this statement: *If someone is a doctor, then that person went to medical school, and if someone went to medical school, then that person is a doctor* to complete this sentence:

    Going to medical school is a _____ condition for being a doctor.

12. Use this statement: *If the vase broke, then it was fragile* to complete this sentence:

    The vase was fragile is a _____ condition for it breaking.

13. Use this statement: *If the police find bloody clothes in Jeff's apartment, then he will be arrested for the murder* to complete this sentence:

Finding bloody clothes in Jeff's apartment is a _____ condition for arresting him for the murder.

14. Based on the information in table 4.9, what is the likely cause of contracting head lice, being at school, in the gym, at the airport, in the theater, or in the diner? Is this cause a necessary condition, a sufficient condition, or a necessary and sufficient condition for contracting head lice?

15. Based on the information in table 4.10, what is the likely cause of contracting Bolivian hemorrhagic fever, being in the gym, the basement, the garden, the car, or on the bus? Is this cause a necessary condition, a sufficient condition, or a necessary and sufficient condition for contracting Bolivian hemorrhagic fever?

16. Based on the information in table 4.11, what is the likely cause of contracting Rocky Mountain spotted fever? Is this cause a necessary condition, a sufficient condition, or a necessary and sufficient condition for contracting Rocky Mountain spotted fever ?

Table 4.9

Cases	Antecedent Circumstances					*head lice*
	school	gym	airport	theater	diner	
Jeff	yes	yes	—	yes	—	yes
Claire	yes	—	yes	yes	—	—
Mary	yes	—	—	—	yes	—

Table 4.10

Cases	Antecedent Circumstances					*Bolivian hemorrhagic fever*
	gym	basement	garden	car	bus	
Elena	yes	yes	yes	yes	—	yes
Tony	—	—	yes	yes	—	yes
Mateo	yes	—	yes	—	yes	yes

Table 4.11

Cases	Antecedent Circumstances					Rocky Mountain spotted fever
	locker room	basketball court	pool	school	diner	
Jeff	yes	yes	—	yes	—	yes
Jon	—	—	—	yes	—	—
Phil	yes	yes	—	—	yes	yes
Tom	yes	—	yes	—	yes	yes
Mike	—	—	—	yes	yes	—

Table 4.12

Cases	Antecedent Circumstances					trench fever
	hospital	homeless shelter	park	school	gym	
Mateo	yes	yes	—	yes	—	yes
Kiley	—	—	yes	yes	—	—
Elena	—	yes	—	yes	yes	yes
Charlotte	—	—	yes	yes	—	yes
Jack	yes	yes	—	yes	yes	yes

Table 4.13

Cases	Antecedent Circumstances					food poisoning
	coffee	soup	salad	pasta	turkey	
Willie	yes	yes	—	yes	—	—
Morgan	yes	—	yes	yes	—	yes
Stuart	yes	yes	—	—	yes	—

17. Based on the information in table 4.12, what is the likely cause of contracting trench fever? Is this cause a necessary condition, a sufficient condition, or a necessary and sufficient condition for contracting trench fever?

18. Based on the information in table 4.13, what conclusion can be drawn about the cause of the food poisoning? Which of Mill's methods is used to draw this conclusion?

19. Based on the information in table 4.14, what conclusion can be drawn about the cause of the food poisoning? Which of Mill's methods is used to draw this conclusion?

Table 4.14

Cases	Antecedent Circumstances					food poisoning
	iced tea	water	soup	chicken	lasagna	
Joshua	yes	yes	—	yes	—	yes
Matthew	yes	—	yes	—	yes	yes
Kiley	yes	yes	yes	—	yes	yes

Table 4.15

Cases	Antecedent Circumstances					food poisoning
	water	iced tea	salad	chicken	tuna	
Sarah	—	yes	—	yes	—	—
Amy	yes	—	yes	yes	—	yes
Kate	—	yes	—	—	yes	—
Omar	—	yes	yes	—	yes	—
Sam	—	yes	yes	yes	—	—

Table 4.16

Cases	Antecedent Circumstances					food poisoning
	iced tea	coffee	pasta	fish	steak	
Jeff	—	yes	—	yes	—	—
Claire	yes	—	yes	—	—	yes
Erika	—	—	—	—	yes	—
Mary	yes	—	yes	—	—	yes
Omar	—	yes	yes	—	—	yes
Tom	yes	—	—	—	yes	—

20. Based on the information in table 4.15, what conclusion can be drawn about the cause of the food poisoning? Which of Mill's methods is used to draw this conclusion?

21. Based on the information in table 4.16, what conclusion can be drawn about the cause of the food poisoning? What method is used to draw this conclusion?

22. Based on the information in table 4.17, what conclusion can be drawn about the cause of the food poisoning? What method is used to draw this conclusion?

Table 4.17

Cases	Antecedent Circumstances					
	water	wine	salad	salmon	steak	food poisoning
Sarah	yes	yes	yes	yes	—	—
Josh	yes	yes	yes	yes	—	yes
Mike	yes	—	yes	—	—	yes
Matt	—	—	yes	—	yes	yes

23. A set of identical twins, Jill and Jane, go to a restaurant. They both order salad, pasta, and ice cream. Jill orders the soup, and Jane does not. Later Jill contracts shigellosis, and Jane does not.

    Create a table for this information about Jill and Jane. What is the probable cause of the shigellosis? What method is used to identify that cause?

24. Write out the argument contained in this passage. What method is used to draw the conclusion?

    Although it was January and Tom lived in Maine, his apartment was very hot: 104 degrees. He knew that some of the heat was a result of the cooking that he had been doing all day. Some of the heat was the result of the radiators, which were broken and stuck on high. And some of the heat was from the traditional Finnish sauna that his wife had built in their spare bedroom. The next day, Tom didn't do any cooking, fixed the radiators and turned them off, and turned off the stove in the sauna. Although his apartment was not hot anymore, it was still pretty warm: 78 degrees. Tom figured that this was the result of heat from the apartment below his, which was occupied by an elderly couple who had just moved from Arizona.

25. Create a table that contains the information in the following passage. Based on this information, what conclusion can be drawn? Which of Mill's methods is used to draw this conclusion?

    A small apartment building has six elderly residents: Sarah, Amy, Kate, Chris, Omar, and Sam. Three of them—Sarah, Kate, and Omar—have a rare form of cancer. All six of the residents have worked several different jobs in the past, and it is likely that the cancer resulted from an exposure at one of the jobs.

    Right out of college, Sarah, Amy, and Chris worked in a factory manufacturing asbestos. After a number of years there, Sarah left and went to work in a uranium mine. Sometime later, Sarah and Kate found jobs at a factory that manufactured biological weapons. Just as Sarah and Kate were getting started at the bio-weapons factory, Chris and Omar began working in a small factory painting toys with lead-based paint. A few years after that, Kate left her factory job and went to work in the uranium mine, Sam decided to take a job in the small factory painting toys with lead-based paint, and Amy went to work in the factory that manufactured biological weapons. Many years later, Omar became dissatisfied with the toy-painting job and left to work in the uranium mine. At the same time Kate was beginning a new job in the radiology department at a large hospital. Finally, at the end of their careers, Amy and Omar worked together in a library, Sam worked for a company that repaired cell-phone towers, and Sarah and Chris worked in the radiology department at the large hospital.

26. Create a table that contains the information in the following passage. Based on this information, what conclusion can be drawn? Which of Mill's methods is used to draw this conclusion?

On a Tuesday morning, Jeff shows up in the emergency room with an unusual type of infection on his arm. Two days later, Claire goes to the emergency room and doctors find the same infection on her leg. After some investigation, it turns out that Jeff and Claire both live in the same apartment building. It is a small building, and, besides Jeff and Claire, there are four other residents: Jack, Tom, Nicole, and Mary. All six residents have their own apartment. The doctors believe that the cause of the infection is probably somewhere in the apartment building, and so they search it thoroughly.

In Jeff's apartment, they find a significant amount of mold in the kitchen and bathroom; they also find a gas leak. In Jack's apartment, they find ticks and another gas leak. In Tom's apartment, there is the mold, a rat's nest that looks new, and the ticks. Nicole's apartment has the ticks and a gas leak. Mary's has a rat's nest, some of the mold, and the ticks.

While Mary's apartment is being searched, Tom and Nicole go to the emergency room with the same infection. When Claire's apartment is examined, the doctors find mold in the kitchen and several fresh-looking rats' nests. As they are leaving, the doctors notice that leading up to the rear door of the apartment building are stairs covered with pigeon droppings. They return inside to question the remaining residents. Jack says that he regularly uses the back door and Tom and Claire do also. While they are inside Jack's apartment, the doctors see some mold in his apartment that they hadn't noticed before. They then knock on Mary's door. She limps to the door and shows the doctors the infection on her ankle. She tells them that she doesn't use the back door, and she is sure that Nicole and Jeff don't either. Before the doctors leave—with Mary now in tow—they return to Nicole's apartment, which somehow in all of the commotion was left unlocked. They look around again and find a little bit of the mold and a rat's nest.

27. Write out the argument contained in the passage below. This is the first premise:

> **P1** The density of snags was three times higher in stands with no history of timber harvest (compared to stands that had been selectively harvested for timber).

Which of Mill's methods is used in this argument?

> Many species of vertebrates depend on snags (standing dead trees) for persistence, and limited research suggests that snag density is lower in areas of intensive timber harvest and increased human access. While intensive timber harvest is one source of potential snag loss, ease of human access to forest stands may also facilitate loss via firewood cutting of snags. Accordingly, we hypothesized that density of snags (number of snags per hectare) would decline in forest stands with increasing intensity of timber harvest and increasing ease of human access. We tested our hypothesis by sampling stands [*def.* stand: a group of trees], under varying levels of timber harvest and access, on National Forest land in the northwestern United States. Stands with no history of timber harvest had 3 times the density of snags as stands selectively harvested, and 19 times the density as stands having undergone complete harvest. Stands not adjacent to roads had almost 3 times the density of snags as stands adjacent to roads. Unharvested stands adjacent to non-federal lands and closer to towns had lower snag density, as did stands with flat terrain in relation to the nearest road. Our findings demonstrate that timber harvest and human access can have substantial effects on snag density.

28.   Jeff's boat can hold up to 450 pounds safely. If the weight of the passengers and their stuff exceeds 450 pounds, the boat will begin to take on water. Sunday morning Jeff, who weighs 190 pounds, Jon, who weighs 210 pounds, and Jon's dog, Rascal, who weighs 40 pounds, all got into the boat. Right before they were about to take off, Jeff remembered the cooler full of sandwiches and drinks. He retrieved the cooler from his car, put it in the boat, and they took off. Immediately the boat began to sink.

What conclusion can be drawn about the weight of the cooler? Write out the whole argument. Which of Mill's methods is used here?

29. Based on the information in this passage, what conclusion can be drawn? Which of Mill's methods is used to draw this conclusion?

> It is scarcely necessary to give examples of a logical process to which we owe almost all the inductive conclusions we draw in daily life. When a man is shot through the heart, it is by this method we know that it was the

gun-shot which killed him: for he was in the fullness of life immediately before, all circumstances being the same except the wound.[15]

30.   Let us now suppose the question to be, what influence the moon exerts on the surface of the earth. We cannot try an experiment in the absence of the moon, so as to observe what terrestrial phenomena her annihilation would put an end to; but when we find that all the variations in the position of the moon are followed by corresponding variations in the time and place of high water, the place being always either the part of the earth which is nearest to, or that which is most remote from, the moon, we have ample evidence that the moon is, wholly or partially, the cause which determines the tides.[16]

Based on the information in this passage, what conclusion can be drawn? Which of Mill's methods is used to draw this conclusion?

Source

Michael J. Wisdom and Lisa J. Bate. "Snag Density Varies with Intensity of Timber Harvest and Human Access." *Forest Ecology and Management* 255 (2008): 2085–2093.

4.6 Answers

1. Sufficient condition

2. Necessary condition

3. Sufficient condition

4. Sufficient condition

5. Necessary and sufficient condition

6. Necessary condition

7. Necessary and sufficient condition

8. This has more than one correct answer—in fact, with the proper explanation, any answer is correct.

    A sufficient condition is, probably, the most likely answer. This means that if someone is in a costume on October 31, then that person is celebrating Halloween. If it is just a sufficient condition, though—and not a necessary and sufficient condition—then a person can celebrate

---

15. Mill, *A System of Logic*, 280.
16. Mill, *A System of Logic*, 287.

Halloween without putting on a costume as long as some other sufficient condition is satisfied—for instance, perhaps displaying a carved
pumpkin.

Wearing a costume could also be a necessary condition for celebrating
Halloween. This means that a person cannot be celebrating Halloween
unless he or she is in a costume. But if it is only a necessary condition—
and not a necessary and sufficient condition—then, to be celebrating
Halloween, some other action must also be taken (e.g., displaying a
carved pumpkin or giving out candy).

Finally, if this is a necessary and sufficient condition, then wearing
a costume is required (because it is a necessary condition). It is all that
is required (because it is the only necessary condition). And it will
bring about the result, celebrating Halloween (because it is a sufficient
condition).

9. *Mary went to the store* is a sufficient condition.

10. *Having gone to medical school* is a necessary condition.

11. *Having gone to medical school* is a necessary and sufficient condition for
being a doctor.

12. *The vase was fragile* is a necessary condition for it breaking.

13. *Finding bloody clothes in Jeff's apartment* is a sufficient condition for
arresting him for the murder.

14. Based on the information in table 4.9, this conclusion is drawn:

    C Contracting head lice was probably caused by being in the gym.

    Since the method of difference is used to draw this conclusion, going to
    the gym is a sufficient condition for contracting head lice. None of the
    other antecedent circumstances can be a sufficient condition because all
    are present for either Claire or Mary (or both of them), and neither of
    them contracted head lice.

15. Based on the information in table 4.10, this conclusion is drawn:

    C Contracting Bolivian hemorrhagic fever was probably caused by
       being in the garden.

    This conclusion is drawn using the method of agreement, and so being in
    the garden is a necessary condition for contracting Bolivian hemorrhagic

fever. None of the other antecedent circumstances can be necessary conditions because all are absent in cases where Bolivian hemorrhagic fever is present.

16. Based on the information in table 4.11, the conclusion is

    C Contracting Rocky Mountain spotted fever was probably caused by being in the locker room.

    This conclusion is drawn using the joint method of agreement and difference. Thus, being in the locker room is a necessary and sufficient condition for contracting Rocky Mountain spotted fever.

17. Based on the information in table 4.12, the conclusion is

    C Contracting trench fever was probably caused by being at school.

    Since the method of agreement is used to make this inference, being at the school is a necessary condition for contracting trench fever.

18. Given the information in table 4.13, the method of difference is used to draw this conclusion:

    C Therefore, the salad probably caused the food poisoning.

19. Given the information in table 4.14, the method of agreement is used to draw this conclusion:

    C Therefore, the iced tea probably caused the food poisoning.

20. Given the information in table 4.15, the method of difference is used to draw this conclusion:

    C Therefore, the water probably caused the food poisoning.

21. Given the information in table 4.16, the joint method of agreement and difference is used to draw this conclusion:

    C Therefore, the pasta probably caused the food poisoning.

22. Given the information in table 4.17, the method of agreement is used to draw this conclusion:

    C Therefore, the salad probably caused the food poisoning.

23. The information given in the question is in table 4.18. The method of difference is used to draw this conclusion: Therefore, the soup is the probable cause of the shigellosis.

Table 4.18

Cases	Antecedent Circumstances				shigellosis
	salad	pasta	ice cream	soup	
Jill	yes	yes	yes	yes	yes
Jane	yes	yes	yes	no	no

Table 4.19

Cases	Antecedent Circumstances							cancer
	asbestos factory	uranium mine	biological weapons factory	exposed to lead paint	radiology depart-ment	library	cell phone towers	
Sarah	yes	yes	yes	—	yes	—	—	yes
Amy	yes	—	yes	—	—	yes	—	—
Kate	—	yes	yes	—	yes	—	—	yes
Chris	yes	—	—	yes	yes	—	—	—
Omar	—	yes	—	yes	—	yes	—	yes
Sam	—	—	—	yes	—	—	yes	—

24. This argument uses the method of residues.

    P1 The 104 degree temperature in Tom's apartment is caused by cooking, the radiators, the sauna, and the heat in his downstairs neighbors' apartment.

    P2 Raising the temperature from 78 degrees to 104 degrees is caused by the cooking, the radiators, and the sauna.

    C Therefore, raising the temperature to 78 degrees is caused by the heat in his downstairs neighbors' apartment.

25. Table 4.19 contains the information provided in the passage. The joint method of agreement and difference is used to draw this conclusion:

    C Therefore, working in the uranium mine probably caused the cancer.

26. Table 4.20 contains the information provided in the passage. The method of agreement is used to draw this conclusion:

    C Therefore, the mold probably caused the infection.

Table 4.20

Cases	mold	gas leak	ticks	rats' nests	pigeon droppings	infection
Jeff	yes	yes	—	—	—	yes
Claire	yes	—	—	yes	yes	yes
Jack	yes	yes	yes	—	yes	—
Tom	yes	—	yes	yes	yes	yes
Nicole	yes	yes	yes	yes	—	yes
Mary	yes	—	yes	yes	—	yes

27. This argument uses the method of concomitant variations.

   P1 The density of snags was three times higher in stands with no history of timber harvest (compared to stands that had been selectively harvested for timber).

   P2 The density of snags was nineteen times higher in stands with no history of timber harvest (compared to stands that had been completely harvested for timber).

   P3 The density of snags was almost three times higher in stands that are not adjacent to roads (compared to in stands that are adjacent to roads).

   P4 The density of snags was lower in unharvested stands that are adjacent to non-federal lands and closer to towns.

   P5 The density of snags was lower in stands with flat terrain in relation to the nearest road.

   C Therefore, timber harvesting and easy of human access are probably causally related to snag density.

28. This argument uses the method of residues.

   P1 The combined weight of Jeff, Jon, Rascal, and the cooler is greater than 450 pounds.

   P2 Jeff contributes 190 pounds.

   P3 Jon weighs 210 pounds.

   P4 Rascal weighs 40 pounds.

   C Therefore, the cooler weighs more than 10 pounds.

Table 4.21

Cases	Antecedent Circumstances						dead
	age	height & weight	cholesterol level	wealth	...	shot in the heart	
man, before the shot	same	same	same	same	same	no	no
man, after the shot	same	same	same	same	same	yes	yes

29. The method of difference is used here. As Mill points out, this method is very ingrained in the way we think—so much so that we don't even always realize how we arrived at a conclusion. In this example, the idea is that everything about the man is unchanged between the moment before he was shot and the moment after he was shot, except for the gunshot to the heart and his death. (See table 4.21.) And so this is the conclusion:

    C Therefore, the shot through the heart very likely caused the man's death.

30. The method of concomitant variations is used to draw the conclusion. The conclusion is:

    C The moon is, wholly or partially, the cause which determines the tides.

5 Describing Populations

The central feature of both the proportional syllogism and the inductive generalization is the relationship between an entire population and part of that population. Recall that, in the proportional syllogism, one of the premises contains a description of a population and the conclusion is about an individual who is a member of that population. Meanwhile, in an inductive generalization, one of the premises contains information about part of a population and the conclusion is about the entire population. Table 5.1 illustrates the move that is made in each type of argument from the premise or premises to the conclusion. These are, in a sense, inferences that go in opposite directions.

This chapter explains some of the ways of describing a population and discusses the new information that can be discovered once a population is well described. This, then, is the basis for the next two chapters, which examine the proportional syllogism and inductive generalization in more detail.

Table 5.1
The arrows indicate the "direction" of the inference for each type of argument. Above the arrow is the information contained in the premises; below it is what the conclusion is about.

proportional syllogism	inductive generalization
population	part of the population
⇓	⇓
part of the population	population

5.1   Variables and Their Values

To construct an argument about a population, we must replace the population itself with a ***model of the population***. The model is a description of a population, but this description is one that is well defined in ways that real populations often are not. To see how this works, consider this description of a population: 15 percent of Central City College undergraduates are vegetarians. In this example, the population is Central City College undergraduates, and the population is described in terms of a characteristic that everyone in the population has: *diet*. The diet for 15 percent of this population is *vegetarian*, which means that the diet for the remaining 85 percent is *nonvegetarian*.

The general characteristic that is being used to describe the population is a ***variable***, and the different forms that the variable can take are the ***values of the variable***. In this example, the variable is *diet*; one value of this variable is *vegetarian* and the other is *nonvegetarian*.

Now since it is a model of a population, there are two constraints on the values of the variable. The values must be mutually exclusive and exhaustive.

> Two or more values are ***mutually exclusive*** when having one value prohibits an individual from having any of the other values.

> Two or more values are ***exhaustive*** when an individual must have one of those values.

In the model of Central City College undergraduates, the values *vegetarian* and *nonvegetarian* are mutually exclusive. Therefore, if an individual has the value *vegetarian*, then he or she cannot also be a nonvegetarian. (Maybe in reality a vegetarian in this population might sneak the occasional cheeseburger, but with respect to the model it can be assumed that an individual who has the value *vegetarian* is always a vegetarian.)

And because the values are exhaustive, any individual in this population will have one of the values that has been specified for a particular variable. Because the values are *vegetarian* and *nonvegetarian*, it is obvious that no one in this population will have some other value for the variable *diet*—these two values cover everything. But just as an example, since the values are exhaustive, there will not be a person in this population with the value *vegan*, or the value *kosher*, or the value *none (fasting)*. In short, the values that are given exhaust the available possibilities.

Another example. Consider a jar of marbles in which some of the marbles are red, some are blue, and some are green. In this case, the population is all of the marbles in the jar. The variable is *color*, and this variable has three values: *red*, *blue*, and *green*.

If one of the marbles is red, then—because the values are mutually exclusive—that particular marble cannot be assigned one of the other colors (i.e., blue or green). And because the variable *color* has the values red, blue, and green, no marble can be yellow or even bluish-green—the values that have been specified exhaust the possible values for this variable.

5.2   Describing a Population with Two Variables

Consider the employees of a large factory. Since it opened fifteen years ago, 345 different people have worked in this factory. In their work there, 130 of the employees have been exposed to benzene and the remaining 215 have not. Of the 130 who have been exposed to benzene, 60 have developed cancer, while only 35 of those who have not been exposed to benzene have developed cancer. The diagram in figure 5.1 represents this population in

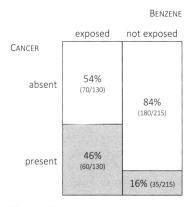

Figure 5.1
In this population, among the individuals who have been exposed to benzene, 46 percent have developed cancer, and 54 percent have not. Among the individuals who have not been exposed to benzene, 16 percent have developed cancer, and 84 percent have not. Note that the population is described in terms of the percentage of individuals that have these characteristics, not the number of individuals who have them.

terms of two variables: *benzene exposure* and *cancer status*. As the diagram shows, each of these variables has two values, which are basically just *yes* and *no*.

What is of interest in this diagram is the difference between (a) the proportion who have cancer among those who have been exposed to benzene and (b) the proportion who have cancer among those who have not been exposed to benzene. As the diagram indicates, a higher proportion of those who have been exposed to benzene have cancer than do those who have not been exposed to benzene: 46 percent versus 16 percent. The difference between these two percentages indicates that, for some reason, in this population, the value *cancer present* has a tendency to go with the value *exposed to benzene* instead of the value *not exposed to benzene*.

Notice that this does not mean that exposure to benzene causes cancer, although it does suggest that as a likely possibility. It is possible, however, that most of the employees who were exposed to benzene also smoked, while most of those who were not exposed to benzene did not smoke. If this is the case, then it may be the smoking that caused the cancer, not the exposure to benzene. But whatever the actual cause is, it is the case that a much higher percentage of the employees who were exposed to benzene developed cancer than did those who were not exposed to benzene.

5.3   Difference in Proportions, Independence, and Association

When examining a population that is described in terms of two variables, three useful concepts are *difference in proportions*, *independence*, and *association*.

5.3.1   Difference in Proportions
Look at figure 5.2. Once a population that is described in terms of two variables is diagrammed, it is possible to see whether there is a difference between the proportions b and d, and whether there is a difference between the proportions a and c (if there is a difference between b and d, then there has to be a difference between a and c, and vice versa). The **difference in proportions** is the difference between the proportion of individuals with x_1 who have y_1 and the proportion of individuals with x_2 who have y_1—so, the difference between b and d. (And the same for y_2.)

For example, in the population in figure 5.1, there is a difference between the proportion of the exposed who have cancer (46 percent) and the

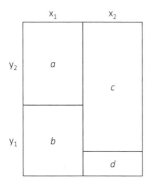

Figure 5.2
In this diagram, y_1 and x_1 are positively associated, as are y_2 and x_2. And y_1 and x_2 are negatively associated, as are y_2 and x_1.

proportion of the nonexposed who have cancer (16 percent). Similarly, there is a difference between the proportion of the exposed who do not have cancer (54 percent) and the proportion of the nonexposed who do not have cancer (84 percent).

5.3.2 Independent and Associated

Now think about a population in which there is no difference between the proportions b and d or between the proportions a and c. This would mean that, for those with x_1 and for those with x_2, the percentage with y_1 is the same (and likewise for y_2). In the population in figure 5.3, for instance, the same percentage of people who have been exposed to fluoride have cancer as do those who have not been exposed to fluoride.

When a population is described in terms of two variables and there is no difference between the proportions b and d (or between a and c), the variables are **independent**. That is to say, there is no special tendency for one value (e.g., y_1) to go with one of the values of the other variable (e.g., x_1). In the population in figure 5.3, the value *cancer present* does not go with *exposed to fluoride* any more than it goes with *not exposed to fluoride*. Hence, the variables *cancer status* and *fluoride exposure* are independent of each other.

On the other hand, if there is a difference in the proportions b and d (and between a and c), then the variables are **associated**. When this is the case, there is a tendency for two of the values to occur together. For example, in the population in figure 5.1, a greater proportion of the people who have been exposed to benzene have cancer than do those who have not been

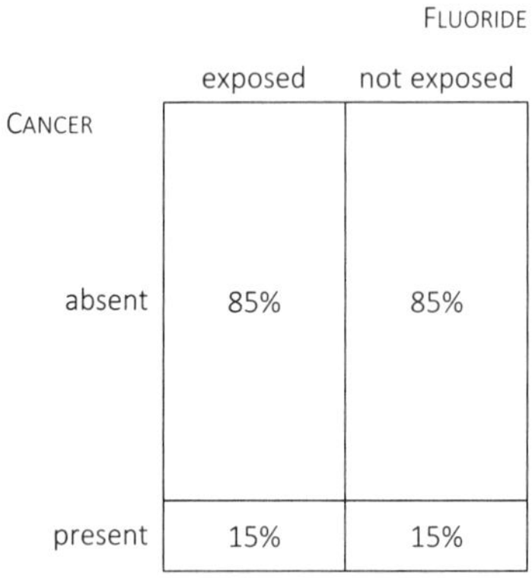

Figure 5.3
In this population, the variables are independent.

exposed to benzene. Therefore, in this population the variables *cancer status* and *benzene exposure* are associated with each other.

When the variables are associated, the values of those variables are either ***positively associated*** or ***negatively associated***.

> If the proportion of individuals who have y_1 is greater among those who have x_1 than those with x_2, then the values x_1 and y_1 are *positively associated*.

> If the proportion of individuals who have y_1 is smaller among those who have x_1 than those with x_2, then the values x_1 and y_1 are *negatively associated*.

A simple way to find a positive association is look at a diagram like the one in figure 5.2 and ask, What does y_1 have a greater tendency to go with, x_1 or x_2? Since the proportion b is larger than the proportion d, the answer is x_1. Thus, y_1 and x_1 are positively associated. The opposite question—What does y_1 have a tendency not to go with, x_1 or x_2?—helps identify the negative association. And then the same can be done for y_2.

5.4   The Strengths of Positive and Negative Associations

Variables are associated as long as there is a difference in proportions, but it is also useful to think about how strongly or weakly the variables are associated. Consider the populations in figure 5.4a and figure 5.4b. In both populations, *vaccination status* and *disease A status* are associated because a higher percentage of people who have not been vaccinated have the disease than do those who have been vaccinated. But the two populations

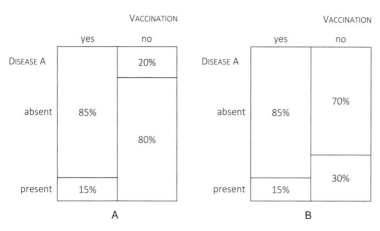

Figure 5.4

are clearly not the same. In the population on the left, a much greater percentage of the unvaccinated have the disease than do the vaccinated (80 percent versus 15 percent). In the population on the right, a greater percentage of the unvaccinated have the disease than do the vaccinated, but not to the same extent (only 30 percent to 15 percent). Calculating the difference between the proportions in each population is one way of specifying how these two populations are different.

In both populations, *disease A present* and *not vaccinated* are positively associated.

> In the population in figure 5.4a, the difference between the proportion of individuals who have the disease among the unvaccinated (.80) and among the vaccinated (.15) is .65 (i.e., .80 – .15 = .65).

> Meanwhile, in the population in figure 5.4b, the difference between the proportion of individuals who have the disease among the unvaccinated (.30) and the vaccinated (.15) is .15 (i.e., .30 – .15 = .15).

Using the difference in proportions as a measure, we find that the **strength of the positive association** between *disease A present* and *not vaccinated* is .65 in the population in figure 5.4a and .15 in the population in figure 5.4b.

When two values are negatively associated, the difference in proportions is a negative value. For example, in the population in figure 5.4a, the difference between the proportion of people who have the disease among the vaccinated (.15) and the proportion with the disease among the unvaccinated (.80) is –.65 (i.e., .15 – .80 = –.65). This means that the strength of the negative association between *disease A present* and *being vaccinated* is –.65.

Table 5.2
The positive and negative associations for the population in figure 5.4a.

The relationship between values	The difference in proportions
Disease A present and *not vaccinated* are positively associated.	The difference between the proportion of people with the disease among the unvaccinated and among the vaccinated: .80 − .15 = .65
Disease A absent and *vaccinated* are positively associated.	The difference between the proportion of people who do not have the disease among the vaccinated and among the unvaccinated: .85 − .20 = .65
Disease A present and *vaccinated* are negatively associated.	The difference between the proportion of people who have the disease among the vaccinated and among the unvaccinated: .15 − .80 = −.65
Disease A absent and *not vaccinated* are negatively associated.	The difference between the proportion of people who do not have the disease among the unvaccinated and among the vaccinated: .20 − .85 = −.65

The difference in proportions, therefore, indicates not only that the variables are associated and which values are positively and negatively associated, but also how strongly the values are associated. The difference in proportions can be any number between +1.0 and −1.0, and when it is zero the variables are independent.

5.5   Information about a Population

What new information can be drawn from a basic description of a population? A good place to start is with the intuitive idea that when two values are positively associated that means that they have a tendency to go together. If a person in the population has one value, then he or she is likely to also have the other value. This idea is on the right track, but a little bit of care is required here. Consider the population in figure 5.5a. In this population, being a scientist is positively associated with having a graduate degree. But being a policy analyst and having a graduate degree also have a tendency to go together—a sizeable majority, 70 percent, of policy analysts have graduate degrees.

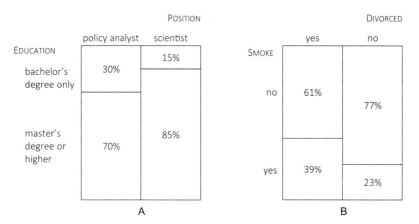

Figure 5.5

The significance of two values being positively associated is not that they have a tendency to go together. Rather, it is that the two values (*scientist* and *graduate degree*) have a greater tendency to go together than the alternative (*policy analyst* and *graduate degree*). Although both policy analysts and scientists tend to have graduate degrees, a greater percentage of scientists have them. That suggests that there is something about the value *scientist* that makes it go with *graduate degree* more than *policy analyst* goes with *graduate degree*.

The population in figure 5.5b is a little bit different. In this population, a minority of the nondivorced are smokers, but also a minority of the divorced are smokers. Nevertheless, *being divorced* is positively associated with *smoking*. And even though a minority of people who are divorced smoke, this positive association is useful information.

Consider these questions about this population.

(a) Imagine mingling with people in this population. You find yourself standing near a person who is divorced and a person who is not divorced. You need a light for your cigarette and, because your lungs have been weakened by years of smoking, you have only enough breath to ask one person. Who are you going to ask for a light, the person who is divorced or the one who is not divorced?

(b) Smoking entails a lot of health risks. If someone is concerned about the health of the people in this population, who are they going to be especially concerned about, people who have been divorced or people who have not been divorced?

Answering these questions requires figuring out which value is positively associated with smoking. But the broader lesson here is that just by organizing the information about a population in the right kind of way, we can easily access new and useful information.

Finally, notice that nothing has been said here about a causal relationship between the two values that are associated—that is, that one of them causes the other to occur. In many cases when there is a positive association, one of the values does, directly or indirectly, cause the other. But a positive association does not always indicate a causal relationship between the two values that are positively associated. That a causal relationship cannot be inferred does not detract from the usefulness of describing a population this way, however. As questions (a) and (b) above demonstrate, even without revealing anything about the cause, the positive association indicates where we should investigate, whether for a light or because we are concerned.

5.6   Measuring the Strength of an Association (Again)

For measuring the strength of a positive or negative association, the difference in proportions is quite easy to use and is generally accurate enough. An alternative, though, is this calculation:

$$\frac{eh - fg}{\sqrt{(e+f)(g+h)(e+g)(f+h)}} \tag{5.1}$$

The letters e, f, g, and h represent the numbers, not the proportions, of individuals with each characteristic. (See table 5.3a.) Table 5.3b is the population described in figure 5.1.

Table 5.3

		variable 1				benzene	
		present	absent			exposed	not exposed
variable 2	present	e	f	cancer	present	60	35
	absent	g	h		absent	70	180

(A)   (B)

By this measure, the strength of the association between *cancer present* and *exposed to benzene* is .32, only slightly different from the value found using the difference in proportion: .30.

$$\frac{(60)(180) - (35)(70)}{\sqrt{(60+35)(70+180)(60+70)(35+180)}} = .32 \tag{5.2}$$

5.7   Exercises

1. Table 5.4 describes the people who work for a small company. Make a diagram of this population. Put the values for the variable *gender* on the top of the diagram. Are the variables *smoking status* and *gender* associated or independent? If the variables are associated, determine which values are positively associated and which values are negatively associated.

Table 5.4

100	males who don't smoke
70	females who don't smoke
100	males who smoke
30	females who don't smoke

2. Table 5.5 describes the people who work for a small company. Make a diagram of this population. Put the values for the variable *gender* at the top of the diagram. Are the variables *smoking status* and *gender* associated or independent? If the variables are associated, determine which values are positively associated and which values are negatively associated.

Table 5.5

60	males who don't smoke
90	females who don't smoke
30	males who smoke
45	females who smoke

3. Table 5.6 describes the contents of a marble jar. The variables *color* and *size* are associated in this population. Construct a diagram of the population, and put the values for the variable *color* at the top of the diagram. Determine which values are positively associated and which are

Table 5.6

40	large red marbles
60	large nonred marbles
80	small red marbles
20	small nonred marbles

negatively associated. Using the difference in proportions as a measure, calculate the strength of each of the positive and negative associations.

4. Construct another diagram of the population described in table 5.6. This time put the values for the variable *size* at the top of the diagram. Determine which values are positively associated and which are negatively associated. Using the difference in proportions as a measure, calculate the strength of each of the positive and negative associations.

5. Does the diagram that you created for question 3 illustrate the same relationship between the values as the diagram that you created for question 4? (That is, are the same values positively associated and are the same values negatively associated?)

6. An assisted living facility has 900 residents. Of these individuals, 500 take medication A292, and 400 do not take this medication. Of those who take medication A292, 90 have a gambling addiction, while the rest who take it do not. As for the others, 10 of the people who are not on medication A292 have a gambling addiction, while the other 390 do not.

    This population is described using two variables, each of which has two values. Construct a diagram that represents this population. Put *taking medication A292* and *not taking medication A292* at the top of the diagram. Are the variables associated or independent?

7. In the population described in the previous question, the variables *gambling habit* and *medication A292* are associated. Which values are positively associated and which values are negatively associated? Use the difference in proportions to measure the strength of each of the positive and negative associations.

8. On September 30, 2009, the Pennsylvania State Senate voted on "2009 Senate Bill 1093," a measure to give $1,563,000 to Drexel University for "instruction and student aid." Forty-nine state senators were present for this vote: 29 Republicans and 20 Democrats. All of these senators voted:

24 of the Republicans and 15 of the Democrats voted for the bill, the rest voted against it.

Create a diagram of this population with *political party* at the top of the diagram. Are the variables *political party* and *vote* associated or independent? If they are associated, (i) determine which values are positively associated and which ones are negatively associated and (ii) use the difference in proportions to find the strengths of the positive and negative associations.

9. On September 29, 2010, the Pennsylvania State Senate voted on "2009 House Bill 400," which establishes criteria for classifying construction workers as employees or as independent contractors. Forty-seven senators voted on this bill: 29 Republicans and 18 Democrats. Sixteen of the Republicans and all of the Democrats voted for it.

   Create a diagram of this population with *political party* at the top of the diagram. The variables *political party* and *vote* are associated. Which values are positively associated and which ones are negatively associated? What are the strengths of these positive and negative associations?

10. On March 31, 2009, the Pennsylvania State Senate voted on "Senate Bill 36." This bill requires the owner of a lost or stolen firearm to file a report within twenty-four hours of discovering it missing. Fifty senators voted on this bill: 30 Republicans and 20 Democrats. All Republicans and all Democrats voted for the bill.

    Create a diagram of this population with *political party* at the top of the diagram. Are the variables *political party* and *vote* associated or independent? Calculate the difference in proportions.

5.8   Answers

1. In this population, diagrammed in figure 5.6, the variables *smoking status* and *gender* are associated. (*Smoke* and *don't smoke* can be in either order, as can *male* and *female*.) *Smoke* and *male* are positively associated; and *don't smoke* and *female* are positively associated. *Smoke* and *female* are negatively associated; and *don't smoke* and *male* are negatively associated.

2. In this population (figure 5.7), the variables *smoking status* and *gender* are independent.

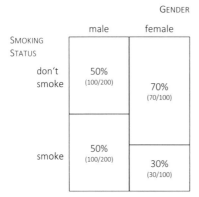

Figure 5.6
Diagram for exercise 1.

GENDER

	male	female
SMOKING STATUS		
don't smoke	67% (60/90)	67% (90/135)
smoke	33% (30/90)	33% (45/135)

Figure 5.7
Diagram for exercise 2.

3. The diagram for this population is in figure 5.8. The values *small* and *red* are positively associated. Using the difference in proportions, we find that the strength of this association is .42. This is calculated by finding the difference between the percentage of red marbles that are small (.67) and the percentage of nonred marbles that are small (.25).

   Large and *nonred* are positively associated. The strength of this positive association is also .42 (i.e., .75 – .33 = .42).

   Small and *nonred* are negatively associated. The strength of this negative association is –.42 (i.e., .25 – .67 = –.42).

   Large and *red* are negatively associated. The strength of this negative association is –.42 (i.e., .33 – 75 = –.42).

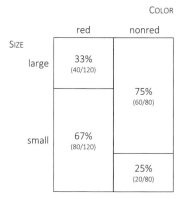

Figure 5.8
Diagram for exercise 3.

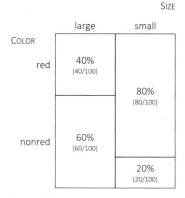

Figure 5.9
Diagram for exercise 4.

4. When the population is diagrammed this way (see figure 5.9), these are the positive and negative associations:

> *Nonred* and *large* are positively associated, and the strength of this positive association is .40. This value is found by doing this calculation: .60 – .20 = .40.
>
> *Red* and *small* are positively associated. The strength of this positive association is also .40 (i.e., .80 – .40 = .40).
>
> For the negative associations, *nonred* and *small* are negatively associated, and the strength of this association is –.40 (i.e., .20 – .60 = –.40).
>
> And *red* and *large* are negatively associated. The strength of this association is also –.40 (i.e., .40 – .80 = –.40).

5. The two diagrams for this population (figures 5.8 and 5.9) do illustrate the same relationship between the values. Both diagrams show that *red* and *small* are positively associated, as are *nonred* and *large*. Both also show that *red* and *large*, and *nonred* and *small*, are negatively associated.

   But the strengths of the positive and negative associations are not quite the same, although they are close. This is unavoidable. It is just a result of using the difference in proportions to measure the strength of a positive or negative association. It does, however, make it important to be clear about how the values for the difference in proportions were found.

6. The information given in the question is in table 5.7, and the diagram of the population is in figure 5.10. In this population, the variables *medication A292* and *gambling habit* are associated. A relatively small percentage of the people on medication A292 have a gambling addiction. Nevertheless, the percentage of people with a gambling addiction among those taking medication A292 is much higher than the percentage of people with a gambling addiction among those who are not taking medication A292 (18 versus 2.5 percent). Hence, there is a positive association between *gambling addiction* and *taking medication A292*.

Table 5.7

taking medication A292 and gambling addiction	90
taking medication A292 and no gambling addiction	410
not taking medication A292 and gambling addiction	10
not taking medication A292 and no gambling addiction	390

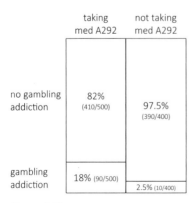

Figure 5.10

7. *Gambling addiction* and *taking medication A292* are positively associated. Using the difference in proportions, the strength of this association is .155 (i.e., .18 – .025 = .155). This value is the difference between (i) the proportion of people with a gambling addiction among those taking the medication (.18) and (ii) the proportion of people with a gambling addiction among those not taking the medication (.025).

No gambling addiction and *not taking medication A292* are also positively associated. The strength of this association is .155 as well (calculation: .975 – .82 = .155).

Gambling addiction and *not taking medication A292* are negatively associated. The strength of this negative association is –.155 (calculation: .025 – .18 = –.155). This value is the difference between (i) the proportion of people with a gambling addiction among those not taking the medication and (ii) the proportion of people with a gambling addiction among those taking the medication.

No gambling addiction and *taking medication A292* are negatively associated. The strength of this negative association is –.155 (calculation: .82 – .975 = –.155).

8. As the diagram in figure 5.11 shows, the variables are associated.

In this population, *voting for the bill* and *Republican* are positively associated. The strength of this positive association is .08 (i.e., .83 – .75 = .08).

Also positively associated are *voting against the bill* and *Democrat*. The strength of this association is .08 (i.e., .25 – .17 = .08).

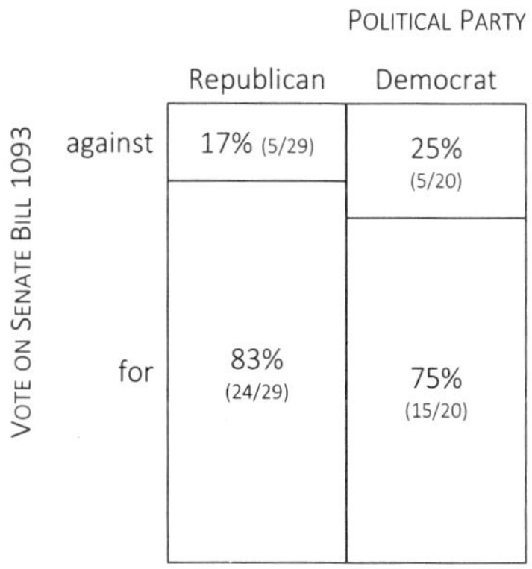

Figure 5.11
Diagram for exercise 8.

For the negative associations, *voting for the bill* and *Democrat* are negatively associated, and *voting against the bill* and *Republican* are negatively associated. The strength of both of these negative associations is –.08.

> *voting for the bill* and *Democrat*: .75 – .83 = –.08
> *voting against the bill* and *Republican*: .17 – .25 = –.08

9. In this case, *voting for the bill* and *Democrat* are positively associated, as are *voting against the bill* and *Republican*. Using the difference in proportions, the strength of both of these positive associations is .45.

> *voting for the bill* and *Democrat*: 1.0 – .55 = .45
> *voting against the bill* and *Republican*: .45 – 0.0 = .45 (0.0 is the percentage, among the Democrats, who voted against the bill).

Voting against the bill and *Democrat* are negatively associated, and the strength of this negative association is –.45 (calculation: 0.0 – .45 = –.45).

Voting for the bill and *Republican* are also negatively associated. The strength of this negative association is –.45 (calculation: .55 – 1.0 = –.45).

10. In this case, the variables *political party* and *voting* are independent.

The percentage of Republicans who voted for the bill is the same as the percentage of Democrats who voted for the bill: 100 percent. When the difference between these two proportions is calculated, the result is zero, i.e., 1.0 – 1.0 = 0, which is what is expected when the variables are independent.

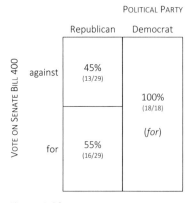

Figure 5.12
Diagram for exercise 9.

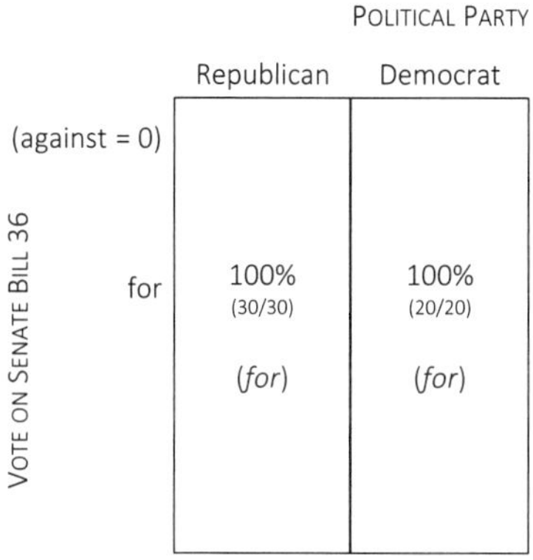

Figure 5.13
Diagram for exercise 10.

These last three problems demonstrate a feature of investigating populations that is sometimes difficult to grasp. Namely, it does not matter—and it does not detract from the accuracy of the results—if a population is small. When looking at only part of a population and using that sample to make an inference about the whole population, the sample should be reasonably large. And even when it is, the inference that is made about the entire population is never precise. But when the entire population has been examined and there is information about every member, the size of the population doesn't matter. The description that is produced is just a picture of that population as it exists. The previous three problems—8, 9, and 10—deal with populations that are pretty small: 49, 47, and 50 individuals. But it is still useful to examine the population and see when the variables *political party* and *vote* are associated and when they are independent. The results provide legitimate and useful information about the populations.

6 The Proportional Syllogism

In chapter 1, the examples of the proportional syllogism had conclusions about a single individual. This type of argument can, however, have a conclusion about more than just one individual, as long as it is less than the whole population. This chapter will focus on some more complex examples of the proportional syllogism, and it will explain the rules we need to follow when making these more complex inferences. First, however, it begins with an introduction to probability.

6.1 Probability and Proportion

In table 6.1a, a population is described in terms of the variable *color*. The values of this variable are red, blue, and green. Because 40 percent of the marbles in this population are red, if one marble is randomly selected, the probability that the marble will be red is 40 percent—and the probability that it will be nonred (that is, blue or green) is 60 percent.

The term *probability* refers to events—the likelihood of something happening. In this chapter and the next, the probability of selecting an individual with a particular property will equal the proportion of individuals in the

Table 6.1

The marbles in the jar		*Notation*
Red marbles	40%	$P(Red) = .40$ or $P(R) = .40$
Blue marbles	25%	Read as: "The probability of selecting a marble that
Green marbles	35%	has the value *red* is .40."
(A)		(B)

population that have that property (i.e., that value).[1] Of course, the selection has to be random—it won't do to look into the jar and search for a red one. That would greatly increase the likelihood of selecting a red one. But, when working with a model of a population, it can be safely assumed that the selections made from the population are random.

6.2   The Theory of Probability

Table 6.2 lists the three basic rules of probability. These rules go some way toward defining the concept *probability*: the probability of an event occurring is some number between zero and one (including zero and one); the probability of an event occurring and the probability of the same event not occurring must add up to 1.0; and the probability of a contradiction is zero.

Beyond these three basic rules, five additional rules of probability are listed in table 6.3. Two of the rules are "conjunction" rules and two of them are "disjunction" rules. Conjunctions and disjunctions are words that are used to combine other words, clauses, or sentences. Most commonly, a conjunction is expressed using "and" and a disjunction is expressed using

Table 6.2

(i)	Every probability is between 0 and 1.
	$0 \leq P(A) \leq 1$
(ii)	The probability of A and the probability of *not A* add up to 1.
	$P(A) + P(not\ A) = 1$, and so $P(not\ A) = 1 - P(A)$
(iii)	The probability of a contradiction is 0.
	$P(A\ \&\ not\ A) = 0$
	And when A and B are mutually exclusive,
	$P(A\ \&\ B) = 0$

---

1. This is not the only way of establishing the probability of an event, but when it is possible, defining probability in terms of a proportion in a population is simple and straightforward. On the other hand, in many cases when probabilities are used, no proportions are available. For example, the probability that it will rain tomorrow or the probability that the Philadelphia Phillies will win the next World Series do not come from the proportions of any populations. But this chapter will focus on probabilities that are set by the proportion in a population.

Table 6.3

(1)	**The General Conjunction Rule**, multiplication for associated (nonindependent) variables $P(A \& B) = P(A) \times P(B \mid A)$
(2)	**The Special Conjunction Rule**, multiplication for independent variables $P(A \& B) = P(A) \times P(B)$
(3)	**The General Disjunction Rule**, addition for nonexclusive values $P(A \text{ or } B) = P(A) + P(B) - P(A \& B)$
(4)	**The Special Disjunction Rule**, addition for exclusive values $P(A \text{ or } B) = P(A) + P(B)$
(5)	**The Conditional Probability Rule** $P(B \mid A) = \dfrac{P(A \& B)}{P(A)}$

"or."[2] Thus, the two conjunction rules are used to combine probability statements with an *and*, while the two disjunction rules combine probabilities statements with an *inclusive or*—"inclusive or" means "either … or … or both". Notice that multiplication is used for the conjunction rules, and addition is used for the disjunction rules.

In addition to the conjunction and disjunction rules, one other rule is included in table 6.3. The conditional probability rule is used to calculate the probability of one event on the condition that another event occurs. Since the general conjunction rule and the conditional probability rule can each be derived from the other, one of the two probabilities—$P(A \& B)$ or $P(B \mid A)$—has to be known in order to find the other one.

Now consider the population described in figure 6.1. Given the proportions for each of these values, the probability of selecting a marble that is red, the probability of selecting one that is nonred, the probability of selecting a large marble, and the probability of selecting a small marble can all be determined. (For example, P(*nonred*) = .60, and P(*large*) = .70.) These probabilities will be used to illustrate the rules that are listed in table 6.3.

---

2. The only conjunction used here will be "and" and the only disjunction will be "or." There are, however, other words that are logically equivalent to "and," namely, "but," "although," "as well as," and "also." Another word that is logically equivalent to "or" is "unless."

The marbles in the jar (200 total)	
80 are red (44L, 36S)	$P(R) = .40$
120 are nonred (96L, 24S)	$P(N) = .60$
140 are large (44R, 96N)	$P(L) = .70$
60 are small (36R, 24N)	$P(S) = .30$

(A)

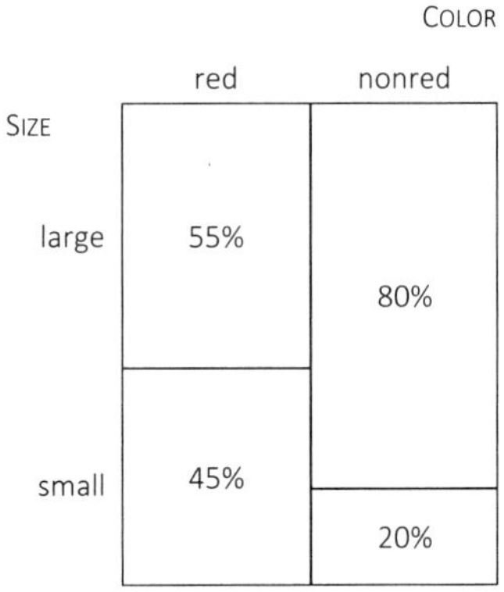

COLOR

	red	nonred
SIZE		
large	55%	80%
small	45%	20%

(B)

Figure 6.1

6.2.1 The General Conjunction Rule

When the variables used to describe a population are associated, we use the general conjunction rule to determine the probability that an individual selected at random will have two specific values. For example, the probability of selecting a marble that is red and large from the jar described in figure 6.1 is

$$P(red \& large) = P(R) \times P(L|R) = .40 \times .55 = .22 \tag{6.1}$$

When using the general conjunction rule, the probability for the first value (in this case, red) is multiplied by a **conditional probability**. A conditional probability is the probability that one event will happen, given that some other event has also happened. The conditional probability in this example is the probability that the marble is large, given that it is red. So, $P(L|R)$ is read as "the probability of being large on the condition that the marble selected is red" or "given that the marble selected is red, the probability that it is large." (It is not "the probability of being large and red," which is what the general conjunction rule is being used to find.)

Since $P(L|R)$ is really just $P(L)$ in a special situation, one easy way of finding the value of $P(L|R)$ is to look at the diagram of the population when the values *red* and *nonred* are the labels at the top, as they are in figure 6.1b. When red is at the top of the diagram, the column that represents the red marbles can, for a moment, be treated as the entire population. In this population (of only red marbles), 45 percent of the marbles are small and 55 percent of them are large. The proportion of marbles that are large, 55 percent, corresponds to the probability that is needed, and so $P(L|R) = .55.^3$

6.2.2 The Conditional Probability Rule

In a situation where $P(R \& L)$ is known, but the conditional probability *large given that it's red* is unknown, we can use the conditional probability rule to find $P(L|R)$. Of course, $P(L|R)$ is known for the population described in figure 6.1, but since $P(R \& L) = .22$ was just found (in equation 6.1), we can implement the conditional probability rule:

$$P(L|R) = \frac{P(R \& L)}{P(R)} = \frac{.22}{.40} = .55 \tag{6.3}$$

Another example. In a normal deck of cards, half the cards are red, half are black, and there are 10 cards (out of 52) that are both red and even numbered. Therefore, the probability of selecting a card that is red and even is about .19 (i.e., $^{10}/_{52}$).

Given that a red card has been selected from a deck, what is the probability that it has an even number? [I.e., what is $P(even|red)$?]

Solution. The probability of selecting a red card from the deck is .50 and $P(red \& even) = .19$. Therefore,

$$P(even|red) = \frac{P(R \& E)}{P(R)} = \frac{.19}{.50} = .38 \tag{6.4}$$

6.2.3 The Special Conjunction Rule

The general conjunction rule must be used when the variables are associated, and it can also be used when the variables are independent. But when the variables are independent, the special conjunction rule is generally preferred because it does not require using a conditional probability.

---

3. The probability of selecting a marble that is red and large [i.e., $P(red \& large)$] can also be calculated by multiplying $P(L)$ and $P(R|L)$. But it's important to be careful that the correct value for this conditional probability is used.

$$P(large \& red) = P(L) \times P(R|L) = .70 \times .3143 = .22 \tag{6.2}$$

In this textbook, the order in which the values are given will indicate the order in which they occur in the calculation, which will then indicate what conditional probability is required.

Consider the population in figure 6.2. In this population, the percentage of individuals who have developed cancer in the exposed group is the same as the percentage of individuals who have developed cancer in the unexposed group. Both are 15 percent. This means that the variables *cancer status* and *fluoride exposure* are independent. Consequently, the probability of selecting an individual from this population who has been exposed to fluoride and has cancer can be calculated with the special conjunction rule.

$$P(exposed \& cancer) = P(E) \times P(C) = .40 \times .15 = .06 \qquad (6.5)$$

The general conjunction rule can also be used here, and it will produce the same result.

$$P(exposed \& cancer) = P(E) \times P(C|E) = .40 \times .15 = .06 \qquad (6.6)$$

These two rules produce the same result in this case because (a) *the probability of having cancer, given that the person selected has been exposed to fluoride, is the same as* (b) *the probability of anyone selected from this population having*

The employees of company A	
120 exposed to fluoride (18C, 102NC)	P(E) = .40
180 not exposed to fluoride (27C, 153NC)	P(NE) = .60
45 have cancer (18E, 27NE)	P(C) = .15
255 do not have cancer (102E, 153NE)	P(NC) = .85

(A)

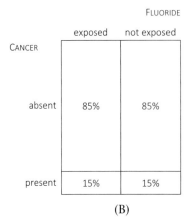

(B)

Figure 6.2

cancer. Since the variables are independent, the chance of developing cancer is the same if a person has been exposed to fluoride or if a person has not been exposed to fluoride, which means that everyone in this population has an equal chance of developing cancer—that is, $P(C|E) = P(C|N) = P(C) = 15$ percent.

This observation gives us a new way of defining *independent* and *associated*.

If $P(y_1|x_1) = P(y_1|x_2)$ (and so $P(y_1) = P(y_1|x_1)$), the variables (for these values) are independent.

If $P(y_1|x_1) \neq P(y_1|x_2)$, the variables are associated.

Another example. If two dice are rolled, how one die lands has no effect on how the other lands. In other words, how the die land are independent of each other. Thus, the special conjunction rule can be used to answer this question: What is the probability of rolling a pair of sixes? In other words, what is the probability that one die lands on six *and* the other die also lands on six?

Solution. Since a die has six sides, the probability of getting any number is .167 (i.e., ¹/₆). Therefore,

$$P(two\ sixes) = P(six) \times P(six) = .167 \times .167 = .028 \qquad (6.7)$$

6.2.4 The Special Disjunction Rule

The remaining two rules are used to combine individual probabilities with an "or." The first of these, the special disjunction rule, can be used only when the values are mutually exclusive—that is, when having one of the values excludes an individual from having the other. *Red* and *nonred* are mutually exclusive, but, since a marble can very well be both red and large, *red* and *large* are not mutually exclusive. Values are only mutually exclusive when they are the values for the same variable. Values that come from different variables are not mutually exclusive.

To calculate the probability of selecting a marble that is red or nonred from the jar described in figure 6.1, we add the probability of selecting a red marble to the probability of selecting a nonred marble:

$$P(red\ or\ nonred) = P(R) + P(N) = .40 + .60 = 1.0 \qquad (6.8)$$

It is, of course, expected that the probability will be 1.0 (i.e., 100 percent). Since all of the marbles in the jar are either red or nonred, there has to be a 100 percent chance that either a red or a nonred marble will be selected. Notice what would happen if we used the special disjunction rule to find the probability of selecting a marble that is red or large:

$$P(red \text{ or } large) = P(R) + P(L) = .40 + .70 = 1.1 \tag{6.9}$$

The result is 110 percent, but it is impossible for there to be a 110 percent chance of selecting a marble from the jar that is red or large. As stated in table 6.2, 100 percent cannot be exceeded, plus there are small nonred marbles in the jar, and there has to be a chance of getting one of them. The mistake here is using the special disjunction rule when the values are not mutually exclusive.

Another example. When one die is rolled, what is the probability of getting an even number?

Solution. Getting an even number means getting a two *or* a four *or* a six. These possible outcomes are mutually exclusive since getting one number (say, a four) excludes the possibility of getting any other. Thus,

$$P(even \ number) = P(two) + P(four) + P(six) =$$
$$.167 + .167 + .167 = .50 \tag{6.10}$$

6.2.5 The General Disjunction Rule

If the values are not mutually exclusive, the general disjunction rule must be used when combining two probability statements with an *or*. To find the probability of selecting a marble that is red or large, we add the probability of selecting a red marble to the probability of selecting a large marble, and then we subtract the probability of selecting a marble that is red and large. Recall that, for this population in figure 6.1, the probability of selecting a marble that is red and large has already been calculated—$P(R \& L) = .22$ (see equation 6.1). Thus,

$$P(red \text{ or } large) = P(R) + P(L) - P(R \& L) = .40 + .70 - .22 = .88 \tag{6.11}$$

6.3 Relative Risk

In sections 6.4 and 6.5, we will apply some of the rules just explained to the task of constructing arguments. But first, we will examine one more new concept.

The difference in proportions, which was explained in chapter 5, is a simple way of gauging the relationship between two values—specifically, it's a way of measuring the strength of a positive or negative association. Another measure of how values are related to each other is *relative risk*.

Consider the population in figure 6.3a. A person in this population who has not been vaccinated is more likely to get the disease than someone who has been vaccinated. But how much more likely? Both vaccinated and unvaccinated have the disease, but how much does a person increase his or her risk of getting the disease when he or she doesn't get the vaccination?[4]

The *relative risk* for two particular values (say, y_1 and x_1) is the probability that an individual who has x_1 will have y_1 relative to the probability

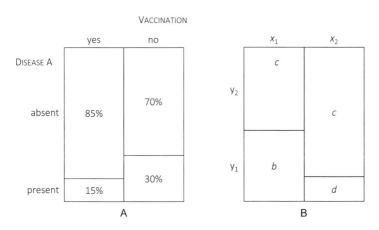

Figure 6.3

4. It is natural when talking about risk and relative risk to have in mind the idea that one variable (the exposure variable) causes, or is at least in some way responsible for, the occurrence of the other variable (the outcome or response variable). And many of the examples used in this chapter fit this format—although not, presumably, color and size. But in the cases where it does fit, the exposure variable is placed at the top of the diagram.

that a person who has x_2 will have y_1. This is the equation for finding the relative risk:

$$RR(y_1 \text{ when } x_1) = \frac{P(y_1 \mid x_1)}{P(y_1 \mid x_2)} \qquad (6.12)$$

So, for the population in figure 6.3a, the relative risk of contracting the disease when a person is not vaccinated is this: the probability that a person has the disease, given that he or she is not vaccinated, relative to the probability that a person has the disease, given that he or she is vaccinated.[5]

$$RR(\textit{disease A when not vaccinated}) = \qquad (6.13)$$
$$\frac{P(\textit{disease A} \mid \textit{not vaccinated})}{P(\textit{disease A} \mid \textit{vaccinated})} = \frac{.30}{.15} = 2.0$$

On the other hand, consider the relative risk of getting the disease when vaccinated:

$$RR(\textit{disease A when vaccinated}) = \qquad (6.14)$$
$$\frac{P(\textit{disease A} \mid \textit{vaccinated})}{P(\textit{disease A} \mid \textit{not vaccinated})} = \frac{.15}{.30} = .50$$

And finally, using the population in figure 6.4, the relative risk of developing cancer when exposed to fluoride is

$$RR(\textit{cancer when exposed}) = \qquad (6.15)$$
$$\frac{P(\textit{cancer} \mid \textit{exposed})}{P(\textit{cancer} \mid \textit{not exposed})} = \frac{.15}{.15} = 1.0$$

These three different results (in equations 6.13, 6.14, and 6.15) illustrate three characteristics of relative risk:

(a) When the relative risk is 1.0, the variables are independent. This means that having x_1 does not change a person's risk of having y_1 (relative to having x_2).

---

5. The terms *risk* and *probability* are in many contexts—including this textbook—interchangeable. Thus, in the population in figure 6.3a, the risk of getting the disease is just the probability of getting it, and the risk of getting the disease given that a person has not been vaccinated is the conditional probability P(*disease A* | *not vaccinated*). Relative risk, however, is not a probability. Rather, it is one conditional probability relative to another conditional probability. Like the difference in proportions, it is a measure of the difference between two conditional probabilities, but instead of measuring the absolute difference (subtraction), it measures the quotient (division).

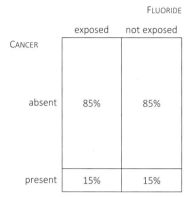

Figure 6.4

(b) When the relative risk is greater than 1.0, having x_1 increases a person's risk of having y_1 (relative to having x_2). And the relative risk indicates how many times more likely a person is to have y_1 when he or she has x_1. For example, the relative risk of 2.0 in equation 6.13 means that a person in this population who has not been vaccinated is twice as likely to have disease A as someone who has been vaccinated.

(c) When the relative risk is less than 1.0, having x_1 decreases a person's risk of having y_1, and the relative risk indicates how much less likely a person is to have y_1 when he or she has x_1. For example, the relative risk of .50 in equation 6.14 means that a person who has been vaccinated is only half as likely to have disease A as someone who has not been vaccinated.

6.4 Calculating the Probability for Multiple Individuals

The examples in section 6.2 all focused on the probability of selecting one individual with some particular collection of properties—the probability of selecting one marble that is red and large, the probability of selecting one marble that is red or large, and so on. This section explains how to calculate the probability that multiple individuals selected from one population will have one specific property—for example, the probability that two marbles selected from a jar will both be red, or the probability that two marbles will be large when three are selected from a jar.

But first, we have to specify two assumptions about how individuals are selected from the population.

1. It has to be the case that each selection is random, which means that every individual has an equal chance of being selected.

2. When one individual is removed from the population another one replaces it, which means that the proportion of individuals with each of the values remains constant.

As long as (1) and (2) are true, then what is obtained for one selection will have no effect on any other selection. Therefore,

3. Each selection is independent of the others.

Now consider a jar of marbles that contains 40 percent red marbles and 60 percent nonred marbles. The probability of getting two red marbles when two selections are made is calculated this way:

$$P(2 \text{ out of } 2 \text{ red}) = P(\text{first is } R) \times P(\text{second is } R) = .40 \times .40 = .16 \qquad (6.16)$$

What's being calculated here is the probability of getting a red marble on the first selection *and* a red marble on the second selection. Because of the *and*, we use one of the conjunction rules, and since the first selection and the second are independent, it's the special conjunction rule.[6]

Before looking at another example, notice that if two marbles are selected from this jar, any of the following scenarios is possible:

1. The first marble selected is red and the second one is red. (R, R)

2. The first marble selected is red and the second one is nonred. (R, N)

3. The first marble selected is nonred and the second one is red. (N, R)

4. The first marble selected is nonred and the second one is nonred. (N, N)

Each of these scenarios is different, although (2) and (3) are similar in that both yield one red and one nonred marble. But nevertheless, they are different scenarios, and it is important to keep this in mind when calculating these probabilities. (Why this is important will become clear in a moment.)

To calculate the probability of getting one (and only one) red marble when two marbles are selected from the jar, we must first find these two probabilities:

---

6. Each selection is being treated as a variable (i.e., the first selection, the second, etc.); the values for each are, in this case, *red* and *nonred*.

(a) A red marble is selected first and a nonred marble is selected second (i.e., R, N)

(b) A nonred marble is selected first and red marble is selected second (i.e., N, R)

The special conjunction rule is used for both:

$$P(R,N) = P(first = R) \times P(second = N) = .40 \times .60 = .24 \tag{6.17}$$

$$P(N,R) = P(first = N) \times P(second = N) = .60 \times .40 = .24 \tag{6.18}$$

The probability of getting one (and only one) red marble when two are selected is the probability of getting (R, N) or (N, R). This *(R, N) or (N, R)* is an "or" statement, and (R, N) and (N, R) are mutually exclusive—getting one of these scenarios excludes the possibility of getting the other one. Thus, we use the special disjunction rule for the last step of this calculation.

$$P(1 \text{ out of } 2 \text{ are red}) = P(R,N) + P(N,R) = .24 + .24 = .48 \tag{6.19}$$

Another example. Consider a different jar of marbles: one that contains 35 percent red marbles and 65 percent nonred marbles. What is the probability of getting exactly two red marbles when three marbles are selected from this jar?

Solution. The first thing that has to be determined is the number of different scenarios that will produce exactly two red marbles when three are selected from the jar. There are three:

(a) The first is red, the second is red, and the third is nonred (R, R, N).

(b) The first is red, the second is nonred, and the third is red (R, N, R).

(c) The first is nonred, the second is red, and the third is red (N, R, R).

Each of these scenarios needs to be part of the calculation when finding the probability of getting two out of three red marbles.

$P(2 \text{ out of } 3 \text{ red marbles}) =$

$P(first \text{ is } R) \times P(second \text{ is } R) \times P(third \text{ is } N) = .35 \times .35 \times .65 = .08$

plus

$P(first \text{ is } R) \times P(second \text{ is } N) \times P(third \text{ is } R) = .35 \times .65 \times .35 = .08 \tag{6.20}$

plus

$P(first \text{ is } N) \times P(second \text{ is } R) \times P(third \text{ is } R) = .65 \times .35 \times .35 = .08$

$= .24$

Hence, the probability of getting exactly two red marbles when three marbles are selected from this jar is 24 percent. Remember that when figuring out these sorts of probabilities the answer is based on all of the scenarios that yield the desired result.

6.5 The Proportional Syllogism

Now back to the proportional syllogism. Here is one of the arguments from chapter 1:

P1 Ninety-four percent of all adolescents in Ohio have received the measles, mumps, and rubella (MMR) vaccine.

P2 Maureen is an adolescent who lives in Ohio.

C Therefore, there is a 94 percent chance that Maureen has received the measles, mumps, and rubella (MMR) vaccine.

argument (1)

It is not too difficult to understand why these premises support this conclusion. As long as there is no other information about Maureen except that she a member of this population, the probability that Maureen has gotten the MMR vaccine comes directly from the proportion of all individuals (in Ohio) who have gotten it. But if instead of a conclusion about one individual, we need a conclusion about multiple individuals, we use the probability rules. For example:

P1 Ninety-four percent of all adolescents in Ohio have received the MMR vaccine.

P2 Maureen and Melissa are adolescents who live in Ohio.

C Therefore, there is an 88 percent chance that Maureen and Melissa have received the MMR vaccine.

argument (2)

Using the information given in the premises, we determine the probability in the conclusion by applying the special conjunction rule:

$$P(both\ MMR) =$$
$$P(Maureen\ MMR) \times P(Melissa\ MMR) = .94 \times .94 = .88$$

(6.21)

Again, we must make the following assumptions in order to use the calculation in equation 6.21:

(a) These girls, Maureen and Melissa, were selected at random. And there is no information indicating that they are more or less likely to have received the MMR vaccine than anyone else in this population.

(b) Their vaccination statuses are independent. That is, one of them being vaccinated (or not) has no effect on whether the other has been vaccinated. In actuality, if they are, say, sisters, or even just from the same community, then their vaccination statuses are probably not independent. For example, if they are sisters and the older one was vaccinated for measles, mumps, and rubella, then there is a greater than 94 percent chance that the younger one was also vaccinated for measles, mumps, and rubella.

Here is another example of the proportional syllogism:

P1   Sixty percent of the marbles in the jar are red.

P2   Two marbles are about to be randomly selected from the jar.

C   There is a 36 percent chance that both of the marbles selected from the jar will be red.

argument (3)

An interesting feature of these arguments is that there is a difference between an argument that is constructed correctly and one that is inductively strong. For any proportional syllogism, a "correct" conclusion is produced by following the probability rules. But following these rules does not always produce a conclusion that is likely to be true if the premises are true.[7] To see this, it is import to understand that the probability in the conclusion indicates how likely it is that some event will occur. In other words, the conclusion in argument (3) is really expressing this idea:

P(Both of the marbles selected from the jar will be red) = .36

The conclusion is just the declarative sentence inside the parentheses, and the probability is the likelihood that the sentence will be true. In

---

7. Recall the definition of inductively strong:

An argument is ***inductively strong*** when it is the case that (1) the argument is not deductively valid, and (2) if the premises are true, then they make it probable that the conclusion is true.

this case, there is a 36 percent chance that this sentence will be true if both premises are true. Thus, even though the conclusion was produced in the correct way, because the premises do not make it very likely that the conclusion will be true, argument (3) is not inductively strong.[8]

It should be obvious, however, that if there is a 36 percent chance that two red marbles will be drawn, then there has to be a 1 − .36 chance that some other number of red marble will be drawn (in this case, one or zero). Therefore, using these same two premises, an argument that is somewhat stronger can be constructed.

P1   Sixty percent of the marbles in the jar are red.

P2   Two marbles are about to be randomly selected from the jar.

 C   There is a 64 percent chance that both marbles will not be red.

argument (4)

We arrive at the conclusion in argument (4), which is stating that one or none of the marbles will be red, by doing this calculation:

$$P(0 \text{ or } 1 R, \ 2 \ selected) =$$

$$P(first \ is \ N) \times P(second \ is \ N) = .40 \times .40 \ = .16$$

$$plus$$

$$P(first \ is \ R) \times P(second \ is \ N) = .60 \times .40 \ = .24 \qquad (6.22)$$

$$plus$$

$$P(first \ is \ N) \times P(second \ is \ R) = .40 \times .60 \ = .24$$

$$= .64$$

In equation 6.22, the probability of getting zero red marbles is computed first and then the probability of getting one red marble is calculated. All of these probabilities are then added together to get the probability that both marbles selected from the jar will not be red, which is 64 percent.

---

8. The entire argument can even be stated as a conditional probability:

P(Both of the marbles selected from the jar will be red | Premise 1 & Premise 2) = .36.

This expresses the idea—which is actually a useful way of thinking about inductive arguments—that the probability of the conclusion, given premises 1 and 2, is 36 percent.

Another example.

P1 Ninety-four percent of all adolescents in Ohio have received the MMR vaccine.

P2 Maureen and Melissa are adolescents who live in Ohio.

C Therefore, at least one of these two has received the MMR vaccine.

argument (5a)

If the premises are true, how likely is it that this conclusion is true?

Solution. "At least one of these two" means *Maureen only, Melissa only,* or *both,* and so these probabilities are needed (M_1 is Maureen, M_2 is Melissa):

$$P(M_1 \ only) = P(M_1 = MMR) \times P(M_2 = not\ MMR) = .94 \times .06 = .056 \quad (6.23)$$

$$P(M_2 \ only) = P(M_1 = not\ MMR) \times P(M_2 = MMR) = .06 \times .94 = .056 \quad (6.24)$$

$$P(M_1 \ \& \ M_2) = P(M_1 = MMR) \times P(M_2 = MMR) = .94 \times .94 = .884 \quad (6.25)$$

And this is the probability that at least one of these two has received the MMR vaccine:

$$P(M_1 \ or \ M_2 \ or \ both) = .056 + .056 + .884 = .996 \quad (6.26)$$

So there is a 99.6 percent chance that the conclusion will be true if the premises are. It's almost certain, but not quite. Adding this information to the conclusion, we can write the argument this way:

P1 94 percent of all adolescents in Ohio have received the MMR vaccine.

P2 Maureen and Melissa are adolescents who live in Ohio.

C Therefore, there is a 99.6 percent chance that at least one of these two has received the MMR vaccine.

argument (5b)

6.5.1 A Note about Evaluating Arguments

It is worth revisiting a point that was made at the end of chapter 1 about evaluating arguments. Arguments like (3) and (4) are deductively invalid, but this is not always obvious upon initial inspection. With respect to argument (3), one might think that, if the premises are true, then it is guaranteed that there is a 36 percent chance that both of the marbles selected from the jar will be red—in other words, the argument is deductively valid. Although this thought is understandable, it is not correct. If it were, then every argument would be valid as long as the conclusion included the word "probably." But that would clearly erode the concept of validity.

One simple way of understanding why these arguments cannot be valid is to consider what it means to claim that argument (3) is deductively valid. To make the point a little clearer, replace "36 percent" with "a small chance." So, to say that argument (3) is valid means that, if the premises are true, then it is guaranteed that there is a small chance that both marbles will be red. But saying "it is guaranteed that there is a small chance" is just the same as saying "there is a small chance." The guarantee adds nothing in the way of certainty, and so the argument cannot meet the standard of a valid argument.

The movie *Anchorman: The Legend of Ron Burgundy* has a joke that is based on this very point. In this scene, Brian Fantana (played by Paul Rudd) is talking with Ron Burgundy (played by Will Ferrell) while preparing to go on a date.

BRIAN FANTANA. Time to musk up. [opens cologne cabinet]

RON BURGUNDY. Wow. Never ceases to amaze me. What cologne you gonna go with? London Gentleman, or wait. No, no, no. Hold on. Blackbeard's Delight.

BRIAN FANTANA. No, she gets a special cologne. It's called Sex Panther by Odeon. It's illegal in nine countries. Yep, it's made with bits of real panther, so you know it's good.

RON BURGUNDY. It's quite pungent.

BRIAN FANTANA. Oh yeah.

RON BURGUNDY. It's a formidable scent. It stings the nostrils. In a good way.

BRIAN FANTANA. Yep.

RON BURGUNDY. Brian, I'm gonna be honest with you, that smells like pure gasoline.

BRIAN FANTANA. They've done studies, you know. Sixty percent of the time, it works every time.

RON BURGUNDY. That doesn't make sense.

The joke, of course, is that Brian Fantana is trying to add certainty to a statement—*the cologne, Sex Panther by Odeon, works*—that is less than certain. It is only true 60 percent of the time.

6.6 Exercises

1. (a) If a marble is taken from the population described in table 6.4, what is the probability that it will be yellow or green?

   (b) If a marble is taken from the population described in table 6.4, what is the probability that it will be blue or yellow?

   (c) Construct a diagram of this population. For the variable *color*, use the values *red* and *nonred*.

   (d) What is the probability that a marble selected from this population will be red and large?

   (e) What is the probability that a marble selected from this population will be red or large?

   (f) What is the probability that a marble selected from this population will be red and small?

   (g) What is the probability that a marble selected from this population will be red or small?

2. (a) Construct a diagram of the population described in table 6.5. For the variable *color*, use the values *red* and *nonred*.

   (b) If a marble is selected from the population described in table 6.5, what is the probability that it will be red and small?

   (c) If a marble is selected from this population, what is the probability that it will be red or small?

Table 6.4
Use this population for exercises 1a through 1g.

The marbles in a jar		
100	red marbles,	of which 40 are large and 60 are small
50	green marbles,	of which 20 are large and 30 are small
30	blue marbles,	of which 15 are large and 15 are small
20	yellow marbles,	of which 5 are large and 15 are small

Table 6.5
Use this population for exercises 2a through 2g.

The marbles in the jar		
100	red marbles,	of which 60 are large and 40 are small
50	green marbles,	of which 10 are large and 40 are small
30	blue marbles,	of which 5 are large and 25 are small
20	yellow marbles,	of which 5 are large and 15 are small

   (d) If a marble is selected from this population, what is the probability that it will be nonred and small?

   (e) If a marble is selected from this population, what is the probability that it will be nonred or small?

   (f) If a marble is selected from this population, what is the probability that it will be yellow and large? Try answering this without creating a diagram.

   (g) If a marble is selected from this population, what is the probability that it will be yellow or large?

3. Here is a description of a population. Forty percent of the individuals in this population are male; 60 percent are female. Sixty percent are smokers, and 40 percent are nonsmokers. Additionally, of the males, half smoke and half do not smoke. Of the females, 67 percent smoke and 33 percent do not.

   (a) Create a diagram of this population. Are the variables *gender* and *smoking status* associated or independent?

   (b) What is the probability of selecting an individual from this population who is male and a smoker?

   (c) What is the probability of selecting an individual from this population who is male or a smoker?

   (d) What is the probability of selecting an individual from this population who is male and a nonsmoker?

   (e) What is the probability of selecting an individual from this population who is male or a nonsmoker?

   (f) What is the probability of selecting an individual from this population who is female and a smoker?

(g) What is the probability of selecting an individual from this population who is female or a smoker?

(h) What is the probability of selecting an individual from this population who is female and a nonsmoker?

(i) What is the probability of selecting an individual from this population who is female or a nonsmoker?

4. There is a 50 percent chance that Joan will enroll at State University next fall. If she does go to State, there is a 60 percent chance that she will make (and play on) the basketball team. What rule is used to figure out the probability that Joan will go to State and play basketball there? What is the probability that Joan will go to State and play basketball?

5. The Smiths are expecting a baby, but they are not yet sure about a name. If the baby is a girl, there is a 70 percent chance that they will name her Kim and a 30 percent chance that they will name her Sarah. If the baby is a boy, there is a 40 percent chance that they will name him Michael, a 30 percent chance that they will name him Willie, and a 30 percent chance that they will name him Thomas. The chance of a boy or a girl is 50–50.

(a) What is the probability that the baby will be named Kim? (That is, what is the probability that the baby will be a girl and named Kim?) What is the probability that the baby will be named Sarah?

(b) What is the probability that the baby will be named Michael? What is the probability that the baby will be named Willie? What is the probability that the baby will be named Thomas?

(c) What is the probability that the baby will be named Kim or Sarah? What is the probability that the baby will be named Kim, Sarah, or Michael? What rule is used to find these probabilities?

6. In a normal deck of cards, half the cards are red and half are black. There are eight cards (out of 52) that are both red and odd numbered. Therefore, the probability of selecting a card that is red and odd is about .154 (i.e., $8/52$).

A red card has been selected from a deck; what is the probability that it has an odd number? That is, what is $P(odd \mid red)$? What rule is used to find this probability?

7. One card has been selected from a normal deck. It is black, and it is not returned to the deck. A second card is about to be selected. The probability of getting a black card and then another black card (without replacing the first card) is 24.5 percent—that is, P(*first* = *B* & *second* = *B*) = .245. The probability of getting a black card and then a red card (again, without replacement) is 25.5 percent.

   (a) What is the probability that the second card will be black, given that the first one was black? That is, what is P(*second* = *B* | *first* = *B*)?

   (b) What is the probability that the second card will be red, given that the first one was black? That is, what is P(*second* = *R* | *first* = *B*)?

8. GDL Manufacturing has a small plant with an equal number of male and female employees. Hence, if an employee is selected at random, P(*M*) = P(*F*) = .50. Some of the employees smoke. If an employee is selected at random, the probability of that employee being a male smoker (i.e., male and a smoker) is 12 percent; the probability of that employee being a female smoker is 18 percent.

   (a) If an employee is selected at random and that employee is male, what is the probability that he smokes? What rule is used to find this probability?

   (b) If an employee is selected at random and that employee is female, what is the probability that she smokes?

9. (a) In the population in figure 6.5, what is the relative risk of being a smoker when not a high school graduate?

   (b) In the population in figure 6.5, what is the relative risk of being a smoker when a high school graduate?

10. In the population in figure 6.6, what is the relative risk of smoking when not a high school graduate?

11. (a) In the population diagrammed in figure 6.7a, what is the relative risk of having the disease when not vaccinated? In the population diagrammed in figure 6.7b, what is the relative risk of having the disease when not vaccinated?

   (b) In both populations (figures 6.7a and 6.7b), *disease A present* and *not vaccinated* are positively associated. Use the difference in proportions to measure the strength of each of these positive associations. When comparing these two populations, why is the difference in

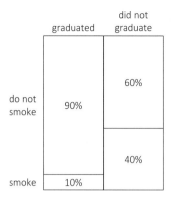

Figure 6.5
Use this population for exercises 9a and 9b.

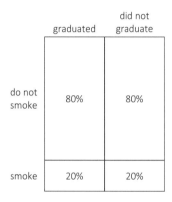

Figure 6.6
Use this population for exercise 10.

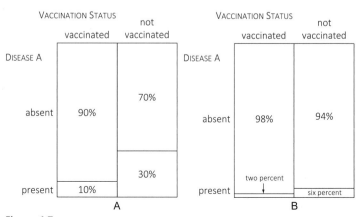

Figure 6.7
Use these populations for exercises 11a and 11b.

proportions an especially useful measure of the relationship between *disease A present* and *not vaccinated*?

12. (a) A jar contains 88 percent red marbles. If three marbles are selected from this jar, what is the probability that all three will be red? (Remember the two assumptions explained at the beginning of section 6.4.)

   (b) If three marbles are selected from the same jar, what is the probability that exactly two will be red?

   (c) If three marbles are selected from this jar, what is the probability that one (and only one) will be red?

   (d) If three marbles are selected from this jar, what is the probability that zero will be red?

13. At the beginning of the summer, Sarah and Chris buy an old Buick Regal and start out on a trip across the country. Because the tires (like the car itself) are old, each one has a 30 percent chance of going flat during the trip.

   (a) What is the probability that all of the tires that they began their trip with will go flat before they reach their destination? What rule is used to find the answer?

   (b) What is the probability that one (and only one) of the tires that they began their trip with will go flat before they reach their destination? What rules are used to find this answer?

14. There is a 40 percent chance that it will rain on Friday, a 50 percent chance that it will rain on Saturday, and a 60 percent chance that it will rain on Sunday. Whether or not it rains on any one of these days has no effect on whether it rains on any other day (i.e., in this problem, each day's weather is independent of the other days' weather).

   (a) How likely is that it will rain on all three of these days?

   (b) How likely is it that it will rain on one and only one of these three days?

   (c) How likely is it that it will rain on at least one of these three days (maybe more)?

15. Complete the conclusion of this argument.

   P1 Seventy percent of the lawyers at the Smith & Brown law firm are from New York.

P2 Kim, Willie, and Morgan are lawyers at Smith & Brown, and they have been (randomly) assigned to work on a case together.

  C There is _____ chance that two (and only two) of these lawyers are from New York.

16. Complete the conclusion of this argument.

    P1 Seventy percent of the lawyers at the Smith & Brown law firm are from New York.

    P2 Kim, Willie, and Morgan are lawyers at Smith & Brown, and they have been (randomly) assigned to work on a case together.

      C There is _____ chance that one or more of these lawyers is from New York.

17. Sarah has a jar of marbles, and 80 percent of the marbles in the jar are red. Josh is about to select three marbles from this jar. What is the probability that all three of the marbles that Josh selects will be red? Use this information to construct an argument. Make the answer to the question the conclusion of the argument.

18. Forty percent of the attorneys at the Jones & Press law firm graduated from a law school in Chicago. Four Jones & Press attorneys live in the same apartment building in Chicago. Use this information to construct two arguments. Make the answers to questions 18a and 18b the conclusions of the arguments.

    (a) What is the probability that all four went to law school in Chicago?

    (b) What is the probability that none of the four went to law school in Chicago?

6.7 Answers

1. (a) To calculate the probability that a marble selected from this jar (table 6.4) will be yellow or green, we need the probability of selecting a yellow marble and the probability of selecting a green marble.

    $P(Y)$ = the proportion of yellow marbles in the jar = $20/200$ = .10

    $P(G)$ = the proportion of green marbles in the population = $50/200$ = .25

Then, to compute the probability that a marble selected from this jar will be yellow or green, we use the special disjunction rule.

$$P(\textit{yellow or green}) = P(Y) + P(G) = .10 + .25 = .35 \qquad (6.27)$$

(b) In the population described in table 6.4, the probability that a marble will be blue or yellow is 25 percent.

$$P(\textit{blue or yellow}) = P(B) + P(Y) = .15 + .10 = .25 \qquad (6.28)$$

(c) The population in table 6.4 can be diagrammed either of the ways that are shown in figures 6.8a and 6.8b. Notice that, in both diagrams, there is the same relationship between the variables *color* and *size*. In this population, color and size are independent.

(d) For the population described in table 6.4, the probability that a marble will be red and large is 20 percent. Since the variables are independent, this is found with the special conjunction rule.

$$P(\textit{red \& large}) = P(R) \times P(L) = .50 \times .40 = .20 \qquad (6.29)$$

(e) The probability that a marble will be red or large is 70 percent.

$$P(\textit{red or large}) = P(R) + P(L) - P(R \& L) = .50 + .40 - .20 = .70 \quad (6.30)$$

(f) The probability that a marble will be red and small is 30 percent.

$$P(\textit{red \& small}) = P(R) \times P(S) = .50 \times .60 = .30 \qquad (6.31)$$

(g) The probability that a marble will be red or small is 80 percent.

$$P(\textit{red or small}) = P(R) + P(S) - P(R \& S) = .50 + .60 - .30 = .80 \quad (6.32)$$

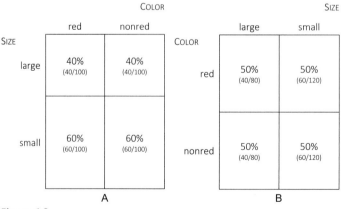

Figure 6.8

2. (a) Whichever way the population is diagrammed, the same relationship occurs between the variables (see figures 6.9a and 6.9b). In this
case, the variables are associated. *Small* and *nonred* are positively associated, and *large* and *red* are positively associated. For the negative
associations, *small* and *red* are negatively associated, and *large* and
nonred are negatively associated.

(b) There is a 20 percent chance of selecting a marble that is red and
small from this population (table 6.5).

$$P(red \& small) = P(R) \times P(S|R) = .50 \times .40 = .20 \qquad (6.33)$$

Now that the population has been diagrammed, we can find $P(S|R)$
by looking at the diagram that has red and nonred at the top. As this
diagram (on the left) shows, if a marble is red, there is a 60 percent
chance that it will be large and a 40 percent chance that it will be
small. Hence, $P(S|R) = .40$.

Equation 6.33 follows the convention of multiplying the two
values in the order that they are given (with the second value as the
first part of the conditional probability). The same probability can
also be calculated as is shown in equation 6.34, in which case figure
6.9b is useful for identifying the conditional probability.

$$P(small \& red) = P(S) \times P(R|S) = .60 \times .33 = .20 \qquad (6.34)$$

(c) The general disjunction rule is used to find the probability of selecting a marble that is red or small. Notice that the result from question

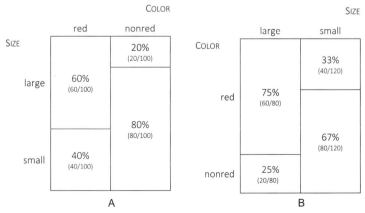

Figure 6.9

2b has to be used in this calculation.

$$P(red \text{ or } small) = P(R) + P(S) - P(R \& S) = .50 + .60 - .20 = .90 \quad (6.35)$$

(d) The probability of selecting a marble that is nonred and small is 40 percent, and this can be found by either of these calculations:

$$P(nonred \& small) = P(N) \times P(S|N) = .50 \times .80 = .40 \quad (6.36)$$

or

$$P(small \& nonred) = P(S) \times P(N|S) = .60 \times .67 = .40 \quad (6.37)$$

(e) The probability of selecting a marble that is nonred or small is 70 percent.

$$P(nonred \text{ or } small) = P(N) + P(S) - P(N \& S) = .50 + .60 - .40 = .70$$
$$(6.38)$$

(f) For this problem, without a diagram of the population to easily figure out if the variables are associated or independent, one approach is just to use the general conjunction rule. This will produce the correct answer even if the special conjunction rule could have been used. The conditional probability that is used for this calculation—the probability of a marble being large if it is yellow—is the percentage of the yellow marbles that are large.

$P(L|Y)$, [i.e., the probability of a marble being large if it is yellow] = $^5/_{20} = .25$

An optional step is to see if this conditional probability is the same as or different from $P(L)$. If $P(L) = P(L|Y)$, then the variables are independent and we can use the special conjunction rule. If $P(L) \neq P(L|Y)$, then the variables are associated and we have to use the general conjunction rule.

There are 200 marbles in this population and 80 of them are large. Therefore,

$P(L) = {}^{80}/_{200} = .40$

Since $P(L) \neq P(L|Y)$, the general conjunction rule must be used. But first we need one more probability:

$P(Y) = {}^{20}/_{200} = .10$

This, then, is the calculation:

$$P(yellow \& large) = P(Y) \times P(L|Y) = .10 \times .25 = .025 \qquad (6.39)$$

And the answer is 2.5 percent.

Notice that the calculation for $P(L \& Y)$ produces the same result.

$$P(large \& yellow) = P(L) \times P(Y|L) = .40 \times .0625 = .025 \qquad (6.40)$$

(g) The probability that a marble selected from the population described in table 6.5 will be yellow or large is 47.5 percent. (Remember that $P(Y \& L)$ was calculated in the previous question.)

$$P(yellow \text{ or } large) = P(Y) + P(L) - P(Y \& L) = .10 + .40 - .025 = .475$$
$$(6.41)$$

3. (a) Given the information provided, the only way to create the diagram is with the values for gender at the top (see figure 6.10). The variables *gender* and *smoking status* are associated.

(b) $P(male \& smoker) = P(M) \times P(S|M) = .40 \times .50 = .20$

(c) $P(male \text{ or } smoker) = P(M) + P(S) - P(M \& S) = .40 + .60 - .20 = .80$

(d) $P(male \& nonsmoker) = P(M) \times P(N|M) = .40 \times .50 = .20$

(e) $P(male \text{ or } nonsmoker) = P(M) + P(N) - P(M \& N) = .40 + .40 - .20 = .60$

(f) $P(female \& smoker) = P(F) \times P(S|F) = .60 \times .67 = .40$

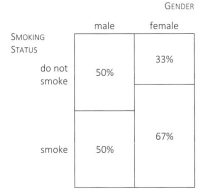

Figure 6.10

(g) P(*female* or *smoker*) = P(F) + P(S) − P(F & S) = .60 + .60 − .40 = .80

(h) P(*female* & *nonsmoker*) = P(F) × P(N|F) = .60 × .33 = .20

(i) P(*female* or *nonsmoker*) = P(F) + P(N) − P(F & N) = .60 + .40 − .20 = .80

4. The general conjunction rule is used to find this answer. The probability that Joan will play basketball if she goes to State University is a conditional probability—it is the probability that she will play basketball on the condition that she goes to State [i.e., $P(B|S) = .60$].

   The probability that Joan will go to State University and play basketball there is .30.

$$P(State \& basketball) = P(S) \times P(B|S) = .50 \times .60 = .30 \qquad (6.42)$$

5. (a) To find the probability that the baby will be named Kim, we have to calculate the probability that the baby is a girl and named Kim. And then do the same for Sarah.

$$P(K) = P(girl \& Kim) = P(G) \times P(K|G) = .50 \times .70 = .35$$
$$P(S) = P(girl \& Sarah) = P(G) \times P(S|G) = .50 \times .30 = .15$$

   (b)

$$P(M) = P(boy \& Michael) = P(B) \times P(M|B) = .50 \times .40 = .20$$
$$P(W) = P(boy \& Willie) = P(B) \times P(W|B) = .50 \times .30 = .15$$
$$P(T) = P(boy \& Thomas) = P(B) \times P(T|B) = .50 \times .30 = .15$$

   (c) The probability that the baby will be named Kim or Sarah is the sum of the two probabilities in 5a. Since *being a girl and named Kim* and *being a girl and named Sarah* are mutually exclusive (i.e., being one excludes the possibility of being the other), the special disjunction rule is used.

$$P(Kim \text{ or } Sarah) = P(G \& K) + P(G \& S) = .35 + .15 = .50$$

   And .50 is, of course, just the probability that the baby will be a girl. The probability that the baby will be named Kim, Sarah, or Michael is .70. Again, we use the special disjunction rule.

$$P(K \text{ or } S \text{ or } M) = P(G \& K) + P(G \& S) + P(B \& M)$$
$$= .35 + .15 + .20 = .70$$

6. The probability of a card, selected at random, being red is .50. The probability of a card, selected at random, being red and odd numbered is 15.4 percent—that is, $P(R \& O) = .154$. Thus, the probability of a card being odd, given that it is red, is 31 percent. This probability is found using the conditional probability rule:

$$P(odd \mid red) = \frac{P(R \& O)}{P(R)} = \frac{.154}{.50} = .31 \tag{6.43}$$

7. (a) Given that the first card selected was black, the probability of the second one being black is 49 percent.

$$P(second = B \mid first = B) = \frac{P(1st = B \& 2nd = B)}{P(1st = B)} = \frac{.245}{.50} = .49 \tag{6.44}$$

(b) Given that the first card selected was black, the probability of the second one being red is 51 percent.

$$P(second = R \mid first = B) = \frac{P(1st = B \& 2nd = R)}{P(1st = B)} = \frac{.255}{.50} = .51 \tag{6.45}$$

8. (a) The conditional probability rule is used to find $P(smokes \mid male)$ when $P(M)$ and $P(M \& S)$ are known.

$$P(smokes \mid male) = \frac{P(M \& S)}{P(M)} = \frac{.12}{.50} = .24 \tag{6.46}$$

(b) The probability of the employee being a smoker, given that she is female, is 36 percent.

$$P(smokes \mid female) = \frac{P(F \& S)}{P(F)} = \frac{.18}{.50} = .36 \tag{6.47}$$

9. (a) In this population, a person is four times more likely to smoke if he or she has not graduated from high school. That is,

$$RR(smoker\ when\ not\ a\ graduate) =$$
$$\frac{P(smoker \mid not\ a\ graduate)}{P(smoker \mid graduate)} = \frac{.40}{.10} = 4.0 \tag{6.48}$$

(b) A person who did graduate from high school is only a quarter as likely (i.e., only .25 times as likely) to smoke as someone who did not graduate.

$$RR(smoker\ when\ a\ graduate) =$$
$$\frac{P(smoker \mid graduate)}{P(smoker \mid didn't\ graduate)} = \frac{.10}{.40} = .25 \tag{6.49}$$

10. In this population, a person who has not graduated is just as likely to smoke as someone who has graduated (i.e., "one time" more likely).

RR(*smoker when not a graduate*) =

$$\frac{P(smoker \mid not\ a\ graduate)}{P(smoker \mid graduate)} = \frac{.20}{.20} = 1.0 \qquad (6.50)$$

11. (a) For the population in figure 6.7a, the relative risk of having the disease when not vaccinated is 3.0.

RR(*having disease A when not vaccinated*) =

$$\frac{P(present \mid not\ vaccinated)}{P(present \mid vaccinated)} = \frac{.30}{.10} = 3.0 \qquad (6.51)$$

For the population diagrammed in figure 6.7b, it is also 3.0.

RR(*having disease A when not vaccinated*) =

$$\frac{P(present \mid not\ vaccinated)}{P(present \mid vaccinated)} = \frac{.06}{.02} = 3.0 \qquad (6.52)$$

In both populations, a person who has not been vaccinated is three times more likely to have the disease than someone who has been vaccinated.

(b) In figure 6.7a, the difference between the proportion of people with the disease among the unvaccinated and among the vaccinated is .20 (that is, .30 − .10 = .20). Using this value as a measure, the strength of the positive association between *disease A present* and *not vaccinated* is .20. In figure 6.7b, again using the difference in proportions, the strength of the positive association between *disease A present* and *not vaccinated* is .04 (i.e., .06 − .02 = .04).

In both populations, *disease A present* is positively associated with *not vaccinated*; and in both populations, a person who has not been vaccinated is three times more likely to have the disease than someone who has been vaccinated. (I.e., the relative risk of having the disease when not vaccinated is 3.0 in both populations.) Nevertheless, the populations are clearly not the same, and looking at the difference in proportions is a good way of explaining the difference. It is the difference in proportions that indicates that the values *disease A present* and *not vaccinated* have a much stronger tendency to go together in the population in figure 6.7a than they do in the population in figure 6.7b.

12. (a) The jar contains 88 percent red marbles. When three are selected from this jar (randomly and with replacement), there is a 68.1 percent chance that all three will be red.

$P(3\ out\ of\ 3\ are\ red) =$

$P(1st = R) \times P(2nd = R) \times P(3rd = R) = .88 \times .88 \times .88 = .681$ (6.53)

(b) When three marbles are selected from this jar, the probability that exactly two will be red is 27.9 percent.

$P(2\ out\ of\ 3\ are\ red) =$

$P(1st = R) \times P(2nd = R) \times P(3rd = N) = .88 \times .88 \times .12 = .093$

plus

$P(1st = R) \times P(2nd = N) \times P(3rd = R) = .88 \times .12 \times .88 = .093$

plus

$P(1st = N) \times P(2nd = R) \times P(3rd = R) = .12 \times .88 \times .88 = .093$

$= .279$

(6.54)

(c) The probability that one (and only one) marble will be red is 3.8 percent.

$P(1\ out\ of\ 3\ is\ red) =$

$P(1st = R) \times P(2nd = N) \times P(3rd = N) = .88 \times .12 \times .12 = .0127$

plus

$P(1st = N) \times P(2nd = R) \times P(3rd = N) = .12 \times .88 \times .12 = .0127$

plus

$P(1st = N) \times P(2nd = N) \times P(3rd = R) = .12 \times .12 \times .88 = .0127$

$= .038$

(6.55)

(d) The probability that no marbles will be red, when three are selected, is 0.2 percent.

$P(0\ out\ of\ 3\ are\ red) =$

$P(1st = N) \times P(2nd = N) \times P(3rd = N) = .12 \times .12 \times .12 = .002$

(6.56)

13. (a) Because one tire going flat does not affect any of the other tires going flat, we use the special conjunction rule for this problem. What we must figure out here is the probability that one of the original tires goes flat *and* then a second one goes flat *and* then a third one goes flat *and* then the last one goes flat.

Even though the probability of each one going flat is 30 percent, the probability that all four tires will go flat is 0.81 percent (i.e., just under 1 percent). FD is *front driver's side tire*, FP is *front passenger's side tire*, etc.

$$P(all\ four\ go\ flat) =$$
$$P(FD = flat) \times P(FP = flat) \times P(RD = flat) \times P(RP = flat) =$$
$$.30 \times .30 \times .30 \times .30 = .0081 \quad (6.57)$$

(b) There is a 41 percent chance that one (and only one) of the four tires will go flat during the trip. We use the special conjunction rule and the special disjunction rule to get this answer.

$$P(only\ one\ of\ the\ four\ goes\ flat) =$$
$$P(FD = F) \times P(FP = N) \times P(RD = N) \times P(RP = N) =$$
$$.30 \times .70 \times .70 \times .70 = .1029$$

plus

$$P(FD = N) \times P(FP = F) \times P(RD = N) \times P(RP = N) =$$
$$.70 \times .30 \times .70 \times .70 = .1029$$

plus $\quad$ (6.58)

$$P(FD = N) \times P(FP = N) \times P(RD = F) \times P(RP = N) =$$
$$.70 \times .70 \times .30 \times .70 = .1029$$

plus

$$P(FD = N) \times P(FP = N) \times P(RD = N) \times P(RP = F) =$$
$$.70 \times .70 \times .70 \times .30 = .1029$$
$$= .412$$

14. (a) There is a 12 percent chance that it will rain on all three of these days.

$$P(3\ out\ of\ 3\ days\ of\ rain) =$$
$$P(Fri = R) \times P(Sat = R) \times P(Sun = R) = .40 \times .50 \times .60 = .12$$

(6.59)

(b) There is a 38 percent chance that it will rain on only one of these three days. Since there are three different ways of getting this result (only one day of rain), three different scenarios must be taken into account.

P(*only* 1 *day of rain*) =

$$P(Fri = R) \times P(Sat = N) \times P(Sun = N) = .40 \times .50 \times .40 = .08$$

plus

$$P(Fri = N) \times P(Sat = R) \times P(Sun = N) = .60 \times .50 \times .40 = .12 \quad (6.60)$$

plus

$$P(Fri = N) \times P(Sat = N) \times P(Sun = R) = .60 \times .50 \times .60 = .18$$

$$= .38$$

(c) There is an 88 percent chance that it will rain on one or more of these three days. What is being calculated here is the probability that it will rain only one day *or* only two days *or* all three days. We have already determined that there is a 12 percent chance that it will rain on all three days and a 38 percent chance that it will rain on only one day. Here is the calculation for two days:

P(2 *out of* 3 *days of rain*) =

$$P(Fri = R) \times P(Sat = R) \times P(Sun = N) = .40 \times .50 \times .40 = .08$$

plus

$$P(Fri = R) \times P(Sat = N) \times P(Sun = R) = .40 \times .50 \times .60 = .12 \quad (6.61)$$

plus

$$P(Fri = N) \times P(Sat = R) \times P(Sun = R) = .60 \times .50 \times .60 = .18$$

$$= .38$$

Thus, the probability that it will rain on one or more of these three days is 88 percent.

P(1 *or more days of rain*) =

$$P(1 \textit{ of } 3) + P(2 \textit{ of } 3) + P(3 \textit{ of } 3) = .38 + .38 + .12 = .88 \qquad (6.62)$$

15. The conclusion of this argument is

   C There is a 44 percent chance that two (and only two) of these lawyers are from New York.

The probability is found this way:

P(2 *out of* 3 *are from NY*) =

P($K = NY$) × P($W = NY$) × P($M = not\ NY$) = .70 × .70 × .30 = .147

plus

P($K = NY$) × P($W = not\ NY$) × P($M = NY$) = .70 × .30 × .70 = .147

plus

P($K = not\ NY$) × P($W = NY$) × P($M = NY$) = .30 × .70 × .70 = .147

= **.441**

(6.63)

16. The conclusion of this argument is

   C There is 97 percent chance that one or more of these lawyers is from New York.

The probability is found by adding the probability from the previous question [P(2 *out of* 3 *from NY*) = .441], the probability that one of the three will be from New York, and the probability that all three are from New York.

P(1 *out of* 3 *is from NY*) =

P($K = NY$) × P($W = not\ NY$) × P($M = not\ NY$) = .70 × .30 × .30 = .063

plus

P($K = not\ NY$) × P($W = NY$) × P($M = not\ NY$) = .30 × .70 × .30 = .063

plus

P($K = not\ NY$) × P($W = not\ NY$) × P($M = NY$) = .30 × .30 × .70 = .063

= **.189**

(6.64)

P(3 *out of* 3 *are from NY*) =

P($K = NY$) × P($W = NY$) × P($M = NY$) = .70 × .70 × .70 = **.343**

(6.65)

P(1 *or more of the* 3 *are from NY*) =

P(1 *of* 3) + P(2 *of* 3) + P(3 *of* 3) = .189 + .441 + .343 = **.973**

(6.66)

17. **P1** Eighty percent of the marbles in Sarah's jar are red.

    P2 Three marbles are about to be selected (randomly and with replacement) from this jar.

    C Therefore, there is a 51 percent chance that all three will be red.

The probability for the conclusion is calculated this way:

$$P(3 \textit{ out of } 3 \textit{ are red}) =$$
$$P(\textit{1st} = R) \times P(\textit{2nd} = R) \times P(\textit{3rd} = R) = .80 \times .80 \times .80 = \textbf{.512}$$
(6.67)

18. (a) This is a case where, in real life, the selections from the population (so to speak) might not be independent. When multiple individuals work together and live in the same building, if one of them went to law school in Chicago, it may be more likely that the others did as well—for instance, maybe they've known each other since they were in law school and that's why they are living in the same building. Nonetheless, right now, they will be treated as if they are independent, and so we use the special conjunction rule.

    P1 Forty percent of the attorneys at the Jones & Press law firm graduated from a law school in Chicago.

    P2 Four residents of an apartment building are Jones & Press attorneys.

    C Therefore, there is a 2.6 percent chance that all four went to law school in Chicago.

Notice that premise 2 is written in this format: *These individuals* are members of *this population*. Writing premise 2 exactly that way isn't mandatory—the relevant information can be expressed other ways—but it does make the argument clearer. This is the calculation needed for the conclusion:

$$P(\textit{all four, law school in Chicago}) =$$
$$P(\textit{first} = C) \times P(\textit{second} = C)$$
$$\times\, P(\textit{third} = C) \times P(\textit{fourth} = C) =$$
$$.40 \times .40 \times .40 \times .40 = .026$$
(6.68)

(b) **P1** Forty percent of the attorneys at the Jones & Press law firm graduated from a law school in Chicago.

    P2 Four residents of an apartment building are Jones & Press attorneys.

    C Therefore, there is a 13 percent chance that none of the four went to law school in Chicago.

$$P(\textit{none of the four, law school in Chicago}) =$$
$$P(\textit{first} = N) \times P(\textit{second} = N)$$
$$\times\ P(\textit{third} = N) \times P(\textit{fourth} = N) =$$
$$.60 \times .60 \times .60 \times .60 = \mathbf{.1296}$$

$$(6.69)$$

7 The Inductive Generalization

7.1 Introduction

Consider a jar of marbles. Forty percent of the marbles in the jar are red. If three marbles are selected from this jar (randomly and with replacement), there is a 6 percent chance that all three will be red; a 29 percent chance that exactly two will be red; a 43 percent chance that only one will be red; and a 22 percent chance that none of the marbles that are selected will be red.

One convenient way of representing this information is in a ***sampling distribution*** like the one in figure 7.1. On the bottom of the chart—on the *x*-axis—are the different possible ***relative frequencies*** of red marbles. When three marbles are about to be selected from the jar, the result may be zero out of three, one out of three, two out of three, or three out of three red marbles—in other words, 0 percent, 33 percent, 67 percent, or 100 percent red marbles. So while the *frequency* of red marbles is the number of red marbles selected (one, two, three, etc.), the *relative frequency* of red marbles is the number of red marbles divided by the total number taken from the jar. On the left side of the chart—on the *y*-axis— are the probabilities, that is, the chance of getting each possible relative frequency.

The sampling distribution is nice to have when thinking about the probabilities for three selections from the jar. But if only three selections are going to be made, the information in the sampling distribution can just as easily be listed, as it is in the first paragraph of this chapter. If, however, we are considering a larger number of selections from the jar, then, to quickly

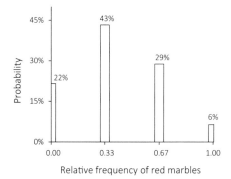

Figure 7.1
When 40 percent of the marbles in the jar are red and three marbles will be selected:
P(0/3 red) = .22
P(1/3 red) = .43
P(2/3 red) = .29
P(3/3 red) = .06

and easily grasp the probability of each possible relative frequency, the sampling distribution is really essential.

For the five sampling distributions in figures 7.1 and 7.2a through 7.2d, the probability of selecting one red marble is the same; for each one P(R) = .40. So, let's say that all of the distributions represent information for the same jar of marbles—a jar in which 40 percent of the marbles are red. Each distribution just contains information for a different situation: in the first situation three marbles will be selected from the jar, in the next situation five will be selected, then 10, 50, and 100.

By looking at these five sampling distributions carefully, we can see the following:

(a) In figures 7.2a – 7.2d, the ***most probable relative frequency***—that is, the relative frequency that someone is most likely to get—is .40, which is the same as the percentage of red marbles in the jar. In figure 7.1, the most probable relative frequency is as close to .40 as is possible when three marbles will be selected.

(b) As the number of selections from the population increases, the probability of the most probable relative frequency goes down. The most probable relative frequency for each scenario is also listed in table 7.1.

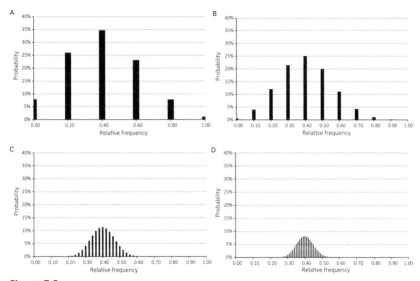

Figure 7.2
Sampling distributions for selections from a jar containing 40 percent red marbles.
(A) 5 selections. (B) 10 selections. (C) 50 selections. (D) 100 selections. On the bottom
of each chart (on the x-axis) is the relative frequency of red marbles. On the side of
each (on the y-axis) is the probability of getting each relative frequency.

Table 7.1
The probabilities for the most likely relative frequency when 3, 5, 10, 50, and 100
marbles will be selected from a jar that contains 40 percent red marbles. The information in each row can be read as, for instance, "When five marbles are selected from
this jar, there is a 35 percent chance of getting 40 percent red marbles (i.e., 2 out of 5),
and that is the most likely outcome."

Marbles selected	Probability	Most probable relative frequency
3	43% chance	33% red marbles
5	35% chance	40% red marbles
10	25% chance	40% red marbles
50	11% chance	40% red marbles
100	8% chance	40% red marbles

7.2   Calculating the Probability of an Interval

Imagine being offered the following deal. One hundred marbles are about
to be selected (randomly and with replacement) from a jar that contains

40 percent red marbles.[1] If you correctly guess the number of red marbles that are selected, you will win $200. The most reasonable guess is *40 percent of the marbles that are selected will be red*. But the chance of this guess being correct is pretty small—only 8 percent (see figures 7.2d and 7.3). A safer guess would be one like this: *between 39 percent and 41 percent of the marbles will be red*. As it turns out, there is a 24 percent chance that, when 100 marbles are selected from the jar, 39 percent, 40 percent, or 41 percent of them will be red.

Let's say that you are allowed to guess three numbers, although if you guess three and one of them is correct, you will only win $150. The possible reward is less than before, but by guessing this range, the chance of winning has increased from less than one in ten to almost one in four.

So, how is the probability of getting 39 percent, 40 percent, or 41 percent red marbles (when 100 are selected) determined? We use the special disjunction rule:

$$P(.39R \text{ or } .40R \text{ or } .41R) =$$
$$P(.39R) + P(.40R) + P(.41R) = .08 + .081 + .079 = .24 \tag{7.1}$$

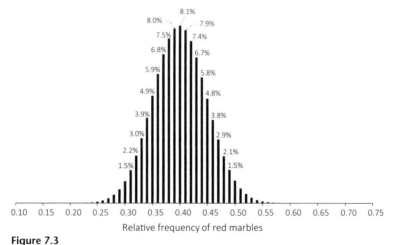

Figure 7.3
A sampling distribution for 100 selections from a jar containing 40 percent red marbles.

1. For all of the examples in this chapter, it will be assumed that the selections are made randomly and, when one individual is selected from a population, another one replaces it so that the proportions (and, hence, the probabilities) stay constant.

What is being computed here is the probability of selecting 39 percent red marbles *or* 40 percent red marbles *or* 41 percent red marbles. Each of these relative frequencies is mutually exclusive—getting one of them excludes you from getting any of the others. Thus, we use the special disjunction rule.

A guess that has a 24 percent chance of being correct is not bad, but there is a simple way to make it even more likely that the guess will be correct, namely, include more relative frequencies. For example, someone who guesses that between 31 percent and 49 percent of the marbles that are selected will be red has a 95 percent chance of being correct. In other words, there is a 95 percent chance that the actual number of red marbles that are selected will be somewhere within this interval: .31–.49 red marbles. The probabilities are given in figure 7.3, and, using the special disjunction rule again, the probability of getting each relative frequency between .31 and .49 are added together.

$$0.015 + 0.022 + 0.030 + 0.039 + 0.049 +$$
$$0.059 + 0.068 + 0.075 + 0.080 + 0.081 +$$
$$0.079 + 0.074 + 0.067 + 0.058 + 0.048 +$$
$$0.038 + 0.029 + 0.021 + 0.015 = \quad 0.947$$

$$(7.2)$$

7.3 The 95 Percent Interval

When the proportions in a population are known, an interval like the one just created is useful for understanding what the outcome will most likely be if a certain number of selections are made from the population. Four different populations are represented in figures 7.4 through 7.7. Each sampling distribution shows the probability for every relative frequency of red marbles when 100 marbles are going to be selected. In each, the bars that are colored black represent probabilities that add up to 95 percent.

In figure 7.4, the sampling distribution represents selections from a population in which 40 percent of the marbles are red. In figure 7.5, it's 50 percent; in figure 7.6, 60 percent; and in the last, 70 percent. Notice that in each, the most probable relative frequency matches the proportion of red marbles in the population—and, as a result, also matches $P(R)$. Since the most probable relative frequency occurs in different places, the "curve"

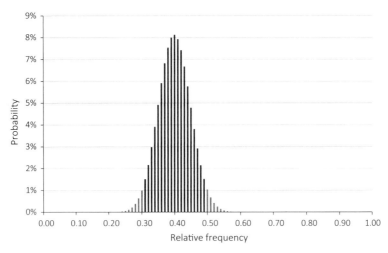

Figure 7.4
A sampling distribution for 100 selections from a jar containing 40 percent red marbles.

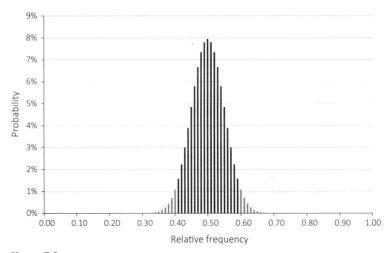

Figure 7.5
A sampling distribution for 100 selections from a jar containing 50 percent red marbles.

that is created by all of the probabilities moves around. But while this curve is shifting around, one thing is staying almost exactly the same. The size of the interval that contains about 95 percent of the probabilities, colored

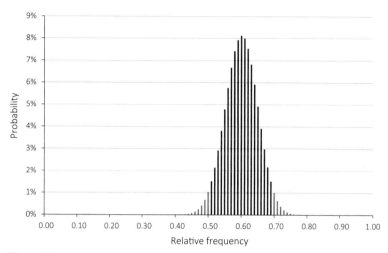

Figure 7.6
A sampling distribution for 100 selections from a jar containing 60 percent red marbles.

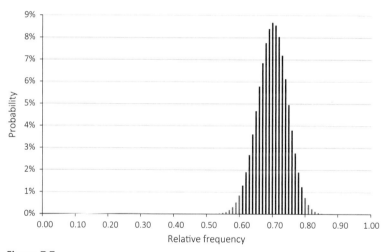

Figure 7.7
A sampling distribution for 100 selections from a jar containing 70 percent red marbles.

in black, remains at .18 (see also table 7.2). Let's call this the ***95 percent probability interval***. This interval is useful, not only for predicting what will happen when marbles are about to be selected from the jar, but also when trying to understand the population itself.

Table 7.2
The .95 interval for populations containing 40 percent, 50 percent, 60 percent, and 70 percent red marbles

Population	Interval	Sum of the probabilities
$P(R) = 0.40$	.31 to .49	94.81%
$P(R) = 0.50$	.41 to .59	94.31%
$P(R) = 0.60$	.51 to .69	94.81%
$P(R) = 0.70$	.61 to .79	96.25%

7.4   An Example of an Inductive Generalization

Imagine that there is a jar of marbles, but the proportion of red marbles in the jar is unknown (as is the proportion of any other color). One hundred marbles are selected (randomly and with replacement), 45 are red, and 55 are nonred. The *observed relative frequency* of red marbles in this sample is .45 (i.e., $45/100$). This sample is the only available information about the population. Still, it should not be inferred that 45 percent of the marbles in the jar are red. It's possible that 45 percent of the marbles in the jar are red, but, as noted earlier, when 100 marbles are selected from a population, there is only a small chance (around 8 percent) that the observed relative frequency will match the proportion of red marbles in the population. Thus, it is much safer to draw the conclusion that the proportion of red marbles in the jar is somewhere around 45 percent. But let's be more specific.

The jar, of course, contains some specific percentage of red marbles. Call that percentage r. And r corresponds to the most probable relative frequency, so let's call the most probable relative frequency r also. Therefore, when 100 marbles are selected from the jar, there is a 95 percent chance of getting between

$(r - .09)$ and $(r + .09)$ red marbles.

(Recall from the previous section that when a sample contains 100 individuals there is a 95 percent chance of getting a relative frequency that is somewhere within an interval .18 wide; and the most probable frequency—in this case, r—is at the center of this interval.)

So, the sample contains 45 percent red marbles (45 out of 100), and, most likely, .45 is within this range: $r - .09$ to $r + .09$ red marbles. In fact, there is a 95 percent chance that .45 is within this range. But where in this range? And, more importantly, what is r? Let's consider these possible values for r:

(a) 25 percent of the marbles in the jar are red.

(b) 36 percent of the marbles in the jar are red.

(c) 49 percent of the marbles in the jar are red.

(d) 54 percent of the marbles in the jar are red.

(e) 62 percent of the marbles in the jar are red.

Using the .18 guideline [i.e., $(r - .09)$ and $(r + .09)$], the following holds for each of these five possibilities.

(a) If 25 percent of the marbles in the jar are red, when 100 are selected, there is a 95 percent chance of getting between 16 and 34 percent red marbles.

(b) If 36 percent of the marbles in the jar are red, when 100 are selected, there is a 95 percent chance of getting between 27 and 45 percent red marbles.

(c) If 49 percent of the marbles in the jar are red, when 100 are selected, there is a 95 percent chance of getting between 40 and 58 percent red marbles.

(d) If 54 percent of the marbles in the jar are red, when 100 are selected, there is a 95 percent chance of getting between 45 and 63 percent red marbles.

(e) If 62 percent of the marbles in the jar are red, when 100 are selected, there is a 95 percent chance of getting between 53 and 71 percent red marbles.

For some of these, 45 percent red marbles falls within the 95 percent probability interval. For some of them, it does not. If 25 percent of the marbles in the jar are red, it is very unlikely that, when 100 are selected, 45 percent of those 100 will be red. If the jar contains 36 percent, 49 percent, or 54 percent red marbles, then it is likely (or, at least, not unlikely) that 45 percent red marbles would have been selected. (I.e., .45 falls within the range for each of them.) If the jar contains 62 percent red marbles, then, again, it's unlikely that 45 percent red marbles would have been selected.

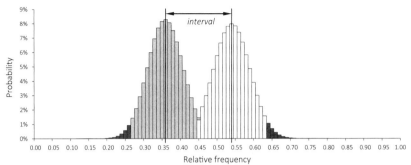

Figure 7.8
One hundred marbles have been selected from a jar and 45 percent of them are red. It is possible that 36 percent of the marbles in the jar are red and the observed relative frequency (.45) is on the right outer edge of the 95 percent interval. This interval is light gray. Another possibility is that 54 percent of the marbles in the jar are red and the observed relative frequency is on the left edge of this 95 percent interval. This interval is white. And of course, it is also possible that the percentage of red marbles in the jar is somewhere else between .36 and .54.

It is unlikely, however, that the percentage of red marbles in the jar is less than 36 percent or more than 54 percent—if it were, then it is very unlikely that the observed relative frequency would have been .45. Given these possibilities, there is a 95 percent chance that this statement is true: *The percentage of red marbles in the jar is between 36 percent and 54 percent.*

We can easily extend this line of thought. If the jar contains 36 percent red marbles, then selecting 45 percent red marbles is "likely" (just barely). But if the jar contains 35 percent red marbles, then selecting 45 percent red marbles becomes "unlikely" (that is, it falls outside the ±.09 range around .35). Likewise, if the jar contains 54 percent red marbles, then selecting 45 percent red marbles is "likely," but if the jar contains 55 percent red marbles, then selecting 45 percent red is "unlikely." Thus, at one extreme, .36 is possible. At the other extreme, .54 is possible. (That the jar contains less than 36 percent or more than 54 percent red marbles is not impossible, but anything below 36 percent or above 54 percent won't include .45 in its 95 percent probability interval.) And so, to have a 95 percent chance of being correct, our guess about the actual proportion of marbles in the jar has to be: *The actual proportion of red marbles in the jar is somewhere between .36 and .54.*

We found that range, basically, by trial and error. We considered different values for *r* until satisfactory ones turned up. But, it's not hard to see that trial and error isn't required. Rather, adding and subtracting .09 from .45 also works. That produces a range from .36 to .54.

This section started with a jar containing an unknown percentage of red marbles. On the basis of information about some of the marbles in the jar—the 100 that were selected—we made an inference about the entire population. Recall that the type of argument that begins with information about part of the population and has a conclusion about the entire population is an inductive generalization. Thus, this argument is an inductive generalization:

P1 One hundred marbles were selected from the jar.

P2 Forty-five percent of these marbles are red.

C   Therefore, there is a 95 percent chance that the jar contains between 36 percent and 54 percent red marbles.

argument (1)

One premise reports the number of individuals that were selected from the population, that is, the size of the sample. Another reports the observed relative frequency—that is, the percentage of individuals that have the property of interest.

The conclusion in this argument can be made more specific; that is, the range can be narrowed. For example, this is another conclusion for argument (1):

C   Therefore, the jar contains between 42 percent and 48 percent red marbles.

This conclusion is, however, less likely to be correct. Given the information in the premises, there is only about a 52 percent chance that the jar contains between 42 percent and 48 percent red marbles. Hence, there is a trade-off between how specific the conclusion is and how likely it is to be correct. Generally, a conclusion that has a higher chance of being correct is preferred, at least until that level reaches 95 percent, which is usually taken to be certain enough.

It is also easy to see that argument (1)—with its original conclusion—is inductively strong. Recall that an argument is inductively strong when it is the case that if the premises are true, then that makes it likely that the conclusion is true. In argument (1), if the premises are true, then there is a 95 percent chance that the conclusion, *the jar contains between 36 percent and 54 percent red marbles*, is true.[2] That's pretty likely, and so the argument is inductively strong.

7.5   The Conclusion of an Inductive Generalization

The argument discussed in the previous section relies on the information in figure 7.8 and equations like 7.2. It is not too convenient, however, to go through all of the calculations that are needed to generate that information simply to create the conclusion of an inductive generalization. There are fairly simple equations that can be used to identify the appropriate interval (given a sample size and an observed relative frequency), but it will suffice for the purpose of thinking about the inductive generalization to use the information in table 7.3.

In the center column of this table ("Probability interval") is the range that contains about 95 percent of the probabilities when the proportion (of whatever value) in the population is .50 (for example, 50 percent of the marbles are red). The column on the right reports the size of this interval (the full size and also the interval in plus-minus form).

Table 7.3
Ninety-five percent probability intervals for an observed relative frequency of .50

Sample size	Probability interval	Size of the interval
50	0.36 to 0.64	0.28, ±.14
100	0.41 to 0.59	0.18, ±.09
250	0.44 to 0.56	0.12, ±.06
500	0.46 to 0.54	0.08, ±.04
1,000	0.47 to 0.53	0.06, ±.03
2,000	0.48 to 0.52	0.04, ±.02
10,000	0.49 to 0.51	0.02, ±.01

---

2. As was explained in the previous chapter, the conclusion of this argument is really expressing this idea: P(the jar contains between 36 percent and 54 percent red marbles) = .95. Or this whole argument can be thought of as a conditional probability:

P(the jar contains between 36 percent and 54 percent red marbles | 100 marbles were randomly selected, and the observed relative frequency is .45) = .95.

When the number of individuals that have been selected from a population matches one of the sample sizes in the table (50, 100, 250, etc.), and the observed relative frequency is known, then table 7.3 can be used to make an inference about the population. The interval just has to be shifted so that the observed relative frequency is at the center.

Example. A jar of marbles contains an unknown percentage of green marbles. Two hundred fifty marbles are selected from this jar. Of these 250 marbles, 150 are green and the rest are nongreen. What is the proportion of green marbles in the population?

Solution. In this problem, the observed relative frequency is .60 ($^{150}/_{250}$ = .60). And, as table 7.3 indicates, when the sample size is 250, the 95 percent probability interval is .12 wide. If the observed relative frequency (.60) is placed at the center of this interval, then the interval is .54 to .66. With that, we can say the following about this population: there is a 95 percent chance that the percentage of green marbles in this jar is between 54 percent and 66 percent.

The purpose of table 7.3 is to simplify the process of solving these types of problems. In actuality, the size of the interval will change a little bit depending on the observed relative frequency (e.g., .50 or .60 or .70). But as long as the observed relative frequency is above .10 and below .90, it doesn't change too much, and so the values in table 7.3 can be used to quickly and easily come up with an answer.

As mentioned in the previous section, a conclusion about a population can be made more specific—that is, can include a narrower range—but when the range is made narrower, there is a lower chance that it will be correct (i.e., that it will contain the true proportion in the population). But as table 7.3 shows, there is another way to make the conclusion about a population more specific: increase the sample size. For example, if 100 marbles are selected from the jar and 50 of them are red, then there is a 95 percent chance that the percentage of red marbles in this jar is between 41 percent and 59 percent. But if 1,000 marbles are selected from the jar and 500 of them are red, then there is a 95 percent chance that the percentage of red marbles in this jar is somewhere within a much smaller interval, namely, between 47 percent and 53 percent.

7.6 Inductive Strength

Once the answer is supplied, the example from the previous section is an argument.

P1 Two hundred fifty marbles were selected from the jar.

P2 Sixty percent of the marbles that were selected are green.

C Therefore, there is a 95 percent chance that the jar contains between 54 percent and 66 percent green marbles.

argument (2)

Again, notice that one premise reports the size of the sample—that is, the part of the population that has been randomly selected and examined. A second premise reports the observed relative frequency for the property of interest—in this case, being green.

One important point that must be emphasized about any inductive generalization is that the conclusion has to contain an interval. Because the observed relative frequency is unlikely to match the actual proportion in the population, if an interval is not included, then the conclusion is most likely going to be false. And if the conclusion is likely to be false even if the premises are true, the argument is inductively weak. Consider these two arguments, which have the same premises.

P1 Two hundred fifty marbles were selected from the jar.

P2 Thirty-eight percent of the marbles that were selected are green.

C Therefore, the jar contains 38 percent green marbles.

argument (3)

P1 Two hundred fifty marbles were selected from the jar.

P2 Thirty-eight percent of the marbles that were selected are green.

C Therefore, the jar contains between 32 percent and 46 percent green marbles.

argument (4)

In argument (3), if the premises are true, there is only a 5 percent chance that the conclusion will be true, which is not too likely. Thus, this argument (with this conclusion) is inductively weak. In contrast, if the premises are true in argument (4), then there is a 95 percent chance that the conclusion is true, so that's an inductively strong argument.

Hence, to create a satisfactory inductive generalization, the conclusion must be phrased as a range, or, at the very least, it must include wording that indicates that the actual proportion in the population is not necessarily the same as the observed frequency (for example, using words like "around" or "near"). But in this chapter, specific intervals are expected.

The inductive generalization draws attention to an interesting feature of the way we think. On the one hand, people have an easy time drawing a conclusion about an entire population based on information about only part of that population. Humans seem to be born ready to make this kind of inference. But, on the other hand, humans are very poor at putting together strong inductive generalizations. For whatever reason, it is difficult to grasp the idea that the conclusion must contain an interval to have a reasonable chance of being correct.

For example, if we're told that 65 percent of the individuals who were questioned support a particular proposal, the thought that 65 percent of all individuals support the proposal immediately jumps to mind. Or, if a recent survey of likely voters indicates that around 51 percent of voters intend to vote for Smith and around 49 percent intend to vote for Jones, there is an overwhelming tendency for people to think that Smith has a small but real advantage over Jones, which may or may not be true. We can avoid these mistakes by remembering that the conclusion of an inductive generalization must contain an interval.

7.7   Exercises

1. (a) Amy has a jar that contains 40 percent red marbles. (See figure 7.9.) If she selects five marbles from this jar, what *number* of red marbles is she most likely to get? How likely is it that she will get this number of red marbles?

   (b) What is the probability that Amy will get one or two red marbles when she selects five marbles from this population?

   (c) What is the probability that Amy will get three, four, or five red marbles when she selects five marbles from this jar?

2. (a) If Sarah is about to select four marbles from a jar that contains 35 percent red marbles, what is the chance that she will get either no red marbles or all red marbles? (See figure 7.10.)

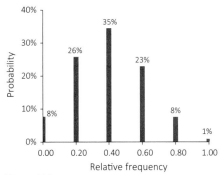

Figure 7.9

P(R) = .40, 5 selections.

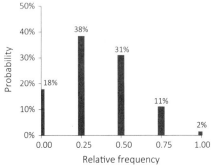

Figure 7.10

P(R) = .35, 4 selections.

(b) If instead of selecting four marbles from this jar that contains 35 percent red marbles, Sarah selected 30 marbles, would the probability for the number of marbles that she is most likely to get (i.e., the probability for the most probable frequency) increase, decrease, or stay the same?

3. (a) When the probability of selecting one red marble is .60 and 25 selections are about to be made from the jar, what is the probability of selecting exactly 60 percent red marbles? (See figure 7.11.)

   (b) What is the probability of selecting 56 percent, 60 percent, or 64 percent red marbles when P(R) = .60 and 25 selections are about to be made?

   (c) What is the probability of getting 12, 13, 14, 15, 16, 17, or 18 red marbles when P(R) = .60 and 25 marbles are about to be selected from the jar? What rule do you use to find the answer?

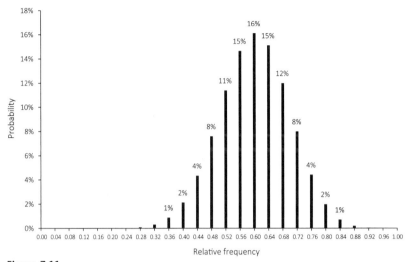

Figure 7.11

$P(R) = .60$, 25 selections.

(d) From this jar, there is a 93 percent chance of selecting between _____ percent red marbles and _____ percent red marbles.

4. (a) If Kate is selecting 50 marbles from a jar and $P(R) = .60$, how likely is it that she will get the relative frequency that is exactly the same as $P(R)$? Use the sampling distribution in figure 7.12 to answer this question.

(b) When Kate makes these selections, she has (about) a 95 percent chance of selecting a certain number of red marbles that falls within what range? (I.e., she has a 95 percent chance of getting between *what* and *what* red marbles?) Although it is possible to answer this question using table 7.3, try to answer it using just the distribution in figure 7.12.

5. Use table 7.3 to complete the conclusion of this argument.

P1 As they checked out of hotels, bed and breakfasts, and hostels, 2,000 tourists were briefly questioned about Montreal's subway system.

P2 Seventy-nine percent stated that they were very satisfied with the subway system.

C Therefore, there is a 95 percent chance that between _____ and _____ of all tourists are very satisfied with Montreal's subway system.

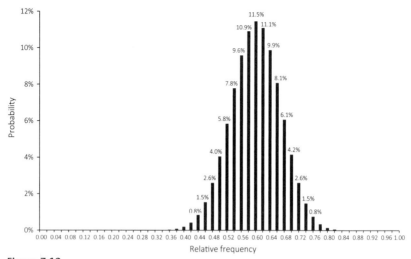

Figure 7.12
$P(R) = .60$, 50 selections.

6. 500 marbles have been selected from a jar (randomly and with replacement). Of these, 125 are red, 200 are blue, and 175 are green. What percentage of the marbles in the jar are red, blue, and green?

7. Mary, randomly and with replacement, selected 250 marbles from a jar. Of the marbles that she selected, 160 are red. What conclusion can Mary draw about the percentage of red marbles in the jar? Write this as an argument. (Use the arguments in this chapter as a model.)

8. The State University chapter of the American Medical Student Association wanted to know how many students at State University use the school's recreational facilities. To find out, they contacted 1,000 randomly selected State University students and asked them how often they used any of the recreational facilities on campus. Of these students, 380 said that they used the recreational facilities at least once a week. What can the AMSA conclude about all students at State University? Write this as an argument and make the answer to the question the conclusion.

9. The Hospitality Division of the Garcia-Brown Hotel wanted to determine how satisfied their customers were with the hotel's towels. Five hundred customers were randomly selected as they checked out of the hotel and asked how they had liked the towels. Of these customers, 360 said that they were satisfied with the hotel's towels.

What can the Hospitality Division conclude about all of the Garcia-Brown Hotel's customers? Write this as an argument and make the answer to the question the conclusion.

10. Seventy percent of State University undergraduates use the cafeteria. Jeff has been assigned to a study group with three other students and, if possible, he would like to study with them in the cafeteria. How likely is it that all three of Jeff's study partners use the cafeteria? Write this as an argument and make the answer to the question the conclusion.

7.8 Answers

1. (a) The most likely outcome is getting two red marbles (that is, 40 percent red marbles). She has a 35 percent chance of getting two out of five.

   (b) Getting one red marble when five are selected from the jar is a relative frequency of .20 (i.e., $1/5 = .20$), and getting two red marbles when five are selected from the jar is a relative frequency of .40 (i.e., $2/5 = .40$). As the sampling distribution shows, she has a 26 percent chance of getting 20 percent red marbles and a 35 percent chance of getting 40 percent red marbles. Therefore, the probability of getting 20 percent or 40 percent red marbles (when five are selected and $P(R) = .40$) is 61 percent. This is calculated using the special disjunction rule.

   $$P(.20R \text{ or } .40R) = P(.20R) + P(.40R) = .26 + .35 = .61 \qquad (7.3)$$

   (c) If five marbles are about to be selected and $P(R) = .40$, the probability of getting three, four, or five red marbles is 32 percent.

   $$P(.60R \text{ or } .80R \text{ or } 1.0R) = \qquad (7.4)$$
   $$P(.60R) + P(.80R) + P(1.0R) = .23 + .08 + .01 = .32$$

2. (a) When selecting four marbles from a jar that contains 35 percent red marbles, Sarah has a 20 percent chance of getting either no red marbles or all red marbles.

   $$P(0R \text{ or } 1R) = P(0.0R) + P(1.0R) = .18 + .02 = .20 \qquad (7.5)$$

   (b) As the number of selections increases from four to thirty, the probability of the most probable relative frequency goes down. When four are selected, the most probable relative frequency is .25 (i.e., one out of four red marbles) and there is a 38 percent chance that Sarah will get this relative frequency. The sampling distribution in figure 7.13 shows that when 30 marbles are selected from this same population, the most probable relative frequency is .33 (i.e., 10 out of 30), and Sarah has a 15 percent chance of getting this relative frequency. Thus, the probability of the most probable relative frequency has dropped from 38 percent to 15 percent.

This result is the same for all cases: when the sample size increases, the probability of the most probable relative frequency gets smaller.

3. (a) The chance of getting exactly 60 percent red marbles—when $P(R) = .60$ and 25 marbles are about to be selected from the jar—is 16 percent.

   (b) The probability of getting .56, .60, or .64 is 46 percent. We use the special disjunction rule to find this answer.

$$P(.56R \text{ or } .60R \text{ or } .64R) =$$
$$P(.56R) + P(.60R) + P(.64R) = \qquad (7.6)$$
$$.15 + .16 + .15 = .46$$

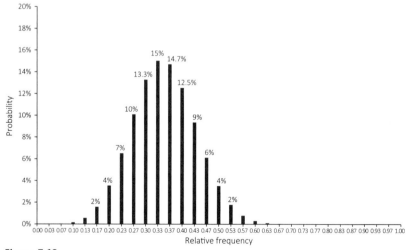

Figure 7.13
$P(R) = .35$, 30 selections.

(c) When selecting 25 marbles from a jar that contains 60 percent red marbles, the probability of getting between 12 and 18 red marbles is 85 percent.

To figure this out, first, we must determine the relative frequencies that correspond to 12, 13, 14, 15, 16, 17, and 18 red marbles— $12/25 = .48$, $13/25 = .52$, $14/25 = .56$, and so forth. Next, we use the sampling distribution given in the question (see figure 7.11) to identify the probability of getting each of these relative frequencies. Finally, we add these probabilities up using the special disjunction rule.

$$P(getting\ between\ .48\ and\ .72\ red\ marbles) =$$
$$P(.48R) + P(.52R) + P(.56R)$$
$$+ P(.60R) + P(.64R) + P(.68R) + P(.72R) =$$
$$.08 + .11 + .15 + .16 + .15 + .12 + .08 = .85$$

(7.7)

What's being calculated here is the probability of getting 48 percent red marbles, or 52 percent red marbles, or 56 percent, or 60 percent, or 64 percent, or 68 percent, or 72 percent red marbles. We use the special disjunction rule because these relative frequencies are mutually exclusive—getting one of them (once the selections from the jar are made) excludes a person from getting any other one.

(d) There is a 93 percent chance of selecting between 44 percent red marbles and 76 percent red marbles.

To find the range for a 93 percent chance, we add the probability of selecting 44 percent red marbles, .04, and the probability of selecting .76 red marbles, also .04, to the 85 percent from the previous question (i.e., the probability of getting between 48 percent and 72 percent red marbles).

4. (a) Although 60 percent of the marbles in the jar are red, if Kate selects 50 marbles from the jar, she has only an 11.5 percent chance of getting exactly 60 percent red marbles (i.e., of getting 30 out of 50 red marbles).

(b) Kate has a 94.2 percent chance of getting between 48 and 72 percent red marbles (that is, between 24 and 36 red marbles). Another acceptable answer is that she has a 97.2 percent chance of getting between 46 and 74 percent red marbles. It turns out that it is not possible to have a range that contains exactly 95 percent of the probabilities (at least not one that is the same size on both sides of the most probable frequency), and so either answer is correct.

5. This conclusion can easily be completed by using the information in table 7.3. When the sample size is 2,000, the 95 percent probability interval is .04 wide. Thus, .02 is added to the observed relative frequency (.79) and .02 is subtracted from it. This produces the range .77 to .81.

> P1 Two thousand tourists were briefly questioned about Montreal's subway system.
>
> P2 Seventy-nine percent stated that they were very satisfied with the subway system.
>
> C Therefore, there is a 95 percent chance that between 77 and 81 percent of all tourists are very satisfied with Montreal's subway system.

6. The information given in the question is about part of the population, and the goal is to describe the population itself. In this situation, it is not possible to determine the exact percentages of red, blue, and green marbles in the jar. Instead, the answer must take the form of three intervals. For each interval, there is a 95 percent chance that it contains the actual percentage of red, blue, or green marbles.

The percentage of red marbles in the jar is somewhere between 21 and 29 percent. The percentage of blue marbles is somewhere between 36 and 44 percent. And the percentage of green marbles is between 31 and 39 percent.

These ranges were found by first finding the observed relative frequency of red, blue, and green marbles. For red it is .25 ($^{125}/_{500}$), for blue it is .40 ($^{200}/_{500}$), and for green it is .35 ($^{175}/_{500}$). Next, table 7.3 is used to find the size of the interval. Since the sample size is 500, the interval has to be .08 wide. Each observed relative frequency is placed in the middle of the interval and the boundaries of the interval are then identified (.04 in each direction).

7. P1 Two hundred fifty marbles have been selected from the jar.

P2 Sixty-four percent ($^{160}/_{250}$) of these marbles are red.

C Therefore, there is a 95 percent chance that between 58 percent and 70 percent of the marbles in the jar are red.

8. **P1** One thousand randomly selected State University students were contacted.

   P2 Thirty-eight percent of these students use the recreational facilities at least once a week.

   C Therefore, there is a 95 percent chance that between 35 percent and 41 percent of all State University students use the recreational facilities at least once a week.

   Notice that the first sentence in the description of this problem is not included in the argument ("The State University chapter of the American Medical Student Association wanted to know how many students at State University use the school's recreational facilities"). There can sometimes be more than one correct way to write out an argument, but ideally only premises that are supporting the conclusion are included.

9. **P1** Five hundred Garcia-Brown Hotel customers were randomly selected.

   P2 Seventy-two percent of these customers said that they were satisfied with the hotel's towels.

   C Therefore, it is very likely (i.e., there is a 95 percent chance) that between .68 and .76 of all Garcia-Brown Hotel customers are satisfied with the hotel's towels.

10. This argument is a proportional syllogism (discussed in the previous chapter), not an inductive generalization. This problem is included here as a reminder. It is important to be able to identify the type of inference needed based on the information given and the desired conclusion.

   P1 Seventy percent of State University undergraduates use the cafeteria.

   P2 Jeff's three study partners are State University undergraduates.

   C Therefore, there is a 34.3 percent chance that all three of Jeff's study partners use the cafeteria.

   We determine the probability for the conclusion by doing this calculation:

$$\text{P}(all\ 3\ use\ the\ cafeteria) =$$
$$\text{P}(first = C) \times \text{P}(second = C) \times \text{P}(third = C) = \qquad (7.8)$$
$$.70 \times .70 \times .70 = .343$$

8 Bayes' Rule

8.1 Bayes' Rule

Bayes' rule (sometimes called Bayes' theorem) is named for the English minister Thomas Bayes who first developed the idea in his "An Essay towards Solving a Problem in the Doctrine of Chances," published in 1763, two years after his death. This is Bayes' rule:

$$P(A|B) = \frac{P(A) \times P(B|A)}{[P(A) \times P(B|A)] + [P(not\ A) \times P(B|not\ A)]} \tag{8.1}$$

To begin thinking about this equation, notice that the expression in the numerator, $P(A) \times P(B|A)$, is equivalent to the probability of A and B both occurring (recall that $P(A\ \&\ B) = P(A) \times P(B|A)$). The denominator, meanwhile, is equivalent to: the probability of $A\ \&\ B$ or $not\ A\ \&\ B$. The equation, then, can be rewritten as:

$$P(A|B) = \frac{P(A\ \&\ B)}{P(A\ \&\ B) + P(not\ A\ \&\ B)} \tag{8.2}$$

Going a step further, the denominator in equation 8.2, $P(A\ \&\ B)$ or $P(not\ A\ \&\ B)$, is equal to just $P(B)$. Hence, Bayes' rule reduces to the conditional probability rule:

$$P(A|B) = \frac{P(A\ \&\ B)}{P(B)} \tag{8.3}$$

There are reasons, however, for using equation 8.1 when possible. And, although it may look a bit daunting, Bayes' rule is pretty easy to use. It requires a grasp of conditional probabilities (see section 6.2.1 in chapter 6), but otherwise, the calculations are straightforward.

Bayes' rule has two especially useful features. One is its ability to get a conditional probability, say, P(H|E), when P(E|H) and P(E|not H) are known. (Notice how the placement of H and E switch there.) The second is that it provides a way of updating probabilities as more evidence becomes available. P(A) is on the right side of equation 8.1 That probability is the starting point, and it's referred to as the *prior probability*. But then event B occurs. Bayes' rule updates P(A) in light of B having happened. In essence, P(A|B)—the probability on the left side of equation 8.1—replaces P(A). P(A|B) is, therefore, called the *posterior probability*.

Having already covered the theory of probability in chapter 6, the best way to become familiar with Bayes' rule is simply to go through several different kinds of examples where it is used, and so most of this chapter does just that. In section 8.4, we discuss the argument that results from applying Bayes' rule.

8.2 Example 1: Two Jars of Marbles

There are two jars of marbles. In the first jar, 75 percent of the marbles are red, and 25 percent are nonred. In the second jar, 40 percent are red, and 60 percent are nonred. A fair coin is going to be flipped. If the coin lands heads up, a marble will be selected from the first jar. If the coin lands tails up, the marble will be taken from the second jar.

The coin is flipped, and a marble is randomly selected from one of the two jars—but how the coin landed is not revealed. Before this marble is inspected, there is an equal chance that it came from either jar. (Because it is based on a coin toss, there's a 50 percent chance that it came from the first jar and a 50 percent chance that it came from the second jar.) Now the marble is displayed: it's red. What is the probability that the marble came from the first jar, given that it's red? That is, what is P(*jar 1*|*red*)?

Table 8.1

	heads this jar Jar 1	tails this jar Jar 2
red	75%	40%
nonred	25%	60%

These probabilities are known:

P(*jar* 1) = .50

P(*jar* 2) = .50

P(*red*|*jar* 1) = .75

P(*red*|*jar* 2) = P(*red*|*not jar* 1) = .40

And they are all we need for Bayes' rule.

$$P(jar\ 1|red) = \frac{P(jar\ 1) \times P(red|jar\ 1)}{[P(jar\ 1) \times P(red|jar\ 1)] + [P(jar\ 2) \times P(red|jar\ 2)]}$$

$$P(jar\ 1|red) = \frac{.50 \times .75}{(.50 \times .75) + (.50 \times .40)} = \frac{.375}{.575} \tag{8.4}$$

$$P(jar\ 1|red) = .652$$

Since the marble is red, there is a 65 percent chance that it came from the first jar.

The probability that the marble came from the second jar is calculated in the same way. (Now P(*red*|*jar* 1) = P(*red*|*not jar* 2).)

$$P(jar\ 2|red) = \frac{P(jar\ 2) \times P(red|jar\ 2)}{[P(jar\ 2) \times P(red|jar\ 2)] + [P(jar\ 1) \times P(red|jar\ 1)]}$$

$$P(jar\ 2|red) = \frac{.50 \times .40}{(.50 \times .40) + (.50 \times .75)} = \frac{.20}{.575} \tag{8.5}$$

$$P(jar\ 2|red) = .348$$

Given that the marble is red, there's only a 35 percent chance that it came from the second jar.

Before the marble was inspected, the probability that it came from the first jar was 50 percent and the probability that it came from the second jar was 50 percent. Those were the prior probabilities. With the information that the marble is red, those prior probabilities are updated to 65 percent and 35 percent.

8.3   Example 2: The Stolen $1.3 Million

Chapter 2 ended with a problem for the induction by confirmation. Sometimes it does not seem as though a hypothesis should be considered false just because the prediction does not match the data. In other words, some predictions are probabilistic. Even if the hypothesis is true, there is only a chance that the prediction will match the data.

In such a situation, Bayes' rule can help. The only difficulty is assigning the probabilities. Here is Bayes' rule again; H stands for hypothesis, and E stands for evidence. So, what's being calculated is the probability that the hypothesis is correct, given the evidence.

$$P(H \mid E) = \frac{P(H) \times P(E \mid H))}{[P(H) \times P(E \mid H)] + [P(not\ H) \times P(E \mid not\ H)]} \tag{8.6}$$

This is the example from the end of chapter 2.

A detective begins with a little bit of data. $1.3 million is missing from the company where John works. John had access to the money, and John has broken the law in the past. Based on these data, the detective forms this hypothesis: John stole the $1.3 million from his company. The detective now needs to confirm this hypothesis. As it stands, the hypothesis should not be accepted as true, and no court is going to convict John. The detective formulates this prediction: John will have a secret bank account. But the data that the detective uncovers do not match this prediction.

As an induction by confirmation, the inference looks like this:

P1   If John stole the $1.3 million, then the detective will find that John has a secret bank account.

P2   The detective did not find a secret bank account.

C   Therefore, the hypothesis is false. (That is, John did not steal the $1.3 million.)

argument (1)

To use Bayes' rule, the detective thinks about the case and other similar cases and assigns the probabilities below. Someone else might have assigned slightly different probabilities, but the detective needs to start somewhere, and so he uses his informed opinion. (The evidence is that there is no secret bank account; *SBA* stands for *secret bank account*.)

$P(H) = P(stole) = .67$

$P(E \mid H) = P(no\ SBA \mid stole) = .45$

$P(E \mid not\ H) = P(no\ SBA \mid didn't\ steal) = .90$

The probability to be found, then, is $P(H|E)$, the probability that John stole the $1.3 million, given that there is no secret bank account.

$$P(H|E) = \frac{.67 \times .45}{(.67 \times .45) + (.33 \times .90)} = \frac{.302}{.599} = .504 \tag{8.7}$$

Initially, the probability of the hypothesis being true was 67 percent, and not finding a secret bank account has lowered that probability to 50 percent. But, according to Bayes' rule, not finding a secret bank account does not drop the probability that the hypothesis is true to zero.

What happens when the evidence confirms rather than disconfirms the hypothesis? That is, when the detective finds a secret bank account of John's? These are the probabilities:

$$P(H) = P(stole) = .67$$
$$P(E|H) = P(SBA|stole) = .55$$
$$P(E|not\ H) = P(SBA|didn't\ steal) = .10$$

With these probabilities and with $P(H|E)$ being the probability that John stole the $1.3 million, given that he does have a secret bank account, this is the calculation:

$$P(H|E) = \frac{.67 \times .55}{(.67 \times .55) + (.33 \times .10)} = \frac{.369}{.402} = .918 \tag{8.8}$$

And the chance that he stole the money rises to almost 92 percent. As would be expected, finding the secret bank account increased the probability that the hypothesis is correct.

Table 8.2
There is no population here, but a table similar to the diagrams used in chapters 5 and 6 is useful for keeping track of the conditional probabilities in this example. So, for instance, if John stole the money, the probability of finding a secret bank account is 55 percent.

	Stole the money	Didn't steal the money
No secret bank account	45%	90%
Secret bank account	55%	10%

8.4   The Argument Using Bayes' Rule

Like the methods covered in the previous chapters, Bayes' rule is a part of inductive logic. It's a rule that, when followed, will supply a probable conclusion. To see that it is a part of inductive logic, it's helpful to think about the argument, and especially the conclusion, that follows from the application of Bayes' rule. There is no standard way of representing the argument, but let's start with this simple formulation for the stolen $1.3 million example:

P1   John does not have a secret bank account.

  C   Therefore, the probability that John stole the money is 50.4 percent.

argument (2)

This is the bare bones. It is just the two parts of the conditional probability that is on the left side of equation 8.7. *John stole the money* and *John does not have a secret bank account* are split, and one is the premise and the other is the conclusion.

Representing the argument this way has two virtues. First, it is very easy to see that this argument is inductive (i.e., not deductively valid), and it is very easy to tell what its inductive strength is. Although the conclusion in argument (2) contains a probability, the conclusion is just the declarative sentence *John stole the money*. The probability indicates the chance that the conclusion is true, given that John does not have a secret bank account. Since that probability is only 50.4 percent, the argument is not inductively strong.[1]

Second, recall from chapter 1 that the premises and the conclusion have to be statements that can be true or false. The premise and the conclusion

---

1. In the previous two chapters, it was pointed out that an argument can be expressed as a conditional probability, and, in fact, this is a useful way of thinking about inductive arguments. Here is argument (2):

P(John stole the money | John does not have a secret bank account) = .504

This is also the conditional probability on the left side of Bayes' rule (in this case, the left side of equation 8.7). Everything on the right side of the equation, then, can be thought of as the machinery used for making the inference.

in argument (2) clearly satisfy that criteria. There is, however, other information that perhaps should be in the argument, namely,

(a) The initial probability that John stole the money is 67 percent (i.e., $P(H) = .67$).

(b) The probability that John does not have a secret bank account, given that he stole the money, is 45 percent (i.e., $P(E|H) = .45$).

(c) The probability that John does not have a secret bank account, given that he did not steal the money, is 90 percent (i.e., $P(E|not\ H) = .90$).

The reason in favor of including (a), (b), and (c) in the argument is that they are used to make the inference. On the other hand, these do not exactly look like the kinds of statements that, up until this point, have been premises. In the earlier chapters, the premises have included statements about percentages and proportions of various populations (among many other things). But they haven't included probabilities. As a compromise, we can put (a), (b), and (c) in a "preliminary premise," which yields this argument:

P* $P(H) = .67, P(E|H) = .45, P(E|not\ H) = .90$

P1 John does not have a secret bank account.

  C Therefore, the probability that John stole the money is 50.4 percent.

argument (3)

Similarly, this is the first argument in the marble jar example from section 8.2:

P* $P(jar\ 1) = .50, P(red|jar\ 1) = .75, P(red|jar\ 2) = .40$

P1 The marble is red.

  C Therefore, the probability that the first jar was selected is 65 percent.

argument (4)

The most important thing, though, is to see what the conclusion is for this type of inference. Whether the argument has the form used in argument (2) or the one used in argument (3), the conclusion is the same. Notice also that the argument does not include Bayes' rule itself. That's just the rule that is followed to make the inference. But that said, anytime someone is working with Bayes' rule, it is almost always the equation that is given to show how likely the conclusion is.

8.5   Example 3: A Match Made with Bayes' Rule

Consider this scenario. Eric and Linda have both just graduated from college and are new employees at a large company. One Saturday night, Linda is at a bar with some friends and they run into Eric. He says hello, buys Linda a drink, and the two start talking. Is Eric romantically interested in Linda?

Imagine that this scenario unfolds from the perspective of a friend of Linda's, and the probabilities that are assigned are set by that friend—not by Eric, who knows with certainty (let's say) whether or not he is romantically interested in Linda. The friend starts with the following.

P(*Eric is interested in Linda*) = .20
This is the prior probability, P(*H*), in Bayes' equation. Even before buying Linda the drink, there was a chance that Eric was romantically interested in her.

P(*E buys L a drink* | *E is interested*) = .75
This is P(*E*|*H*) in Bayes' equation. Given that Eric is romantically interested in Linda, there is a 75 percent chance that he will buy her a drink. So, if he's interested, there is a good chance that he will buy her a drink, but, for a variety of reasons, it is below 100 percent.

P(*E buys L a drink* | *E is not interested*) = .40
This is P(*E*|*not H*) in Bayes' equation. Even if Eric is not romantically interested in Linda, there is a chance that he will buy her a drink just because he is friendly.

So, now, what is the probability that Eric is romantically interested in Linda? That is, what is P(*E is interested* | *E bought L a drink*)?

$$P(I|D) = \frac{P(I) \times P(D|I)}{[P(I) \times P(D|I)] + [P(not\ I) \times P(D|not\ I)]}$$

$$P(I|D) = \frac{.20 \times .75}{(.20 \times .75) + (.80 \times .40)} = \frac{.15}{.47} \tag{8.9}$$

$$P(I|D) = .319$$

Having bought her the drink, there is just under a 32 percent chance that Eric is interested in Linda, whereas before it was only 20 percent.

But it doesn't end there. Eric and Linda are chatting away, and soon they have ordered another round of drinks, which Eric insists be put on his

tab. These are the probabilities that Linda's friend needs to use Bayes' rule
again.

P(*E is interested*) = .319

P(*E buys L a drink | E is interested*) = .75

P(*E buys L a drink | E is not interested*) = .40

The first probability is the result from the previous calculation. The two
conditional properties have been kept the same. They could have been
changed since this is now the second drink, but they weren't.

Now the probability that Eric is romantically interested is almost 47
percent.

$$P(I|D2) = \frac{P(I) \times P(D2|I)}{[P(I) \times P(D2|I)] + [P(not\ I) \times P(D2|not\ I)]}$$

$$P(I|D2) = \frac{.319 \times .75}{(.319 \times .75) + (.681 \times .40)} = \frac{.239}{.512} \qquad (8.10)$$

$$P(I|D2) = .468$$

Eight years later, Eric and Linda are married. The anniversary of that
first time they hung out at the bar arrives, but Eric doesn't acknowledge it.
Linda is puzzled. Did he forget? Or, did he remember, but ignore it, perhaps
because he no longer cares? Part of Linda is pleased that this anniversary
passed without being mentioned. She has always maintained that it wasn't
a real date since they just ran into each other at that bar. Eric, however,
had always been keen to celebrate their, as he calls it, "first date." Hence,
Linda is also a little concerned that Eric didn't do or say anything about this
anniversary. Maybe Eric is no longer interested in their relationship. She
decides to consult Bayes' rule.

P(*E is interested*) = .95

This is Linda's best estimation of the probability that, prior to this event,
Eric is romantically interested. (It's been updated many times since that
second drink.)

P(*E didn't acknowledge | E is interested*) = .65

If Eric is still romantically interested, the chance that he wouldn't
acknowledge their "first date" is 65 percent.

P(*E didn't acknowledge | E is not interested*) = .98

If Eric is no longer romantically interested, the chance that he wouldn't
acknowledge their "first date" is 98 percent.

What is the probability that Eric is romantically interested in Linda? That is, what is P(*E is interested* | *E didn't acknowledge*)?

$$P(I|DA) = \frac{P(I) \times P(DA|I)}{[P(I) \times P(DA|I)] + [P(not\ I) \times P(DA|not\ I)]}$$

$$P(I|DA) = \frac{.95 \times .65}{(.95 \times .65) + (.05 \times .98)} = \frac{.618}{.667} \tag{8.11}$$

$$P(I|DA) = .926$$

So, that's where it stands. The probability that Eric is still interested in Linda and in their relationship has taken a little bit of a hit, but nothing too severe.

This example was an exercise in updating the probability that Eric is interested as new events occurred and new information became available. It also required coming up with probabilities that only someone familiar with the situation would know. Naturally, for someone else, in a different situation, the probabilities would be different. Additionally, throughout this example, by using both the prior probability, P(*H*), and the probability for the last event under two different conditions—that is, P(*E*|*H*) and P(*E*| *not H*)—Bayes' rule moderates the effect that the last event had on the probability being sought, P(*H*|*E*).

8.6   Example 4: A Positive Mammogram

In addition to updating probabilities, Bayes' rule is also useful in cases where the prior probability is especially significant—particularly large or particularly small. Because Bayes' rule uses that prior probability, the effect of any new event or new information is often much less than might be expected.

The following is an example created by the psychologist Gerd Gigerenzer.[2] A woman is given a mammogram and the result is positive for breast cancer. The woman is, however, a member of a group that has a very small chance of having breast cancer. She is between forty and fifty years old, she has no symptoms associated with breast cancer, and no one in her family has had breast cancer. The probability that a woman in this low-risk group has breast cancer is only .008 (that's just below 1 percent).

Additionally, while there is a 90 percent chance that a woman's mammogram will be positive for breast cancer when she has breast cancer, there is
a 7 percent chance that the mammogram will be positive when a woman
does not have breast cancer. So, given that this woman's mammogram was
positive, what is the probability that she has breast cancer? That is, what is
P(*cancer*|*positive mammogram*)?

These probabilities are stated in the previous paragraph:

P(*cancer*) = .008

P(*pos mammogram*|*cancer*) = .90

P(*pos mammogram*|*no cancer*) = .07

And since P(*cancer*) = .008, P(*no cancer*) has to be .992. This, then, is the
calculation:

$$P(C|Pos) = \frac{P(C) \times P(Pos|C)}{[P(C) \times P(Pos|C)] + [P(not\ C) \times P(Pos|not\ C)]}$$

$$P(C|Pos) = \frac{.008 \times .90}{(.008 \times .90) + (.992 \times .07)} = \frac{.0072}{.0766} \tag{8.12}$$

$$P(C|Pos) = .094$$

Even though this woman had a positive mammogram, there is only a 9.4
percent chance that she has breast cancer—much lower than one might
have guessed based on the positive test.

8.7 Exercises

1. There are two jars of marbles. In the first jar, 75 percent of the marbles
   are red and 25 percent are nonred; in the second jar, 40 percent are red
   and 60 percent are nonred. One die is going to be rolled. If the die lands
   on 1, then a marble is taken from the first jar; if the die lands on any
   other number, then a marble is taken from the second jar.

   (a) A marble has been taken from one of the two jars, and it is red. How
       likely is it that it came from the first jar?

   (b) How likely is it that it came from the second jar?

2. There are two jars of marbles. In the first jar, 70 percent of the marbles are red and 30 percent are nonred; in the second jar, 55 percent are red and 45 percent are nonred. One die is going to be rolled. If the die lands on 1 or 2, then a marble is taken from the first jar; if the die lands on 3, 4, 5, or 6, then a marble is taken from the second jar.

    (a) A marble is taken from one of the two jars, but its color is still unknown. What is the probability that it came from the first jar? What is the probability that it came from the second jar?

    (b) The marble that was taken from one of the two jars is red. What is the probability that it came from the first jar?

    (c) Given that it's red, what is the probability that this marble came from the second jar?

3. Just before leaving for class, Steve goes to the kitchen to get a pop-tart. When he looks in the cupboard, he finds that his last box of pop-tarts is gone. Steve presumes that one of his three roommates has taken them, and it seems most likely that it was Fred. Steve knows that Fred was up late last night watching television; he knows that Fred likes to snack while watching late-night television; and he knows that, in the past, Fred has taken other people's food without asking for permission. Therefore, he estimates that there is an 85 percent chance that Fred took his box of pop-tarts.

   Steve figures that if Fred opened the box of pop-tarts and started eating them while he was watching television, then it is likely that he didn't finish them and took the remaining pop-tarts to his bedroom to save for later. Steve puts this probability at 70 percent. (So, presuming that Fred took them, there is a 30 percent chance that there are not any pop-tarts in his bedroom right now.) He realizes, of course, that if Fred did *not* take the pop-tarts, it is quite unlikely that he will find them in Fred's bedroom—there is only about a 1 percent chance that one of the other roommates took them and stashed them there.

   Steve hurries up to Fred's bedroom, bursts in without knocking, and looks around the room. Although he finds Fred snoring away in bed, Steve does not find any pop-tarts. Annoyed, he leaves for class, buys a pretzel on the way, and is late for his 9:00 am Race, Crime & Justice.

Given that Steve did not find the pop-tarts in Fred's bedroom, what is the probability that Fred took them last night? That is, what is P(*took*| *no pop-tarts*)?

To work through this problem, start by determining what information is needed to apply Bayes' rule. In equation 8.13, *H* is the hypothesis and *E* is the evidence.

$$P(H \mid E) = \frac{P(H) \times P(E \mid H)}{[P(H) \times P(E \mid H)] + [P(not\ H) \times P(E \mid not\ H)]} \qquad (8.13)$$

In this problem, what is the the hypothesis and what is the evidence? What is P(*E*|*H*)? What is P(*E*|*not H*)?

4. There are two jars of marbles. In the first jar, 30 percent of the marbles are red and 70 percent are blue; in the second jar, 75 percent are red and 25 percent are blue. A fair coin is going to be flipped. If the coin is heads, then a marble will be taken from the first jar. If the coin is tails, a marble will be taken from the second jar. After each marble is taken from one of the jars, it is returned to the same jar (so the proportion of red and blue marbles stays the same).

    (a) A marble has been taken from one of the two jars, and it is blue. What is the probability that it came from the first jar?

    (b) A second marble is taken from the same jar (whichever one that is), and it is blue. What is the probability that it came from the first jar? The key step here is using the result from 4(a) to update the probability that the first jar was selected.

    (c) A third marble is taken from the same jar (whichever one that is), and it is blue. What is the probability that it came from the first jar?

    (d) A fourth marble is taken from the same jar (whichever one that is), and it is blue. What is the probability that it came from the first jar?

    (e) A fifth marble is taken from the same jar (whichever one that is), and it is red. What is the probability that it came from the first jar?

5. Look at the example in section 8.5 of this chapter. In the first two parts of this example, Eric bought Linda two drinks. Following that evening, two more relevant events occur. Use them to update the probability that Eric is romantically interested in Linda—that is, P(*E is interested*|*B*). And,

in each case, use the result from the previous iteration of Bayes' rule for P(A).

(a) B = the next day at work, Eric sends Linda a text message asking how her day is going.
P(*texts*|*E is interested*) = .75
P(*texts*|*E is not interested*) = .45

(b) B = two days later, Eric asks Linda if she wants to get dinner with him at a new restaurant not far from their office.
P(*dinner*|*E is interested*) = .85
P(*dinner*|*E is not interested*) = .40

6. Deep in the forest of northern Mississippi, it was a dark and stormy night. A bolt of lightning struck the middle of a swamp. The water bubbled and sparks flew. Suddenly, an arm reached out of the muddy water and grabbed onto a log! The electrical current from the lightning must have rearranged the molecules in the swamp. Swampman—a creature looking just like an adult human male, but created only moments before by the fortuitous shuffling of atoms and ions—was pulling himself onto the shore.

By the next evening, Swampman has cleaned himself up and gotten some clothes. All day he has observed his surroundings. He noticed that it was dark when he crawled out of the swamp, but then the sun rose, moved across the sky, and is now disappearing below the horizon. He wonders if this will happen again. Will the sun rise again the next morning? He forms this hypothesis, which he refers to as *H: The sun will rise tomorrow* (or, equivalently, since each day has a tomorrow, *The sun rises every day*). Since he has no other basis for setting the probability of *H* except to give each possibility—the sun will rise tomorrow or it won't—equal weight, he makes P(H) = .50. He quickly sees that, given *H*—that is, if the sun rises every day—then the probability of the sun rising on any particular morning, including tomorrow morning, is 1.0.

On the other hand, if *H* is false, the sun still might rise on any given morning, but the chance of that happening is less than 100 percent. He has already seen the sun rise once, though, so the probability of the sun rising, given that the sun does not rise every morning, has to be greater than 0. Swampman mulls it over and decides to put P(R|H) at 50 percent also. (*R*, which is the evidence, is *the sun rising in the morning*.)

(a) What are P(H), P(R|H), and P(R|*not H*)? What is the probability that H is correct, given that the sun rose Swampman's first morning? That is, what is P(H|R)?

(b) The next morning, Swampman observes the sun rise again. Now, what is P(H|R)? How many times does Swampman have to observe the sun rising for P(H|R) to be higher than 95 percent?

(c) Going back to Swampman's first day, instead of assigning .50 to the probability of the sun rising, given that the sun does not rise every day [i.e., P(R|*not H*)], he puts this probability at .10. P(H) is still .50. Now, what is P(H|R)? What will P(H|R) be when Swampman sees the sun rise the next morning? And then the following morning?

(d) Going back to Swampman's first day, instead of assigning .50 to the probability of the sun rising, given that the sun does not rise every day [i.e., P(R|*not H*)], he puts this probability at .90. P(H) is still .50. Now, what is P(H|R)? What will this probability be when Swampman sees the sun rise the next morning? And then the following morning? What effect does a higher value for P(R|*not H*) have on P(H|R)? Why does it have this effect?

(e) On his first day, Swampman wasn't sure what probability to assign to H, the hypothesis that the sun rises every day, and so he simply put the probability for both H and *not H* at 50 percent. But what if he had been more conservative? After all, he's existed for less than a day, and he's making a guess about something happening every single day *forever*. If he had started with P(H) = .10—and P(R|H) = 1.0 and P(R|*not H*) = .50—then what is P(H|R)? What will P(H|R) be after Swampman sees the sun rise the next morning? What is P(H|R) when Swampman sees the sun rise on his third, fourth, fifth, sixth, and seventh mornings?

8.8   Answers

1. Begin with these probabilities:

P(*jar* 1) = .167 (i.e., 1/6)

P(*jar* 2) = .833 (i.e., 5/6)

P(*selecting a red marble*|*jar* 1) = .75

P(*selecting a red marble*|*jar* 2) = .40

(a) Given that the marble is red, the probability that it came from the first jar is 27 percent.

$$P(J1|R) = \frac{P(J1) \times P(R|J1)}{[P(J1) \times P(R|J1)] + [P(J2) \times P(R|J2)]}$$

$$P(J1|R) = \frac{.167 \times .75}{(.167 \times .75) + (.833 \times .40)} = \frac{.125}{.458} \qquad (8.14)$$

$$P(J1|R) = .273$$

(b) Since P(jar 1 | red) = .27, the opposite probability, P(jar 2 | red), has to be .73. That probability is found this way:

$$P(J2|R) = \frac{P(J2) \times P(R|J2)}{[P(J2) \times P(R|J2)] + [P(J1) \times P(R|J1)]}$$

$$P(J2|R) = \frac{.833 \times .40}{(.833 \times .40) + (.167 \times .75)} = \frac{.333}{.458} \qquad (8.15)$$

$$P(J2|R) = .727$$

2. (a) Without knowing what color the marble is, the probability that it came from the first jar is .33, and the probability that it came from the second jar is .67.

P(jar 1) = .33

P(jar 2) = .67

(b) These probabilities are also known and needed for Bayes' rule:

P(selecting a red marble | jar 1) = .70

P(selecting a red marble | jar 2) = .55

$$P(J1|R) = \frac{P(J1) \times P(R|J1)}{[P(J1) \times P(R|J1)] + [P(J2) \times P(R|J2)]}$$

$$P(J1|R) = \frac{.33 \times .70}{(.33 \times .70) + (.67 \times .55)} = \frac{.231}{.60} \qquad (8.16)$$

$$P(J1|R) = .385$$

Given that the marble is red, the probability that it came from the first jar is 38.5 percent.

(c) P(*jar 2*|*red*) is calculated this way:

$$P(J2|R) = \frac{P(J2) \times P(R|J2)}{[P(J2) \times P(R|J2)] + [P(J1) \times P(R|J1)]}$$

$$P(J2|R) = \frac{.67 \times .55}{(.67 \times .55) + (.33 \times .70)} = \frac{.369}{.60} \tag{8.17}$$

$$P(J2|R) = .615$$

3. These are P(H), P(E|H), and P(E|*not* H):

P(*Fred took the pop-tarts*) = .85

P(*no pop-tarts*|*took*) = .30

P(*no pop-tarts*|*did not take*) = .99

The probability that Fred did take the pop-tarts is still 63 percent even though Steve did not find any in his bedroom.

$$P(took|no\ pop\text{-}tarts) = \frac{P(T) \times P(no\ PT|T)}{[P(T) \times P(no\ PT|T)] + [P(not\ T) \times P(no\ PT|not\ T)]}$$

$$P(took|no\ pop\text{-}tarts) = \frac{.85 \times .30}{(.85 \times .30) + (.15 \times .99)} = \frac{.255}{.404}$$

$$P(took|no\ pop\text{-}tarts) = .632$$

$$(8.18)$$

4. These are the initial probabilities:

P(*jar 1*) = .50

P(*jar 2*) = .50

P(*selecting a blue marble*|*jar 1*) = .70

P(*selecting a blue marble*|*jar 2*) = .25

(a) Given that the marble is blue, there is a 74 percent chance that it came from the first jar.

$$P(J1|B) = \frac{P(J1) \times P(B|J1)}{[P(J1) \times P(B|J1)] + [P(J2) \times P(B|J2)]}$$

$$P(J1|B) = \frac{.50 \times .70}{(.50 \times .70) + (.50 \times .25)} = \frac{.35}{.475} \tag{8.19}$$

$$P(J1|B) = .737$$

(b) Now P(*jar* 1) = .737, and the probability that the marble came from the first jar, given that it is blue, is 89 percent.

$$P(J1|B) = \frac{P(J1) \times P(B|J1)}{[P(J1) \times P(B|J1)] + [P(J2) \times P(B|J2)]}$$

$$P(J1|B) = \frac{.737 \times .70}{(.737 \times .70) + (.263 \times .25)} = \frac{.516}{.582} \qquad (8.20)$$

$$P(J1|B) = .887$$

(c) Now P(*jar* 1) = .887, and the probability that the marble came from the first jar, given that it is blue, is 96 percent.

$$P(J1|B) = \frac{P(J1) \times P(B|J1)}{[P(J1) \times P(B|J1)] + [P(J2) \times P(B|J2)]}$$

$$P(J1|B) = \frac{.887 \times .70}{(.887 \times .70) + (.113 \times .25)} = \frac{.621}{.649} \qquad (8.21)$$

$$P(J1|B) = .956$$

(d) On this fourth selection, given that the marble is blue, there is a 98 percent chance that it came from the first jar.

$$P(J1|B) = \frac{P(J1) \times P(B|J1)}{[P(J1) \times P(B|J1)] + [P(J2) \times P(B|J2)]}$$

$$P(J1|B) = \frac{.956 \times .70}{(.956 \times .70) + (.044 \times .25)} = \frac{.669}{.68} \qquad (8.22)$$

$$P(J1|B) = .984$$

(e) Again, P(*jar* 1) is updated based on the last draw. But this time the evidence has also changed: a red marble was drawn, not a blue one. So, these are the probabilities needed for Bayes' rule:

P(*jar* 1) = .984

P(*selecting a red marble*|*jar* 1) = .30

P(*selecting a red marble*|*jar* 2) = .75

Even though this marble is red, the probability that it came from the first jar is still high, 96 percent.

$$P(J1|R) = \frac{P(J1) \times P(R|J1)}{[P(J1) \times P(R|J1)] + [P(J2) \times P(R|J2)]}$$

$$P(J1|R) = \frac{.984 \times .30}{(.984 \times .30) + (.016 \times .75)} = \frac{.295}{.307}$$

(8.23)

$$P(J1|R) = .961$$

5. (a) These probabilities are needed to find P(E is interested | texts):

P(E is interested) = .468. This probability is the result of the application of Bayes' rule after Eric bought Linda the second drink. (See section 8.5.)

P(texts | E is interested) = .75

P(texts | E is not interested) = .45

$$P(E \text{ is interested} | texts) = \frac{P(I) \times P(T|I)}{[P(I) \times P(T|I)] + [P(\text{not } I) \times P(T|\text{not } I)]}$$

$$P(E \text{ is interested} | texts) = \frac{.468 \times .75}{(.468 \times .75) + (.532 \times .45)} = \frac{.351}{.351 + .239}$$

$$= \frac{.351}{.590}$$

P(E is interested | texts) = .595

(8.24)

(b) These probabilities are needed to find P(E is interested | dinner):

P(E is interested) = .595

P(dinner | E is interested) = .85

P(dinner | E is not interested) = .40

$$P(E \text{ is interested} | dinner) = \frac{P(I) \times P(D|I)}{[P(I) \times P(D|I)] + [P(\text{not } I) \times P(D|\text{not } I)]}$$

$$P(E \text{ is interested} | dinner) = \frac{.595 \times .85}{(.595 \times .85) + (.405 \times .40)} = \frac{.506}{.506 + .162}$$

$$= \frac{.506}{.668}$$

P(E is interested | dinner) = .757

(8.25)

6. (a) P(H) = .50

P(R|H) = 1.0

P(R|not H) = .50

Given that the sun rose Swampman's first morning, the probability
that H is correct (i.e., the sun rises every day) is 67 percent.

$$P(H|R) = \frac{P(H) \times P(R|H)}{[P(H) \times P(R|H)] + [P(not\ H) \times P(R|not\ H)]}$$

$$P(H|R) = \frac{.50 \times 1.0}{(.50 \times 1.0) + (.50 \times .50)} = \frac{.50}{.75} = .667 \tag{8.26}$$

(b) When Swampman sees the sun rise his second morning, $P(H|R) = .80$.
Then, after the third, fourth, and fifth mornings, the probability is
.889, .941, and .97.

(c) Now $P(R|not\ H) = .10$. Given that the sun rose Swampman's first
morning, the probability that the sun rises every day is 91 percent.

$$P(H|R) = \frac{P(H) \times P(R|H)}{[P(H) \times P(R|H)] + [P(not\ H) \times P(R|not\ H)]}$$

$$P(H|R) = \frac{.50 \times 1.0}{(.50 \times 1.0) + (.50 \times .10)} = \frac{.50}{.550} = .909 \tag{8.27}$$

After Swampman sees the sun rise on his second and third mornings,
$P(H|R) = .99$ and .999.

(d) Now $P(R|not\ H) = .90$, and given that the sun rose Swampman's
first morning, the probability that the sun rises every day is only
53 percent.

$$P(H|R) = \frac{P(H) \times P(R|H)}{[P(H) \times P(R|H)] + [P(not\ H) \times P(R|not\ H)]}$$

$$P(H|R) = \frac{.50 \times 1.0}{(.50 \times 1.0) + (.50 \times .90)} = \frac{.50}{.95} = 526. \tag{8.28}$$

After Swampman sees the sun rise on his second and third mornings,
$P(H|R) = .552$ and .578.

When $P(R|not\ H)$ is high, $P(H|R)$ is lower and rises more slowly
because each occurrence of the sun rising is expected, even if *not H* is
true—that is, even if the sun does not rise every day. That's in contrast
to (c). There, the sun rising is very unexpected if *not H* is true. Hence,
the sun rising increases the likelihood that H is correct quite a bit.

Mathematically, a higher $P(R|not\ H)$ makes the denominator larger,
which makes the result, $P(H|R)$, smaller.

(e) When $P(H) = .10$, $P(H|R) = .182$.

$$P(H|R) = \frac{P(H) \times P(R|H)}{[P(H) \times P(R|H)] + [P(not\ H) \times P(R|not\ H)]}$$

(8.29)

$$P(H|R) = \frac{.10 \times 1.0}{(.10 \times 1.0) + (.90 \times .50)} = \frac{.10}{.55} = .182$$

After the sun rises on his second, third, fourth, fifth, sixth, and seventh mornings, $P(H|R) = .308, .471, .64, .78, .876,$ and $.934$.

In the chapter, two of the examples—the stolen $1.3 million example in section 8.3 and the Eric and Linda example in section 8.5—use subjective probabilities. Those probabilities have to be determined by a person, and they depend, at least in part, on what that person believes. That contrasts with the examples in sections 8.2 and 8.6. Those probabilities— for instance, the probability that a marble is red, given that it came from the first jar, or the probability of a positive mammogram, given that the woman has cancer—are objective. To find objective probabilities, someone just consults the way the world is.

In the Swampman example, the probabilities are subjective. Swampman came up with $P(H)$, the probability that the sun rises every day. He also came up with $P(R|not\ H)$, the probability of the sun rising, given that H is false. ($P(R|H)$, however, is simply a consequence of the hypothesis.) The Swampman example demonstrates that, although those are subjective probabilities, as long as enough evidence is collected and Bayes' rule is repeatedly applied, the result is the same no matter what the initial value is for $P(H)$ or what value is selected for $P(R|not\ H)$. In all cases, $P(H|R)$ will end up over 99 percent.

A A Brief Introduction to Deductive Logic

A.1 Some Rules of Deductive Logic

Recall the definition of deductively valid from chapter 1.

> An argument is **deductively valid** when it is the case that if the premises are true, then the conclusion has to be true.

The most basic rules that uphold the deductively valid standard concern the logical connectives *and*, *or*, and *if-then*. These are "connectives" because they connect two or more statements. For instance, the statements *Socrates is smart* and *Socrates is witty* can be combined into one longer statement with any of these connectives.

> Socrates is smart, and Socrates is witty.
>
> Socrates is smart, or Socrates is witty.
>
> If Socrates is smart, then Socrates is witty.

The rules described in this section define how *and*, *or*, and *if-then* may be used in inferences so that truth is preserved. Thus, when applied correctly, these rules will always produce a deductively valid argument.

A.1.1 *And* and *Or* Rules

When two statements are connected with an *and* to create a single longer statement— for example, *A and B*—the statement *A and B* is true only when *A* is true and *B* is true. That's fairly obvious. When *or* is used, the situation is a little bit less obvious. One option is this: the statement *A or B* is true when (i) *A* is true, or (ii) *B* is true, or (iii) both are true. This use of *or* is called the *inclusive-or*. The other way of interpreting the statement *A or B* is (i) *A* is true, or (ii) *B* is true, but (iii) both are not true. This is called the *exclusive-or*. The inclusive-or and the exclusive-or are both used in everyday speech, but typically deductive logic employs only the inclusive-or, and that is the way that *or* is used here.

There are four basic rules for *and* and *or*.

(1) **Conjunction-introduction rule**. Given two statements, infer a statement that combines the two with an *and*.

P1 *A*.

P2 *B*.

C Therefore, *A* and *B*.

For example:

P1 Mary is at the library.

P2 Jeff is buying coffee.

C Therefore, Mary is at the library and Jeff is buying coffee.

(2) ***Conjunction-elimination rule***. Given a premise containing one statement that has two clauses joined with an *and*, infer either clause by itself.

P1 *A* and *B*.

C Therefore, *A*.

or

C Therefore, *B*.

For example:

P1 Jodie is upstairs and Mary is at the library.

C Therefore, Jodie is upstairs.

(3) ***Disjunction-introduction rule***. Given one statement (e.g., *A*), infer a second statement that is the first statement and another joined with an *or* (e.g., *A* or *X*). The new clause in the *or*-statement can be any statement.

P1 *A*.

C Therefore, *A* or *X*.

For example:

P1 Mary is at the library.

C Therefore, Mary is at the library or Amy is taking a nap.

(4) ***Disjunction-elimination rule***. Given one statement composed of two clauses combined with an or—e.g., *A or B*—and a second statement that is the negation of one of those clauses—e.g., *not A*—infer the other clause in the *or*-statement.

P1 *A* or *B*.

P2 not *A*.

C Therefore, *B*.

For example:

P1 Paul went to the store, or he visited his sister.

P2 He did not go to the store.

C Therefore, Paul visited his sister.

A.1.2 *If-Then* Rules

Understanding how to manipulate a statement containing an *and* or an *or* is relatively straightforward. The *conditional statement* is a little bit more difficult. A conditional statement is one that has the form: If *A*, then *B*. In a conditional statement, each part has a technical name:

> The first part of a conditional statement, the *A* clause in *if A, then B*, is the **antecedent**.
>
> The second part of a conditional statement, the *B* clause in *if A, then B*, is the **consequent**.

So, in the statement, "If Kate went to her office, then she saw the letter," *Kate went to her office* is the antecedent, and *she saw the letter* is the consequent.

Here are four rules for conditional statements.

(5) **Modus ponens**. Given a conditional statement and a second statement that is the antecedent of that conditional, infer the consequent.

> **P1** If *P*, then *Q*.
>
> **P2** *P*.
>
> **C** Therefore, *Q*.

For example:

> **P1** If Kate went to her office, then she saw the letter.
>
> **P2** Kate went to her office.
>
> **C** Therefore, Kate saw the letter.

(6) **Modus tollens**. Given a conditional statement and a second statement that is the negation of the consequent, infer the negation of the antecedent.

> **P1** If *P*, then *Q*.
>
> **P2** not *Q*.
>
> **C** Therefore, not *P*.

For example:

> **P1** If Kate went to her office, then she saw the letter.
>
> **P2** Kate did not see the letter.
>
> **C** Therefore, Kate did not go her office.

(7) **Transposition**. Given a conditional statement, infer a second conditional statement that has, as the antecedent, the negation of the consequent and, as the consequent, the negation of the antecedent.

> **P1** If *Q*, then *P*.
>
> **C** Therefore, if not *P*, then not *Q*.

For example:

P1   If Kate went to her office, then she saw the letter.

C   Therefore, if Kate did not see the letter, then she did not go to her office.

The rule can also be used this way:

P1   If not Q, then not P.

C   Therefore, if P, then Q.

For example:

P1   If Kate did not see the letter, then she did not go to her office.

C   Therefore, if Kate went to her office, then she saw the letter.

(8) *The hypothetical syllogism*. Given two conditional statements, (i) and (ii), when the same clause is the consequent of (i) and the antecedent of (ii), infer a conditional statement that has, as the antecedent, the antecedent of (i) and, as the consequent, the consequent of (ii).

P1   If P, then Q.

P2   If Q, then R.

C   Therefore, if P, then R.

For example:

P1   If Kate went to her office, then she saw the letter.

P2   If Kate saw the letter, then she called her attorney.

C   Therefore, if Kate went to her office, then she called her attorney.

These four rules define how a conditional statement may be manipulated, but it is also helpful to consider, in a little less formal way, what *If A, then B* means.

One way to think about a conditional statement is as a rule that does not get broken. As such, it is a rule stating that if the antecedent happens, then the consequent has to happen. Take the previous example:

If Kate went to her office, then she saw the letter.

Since this statement is a rule, if Kate went to her office, she had to see the letter—for it to be otherwise, the rule would be broken.

The conditional statement will also be true, however (and the rule still in force), when that antecedent does not happen, but the consequent does. For instance, it might be that Kate didn't go to her office, but someone collected the letter and showed it to her outside of the office. The rule isn't being broken; this is just a situation where the rule doesn't apply. This is important, and it is why any argument that has this form is invalid:

P1   If P, then Q.

P2 Q.

C   Therefore, P.

A.2   Categorical Syllogisms

The rules explained in section A.1 are part of modern deductive logic. They are not the only rules, but they are some of the easier ones to grasp, and they give a good sense of the foundations of deductive logic. But before they were set down in the late nineteenth century, logic was mainly based on the theory of the syllogism, which was developed by Aristotle in the fourth century BCE. The term *syllogism* has already been used, of course, for the proportional syllogism, but that usage is relatively new. Traditionally, *syllogism* referred only to categorical syllogisms, a specific kind of deductively valid argument.

A ***categorical syllogism*** is a deductively valid argument with two premises and a conclusion. Both premises and the conclusion must have one of these four forms:

> All *a* are *b*.
>
> No *a* are *b*.
>
> Some *a* are *b*.
>
> Some *a* are not *b*.

And the two premises must have one term (i.e., *a* or *b*) in common.[1]

Most of the 256 syllogisms that can be put together with these four types of statements are deductively invalid. Twenty-four are valid, and below are three examples. The names *Darii, Barbara,* and *Celarent* (which are mnemonics actually) were given to the arguments by medieval logicians.

The Darii form of the categorical syllogism

P1 All *a* are *b*.	**P1** All humans are greedy.
P2 Some *c* are *a*.	**P2** Some mammals are humans.
C Therefore, some *c* are *b*.	C Therefore, some mammals are greedy.

The Barbara form of the categorical syllogism

P1 All *a* are *b*.	**P1** All mammals are animals.
P2 All *c* are *a*.	**P2** All humans are mammals.
C Therefore, all *c* are *b*.	C Therefore, all humans are animals.

The Celarent form of the categorical syllogism

P1 No *a* are *b*.	**P1** No mammals are reptiles.
P2 All *c* are *a*.	**P2** All humans are mammals.
C Therefore, no *c* are *b*.	C Therefore, no humans are reptiles.

---

1. In the previous section, *A* and *B* represented statements (e.g., *Socrates is smart*). Here, when discussing categorical syllogisms, *a* and *b* represent terms (e.g., *men* or *mortal*).

Aristotle's theory of the syllogism does not use statements that have the form "*x* is an *a*" where *x* is one individual. But when such a statement is employed, two more deductively valid arguments that are very similar to a categorical syllogism are possible:

P1 All *a* are *b*.	**P1** All men are moral.
P2 *x* is an *a*.	**P2** Socrates is a man.
C Therefore, *x* is *b*.	**C** Therefore, Socrates is mortal.
P1 No *a* are *b*.	**P1** No man is cold-blooded.
P2 *x* is an *a*.	**P2** Socrates is a man.
C Therefore, *x* is not *b*.	**C** Therefore, Socrates is not cold-blooded.

These two arguments and the proportional syllogism occupy a spectrum. The two deductively valid arguments are the limiting cases, and the deductively invalid proportional syllogism occupies the space between them.

P1 All *a* are *b*.	**P1** *z* percent of *a* are *b*.	**P1** No *a* are *b*.
P2 *x* is an *a*.	**P2** *x* is an *a*.	**P2** *x* is an *a*.
C Therefore, *x* is *b*.	**C** Therefore, there is a *z* percent chance that *x* is *b*.	**C** Therefore, *x* is not *b*.

A.3 Exercises

For problems 1 through 12, determine if the argument is deductively valid or deductively invalid, and if it is valid, identify the rule used.

1. **P1** Paul went to the store, and he bought flour.
   C Therefore, Paul bought flour.

2. **P1** Paul went to the store.
   C Therefore, Paul when to the store or today is Saturday.

3. **P1** Paul went to the store.
   C Therefore, Paul when to the store and today is Saturday.

4. **P1** If Paul went to the store, then he bought flour.
   P2 Paul did not buy flour.
   C Therefore, Paul did not go to the store.

5. If Willie went to the store, then he bought flour. If Willie bought flour, then he will bake a cake. So, if Willie went to the store, he will bake a cake.

6. **P1** If pigs can fly, then Joan is happy.
   P2 Pigs can fly.
   C Therefore, Joan is happy.

7. **P1** If pigs can fly, then Joan is happy.
   P2 Joan is happy.
   C Therefore, pigs can fly.

8. **P1** Both sides agreed to a peace treaty yesterday, or the war will continue.
   P2 Both sides did not agree to a peace treaty yesterday.
   C Therefore, the war will continue.

9. **P1** If pigs can fly, then Joan is happy.
   C Therefore, if Joan is not happy, then pigs cannot fly.

10. **P1** If Paul did not buy flour, then he did not go to the store.
    C Therefore, if Paul went to the store, then he bought flour.

11. **P1** Paul went to the store, or he visited his sister.
    C Therefore, Paul went to the store.

12. **P1** The Magna Carta was created in 1214, or it was created in 1215.
    P2 The Magna Carta was not created in 1214.
    C Therefore, it was created in 1215.

For problems 13 to 28, supply the conclusion that, with the rule that is given, can be inferred from the premise or premises. For problems 29 to 32, using the rule that is given, supply the missing premise and the conclusion.

13. Use the disjunction-elimination rule.

    P1 Either Morgan or Kim spilled the wine.

    P2 Kim did not spill the wine.

    C

14. Use modus ponens.

    P1 If Samuel Clemens was there, then Mark Twain was there.

    P2 Samuel Clemens was there.

    C

15. Use modus tollens.

    P1 If Samuel Clemens was there, then Mark Twain was there.

    P2 Mark Twain was not there.

    C

16. Use the conjunction-elimination rule.

    P1 The cow jumped over the moon, and the dish ran away with the spoon.

    C

17. Use the disjunction-introduction rule.

    P1 Mark Twain was born in Florida, Missouri.

    C

18. Use modus tollens.

    P1 If the Jets do not throw any interceptions, then they will win the game.

    P2 The Jets did not win the game.

    C

19. Use transposition.

   P1 If the detective found the gun, then Ronald went to jail.

   C

20. Use the hypothetical syllogism.

   P1 If Mary goes to law school, then she will move to New York City.

   P2 If Mary moves to New York City, then she will sell the painting.

   C

21. Use transposition.

   P1 If Jack did not make the phone call, then he did not get home before 8:00 p.m.

   C

22. Use the conjunction-introduction rule.

   P1 Cry "Havoc."

   P2 Let slip the dogs of war.

   C

23. Use modus tollens.

   P1 If Jack did not make the phone call, then he did not get home before 8:00 p.m.

   P2 Jack got home before 8:00 p.m.

   C

24. Use the disjunction-elimination rule.

   P1 Either Jones stole the car or Smith forgot where he parked it.

   P2 Smith did not forget where he parked the car.

   C

25. Use the conjunction-elimination rule.

   P1 All the world's a stage, and all the men and women merely players.

   C

26. Use the conjunction-introduction rule.

   P1 Some rise by sin.

   P2 Some by virtue fall.

   C

27. Use modus ponens.

   P1 If Mary was wronged, then she will seek revenge.

   P2 Mary was wronged.

   C

28. Use the hypothetical syllogism.

   P1 If Captain Blight is a cruel tyrant, then his crew will take over the ship.

   P2 If his crew takes over the ship, then they will return to Tahiti.

   C

29. Use the disjunction-elimination rule.

   P1 Either Socrates deserved to die or the jury made a mistake.

   P2

   C

30. Use the hypothetical syllogism.

   P1 If the water is warm, then Sarah is swimming.

   P2

   C

31. Use modus ponens.

   P1 If the water is warm, then Sarah is swimming.

   P2

   C

32. Use modus tollens.

   P1 If the water is warm, then Sarah is swimming.

   P2

   C

For exercises 33 and 34, use the a, b, and c that are given to create the Darii, Barbara, and Celarent forms of the categorical syllogism.

33. a: monsters, b: envious, c: humans

34. a: sanctuaries, b: haunted, c: forests

A.4 Answers

1. This argument is valid. It uses the conjunction-elimination rule.

2. This argument is valid. It uses the disjunction-introduction rule.

3. This argument is invalid.

4. This argument is valid. It uses modus tollens.

5. This argument is valid. It uses the hypothetical syllogism.

6. This argument is valid. It uses modus ponens.

7. This argument is invalid.

8. This argument is valid. It uses the disjunction-elimination rule.

9. This argument is valid. It uses transposition.

10. This argument is valid. It uses transposition.

11. This argument is invalid.

12. This argument is valid. It uses the disjunction-elimination rule.

13. Using the disjunction-elimination rule, this is the conclusion:

    C Therefore, Morgan spilled the wine.

14. Using modus ponens, this is the conclusion:

    C Therefore, Mark Twain was there.

15. Using modus tollens, this is the conclusion:

    C Therefore, Samuel Clemens was not there.

16. Using the conjunction-elimination rule, either of these can be the conclusion:

    C Therefore, the cow jumped over the moon.

    or

    C Therefore, the dish ran away with the spoon.

17. Using the disjunction-introduction rule, this is the conclusion:

    C Therefore, Mark Twain was born in Florida, Missouri or . . . *any statement can go here.*

    The second statement can be anything and the argument will still be valid—for example,

      Mark Twain was born in Florida, Missouri, or today is Thursday.

      Mark Twain was born in Florida, Missouri, or pigs can fly.

      Mark Twain was born in Florida, Missouri, or the United States is a federal republic.

      Mark Twain was born in Florida, Missouri, or the United States is a monarchy.

    Or anything else, as long as *Mark Twain was born in Florida, Missouri*, and an *or* are in it.

18. Using modus tollens, this is the conclusion:

    C Therefore, the Jets did throw one or more interceptions. (I.e., it is not the case that the Jets did not throw any interceptions.)

19. Using transposition, this is the conclusion:

    C Therefore, if Ronald did not go to jail, then the detective did not find the gun.

20. Using the hypothetical syllogism, this is the conclusion:

    C If Mary goes to law school, then she will sell the painting.

21. Using transposition, this is the conclusion:

    C If Jack did get home before 8:00 p.m., then he did make the phone call.

22. Using the conjunction-introduction rule, this is the conclusion:

    C Cry "Havoc," and let slip the dogs of war.

    or

    C Let slip the dogs of war, and cry "Havoc."

23. Using modus tollens, this is the conclusion:

    C Therefore, Jack did make the phone call.

24. Using the disjunction-elimination rule, this is the conclusion:

    C Therefore, Jones stole the car.

25. Using the conjunction-elimination rule, either of these can be the conclusion:

    C All the world's a stage.

    or

    C All the men and women are merely players.

26. Using the conjunction-introduction rule, the conclusion is

    C Some rise by sin, and some by virtue fall.

    or

    C Some by virtue fall, and some rise by sin.

27. Using modus ponens, this is the conclusion:

    C Therefore, Mary will seek revenge.

28. Using the hypothetical syllogism, this is the conclusion:

    C If Captain Blight is a cruel tyrant, then his crew will return to Tahiti.

29. Using the disjunction-elimination rule, the argument can be completed either of these two ways:

    P2 Socrates did not deserve to die.

    C Therefore, the jury made a mistake.

    or

    P2 The jury did not make a mistake.

    C Therefore, Socrates deserved to die.

30. Using the hypothetical syllogism, this is the second premise and the conclusion:

    P2 If Sarah is swimming, then ...B. (B can be any statement.)

    C Therefore, if the water is warm, then ...B.

31. Using modus ponens, this is the second premise and the conclusion:

    P2 The water is warm.

    C Therefore, Sarah is swimming.

32. Using modus tollens, this is the second premise and the conclusion:

    P2 Sarah is not swimming.

    C Therefore, the water is not warm.

33. (a) Darii:

    P1 All monsters are envious.

    P2 Some humans are monsters.

    C Therefore, some humans are envious.

    (b) Barbara:

    P1 All monsters are envious.

    P2 All humans are monsters.

    C Therefore, all humans are envious.

    (c) Celarent:

    P1 No monsters are envious.

    P2 All humans are monsters.

    P3 Therefore, no humans are envious.

34. (a) Darii:

    P1 All sanctuaries are haunted.

    P2 Some forests are sanctuaries.

    C Therefore, some forests are haunted.

    (b) Barbara:

    P1 All sanctuaries are haunted.

    P2 All forests are sanctuaries.

    C Therefore, all forests are haunted.

    (c) Celarent:

    P1 No sanctuaries are haunted.

    P2 All forests are sanctuaries.

    C Therefore, no forests are haunted.

B   Some Further Topics on Probability

B.1   Odds

When talking about chances, people often use a ratio and say things like, "three to one" or "five to two." These are odds, and they are just a different way of stating a probability. Odds are famously used in sports betting, and they are also found in markets where predictions are made about other kinds of future events, for instance, which candidate will win an election or which movie will win Best Picture at the Oscars. But they can be used any time, in place of a probability, to indicate how likely it is that some event will occur.

The odds that an event will occur is the ratio between *the probability that it will not occur* and *the probability that it will occur*. For example, if there is a 25 percent chance that a red marble will be selected from a jar, then the odds of selecting a red marble are .75 to .25 or 3 to 1. If there is a 40 percent chance that a red marble will be selected, then the odds are .60 to .40 or 3 to 2.[1]

---

1. There are actually a number of different ways of representing odds, starting with putting the numbers in the ratio in the opposite order. Instead of having *the probability against the event occurring* first in the ratio, *the probability for the event occurring* can be put first. When *the probability against the event occurring* is first, the odds are called *odds against*, and when the *the probability for the event occurring* is first, the odds are called *odds for* (or *odds in favor*). Most textbooks explain odds using the *odds for* definition, but, generally speaking, *odds against* is more common. (And even though this is a textbook, *odds against* is used here.)

Here is one example of odds against. During the 2015 NCAA men's basketball tournament, David Purdum, writing for ESPN, reported, "The Wildcats (38–0) are looking to become the first team to go undefeated since the 1976 Indiana Hoosiers, a feat that would hand the William Hill sportsbook its largest loss on a single prop bet in the company's three-year history in Nevada. Last summer, William Hill posted Kentucky's odds of going undefeated at 50–1 [i.e., 50 to 1]. Money poured in on the Wildcats, and the book is now facing a mid-six figures liability" (David Purdum, "Vegas Stuck Rooting for Wisconsin," ESPN.com, March 31, 2015, http://espn.go.com/chalk/story/_/id/12584853).

(footnote continues on next page)

Given an odds ratio, a simple way of converting it to a probability is to add the two numbers in the ratio together (so, for three to two, 3 + 2 = 5). This number can be treated as the total number of possible chances. The second number in the ratio is then divided by this total. For three to two, 2 is divided by 5, yielding 40 percent. For this procedure, the formula is

$$a \text{ to } b = \frac{b}{a+b} = probability \qquad\qquad (B.1)$$

Other formulas can be used to convert odds to a probability, but this one sticks very close to the reason why odds are useful when betting on an event. Consider two people, Jeff and Claire, who are going to bet on a horse race. If the horse Little Tony wins the race, then Claire will win the bet. If Little Tony loses, then Jeff will win the bet. Little Tony is a strong and well-rested horse, but the rest of the horses in the race are also pretty fast. Jeff offers to put down $4 if Claire puts down $5. If Little Tony wins the race, then Claire gets all $9, if Little Tony loses, then Jeff gets the $9. In essence, Jeff is proposing 4 to 5 odds on Little Tony winning, which puts the probability at 56 percent.

$$4 \text{ to } 5: \quad \frac{5}{4+5} = .56 \qquad\qquad (B.2)$$

Claire thinks about it and decides that she does not like these odds. Considering how strong the rest of the field is, this bet is too generous toward Jeff—she thinks that the probability of Little Tony winning is less than 56 percent. She suggests that Jeff put down $7 and she will put down $3. If Little Tony wins, Claire gets all $10, and if Little Tony loses, Jeff gets the $10. But now Jeff thinks that the bet is unfair, and so he refuses it. He counters with this: he'll put down $7 if Claire puts down $5. Claire agrees that this is a fair bet, and they both put their money on the table and wait for the race to begin. According to Jeff and Claire, the odds of Little Tony winning are seven to five.

$$7 \text{ to } 5: \quad \frac{5}{7+5} = .42 \qquad\qquad (B.3)$$

The 50 to 1 odds, which were set before the school year began, are odds against and represent a 2 percent probability that the University of Kentucky men's basketball team would end the season undefeated—an event that, at the end of March and with only a couple of games to go, was looking quite a bit more likely.

Beyond the order of the numbers in the ratio, there are many other ways of representing odds. All of the different ways are just various conventions that have taken hold in different places. Odds given as a ratio is the most traditional, but another popular format is explained at the end of this section.

A different, but equivalent, way of representing odds is the *money line*. This style is commonly used for sports betting in the United States and so is sometimes referred to as *American odds*. The money line is either (i) a positive number 100 or larger or (ii) a negative number 100 or smaller. Perhaps counterintuitively, the negative number indicates that the probability is 50 percent or higher, and the positive number indicates that the probability is 50 percent is or lower. (100 and –100 are both equivalent to a 50 percent probability.) Here is an example of the money line on the Cardinals and on the Orioles:

Cardinals: –160

Orioles: 160

The first one means that if someone bets $160 on the Cardinals and the Cardinals win, then that person will get $100 (plus the $160 that he or she bet). For the second one, a $100 bet will pay $160 if the Orioles win (plus the initial $100). Of course, the bet can be for any amount and the payoff will be proportional to the number in the money line and 100.

Since 100 is the basic unit here, converting a money line to traditional odds is relatively easy. When the money line is 160, the traditional odds are 160 to 100. One hundred is the amount bet and 160 is the amount to be won, which is equivalent to 8 to 5. That means that the probability is .38. Note that the order in the ratio is switched when the money line is negative: –160 becomes 100 to 160. One hundred sixty is the amount bet and 100 is the possible winnings, or 5 to 8. (The formulas for converting a money line to a probability are given in table B.1.)

One special feature of odds is that, often when they are used, one of the rules for probabilities is broken: the second rule in table 6.2 in chapter 6. That rule is

The probability of A and the probability of *not A* add up to 1. That is, $P(A) + P(not\ A) = 1$, and so $P(not\ A) = 1 - P(A)$

Sometimes when a probability is represented as odds this rule is followed, but not always. The reason it isn't followed is simple. The bookmaker—the person or organization that takes people's bets—wants to make money.

Consider a horse race again. Two horses are racing, The Wizard of Odds (or The Wiz for short) and Oddsymandias. The best estimate of The Wiz's chance of winning

Table B.1

Money line	Traditional odds	Probability
–180	100 to 180 or 5 to 9	.64
200	200 to 100 or 2 to 1	.33
–x	100 to x	$\dfrac{x}{100+x}$
y	y to 100	$\dfrac{100}{y+100}$

is 45 percent, and so the probability that Oddsymandias will win is 55 percent. That makes the odds on The Wiz 13 to 7 and the odds on Oddsymandias 7 to 13. Again, Jeff and Claire are wagering. Jeff is betting on The Wiz to win; Claire is going with Oddsymandias. But this time, there is a bookmaker involved. Jeff bets $7. If The Wiz wins, then the bookmaker will give Jeff $13 plus his "stake," the $7 he put down. Claire bets $13, and if Oddsymandias wins, she will get $7 plus her stake, the $13 she bet. No one else is betting. The horses race, and Oddsymandias wins. Claire gets $7 plus her $13. Jeff gets nothing. Simple enough, but the bookmaker only handled the transaction. He didn't make or lose any money, and he wants to make money.

Let's redo the example. The bookmaker knows the best estimate of each horse's chances of winning, but he sets the odds this way:

the odds on The Wizard of Odds winning are 13 to 8

the odds on Oddsymandias winning are 7 to 14

These make the implied probabilities 38 percent and 67 percent, for a total of 105 percent. But breaking the rule that mutually exclusive probabilities add up to 1.0 will benefit this bookmaker. Jeff now puts down $8, and Claire puts down $14. So, before the race, the bookmaker is holding $22. The horses race, Oddsymandias wins, and Claire gets $7 plus her $14. That's $21, and so the bookmaker keeps $1.

Of course, it is not always that easy for bookmakers to ensure a profit. To do so, they must carefully gauge the true probabilities—using both their own knowledge and information about how people are betting. Then they try to set the odds, or adjust them if need be, so that no matter the outcome, they will make a little bit of money.

The one thing that bookmakers want to avoid is setting the odds so that someone can put a bet on each possible outcome and be certain of making a profit. This happens when the probabilities given by the odds total less than 1.0. For instance, in a horse race with three horses, if the odds on the first horse to win are 3 to 2, the odds on the second horse are 5 to 3, and the odds on the third horse are 7 to 1, then the probabilities are 40 percent, 37.5 percent, and 12.5 percent, which sum to only 90 percent. Now, if one person bets on all three horses, that bettor can be certain of making money. With the amounts given in table B.2—$64 on horse 1, $60 on horse 2, and $20 on horse 3—no matter which horse wins, the bettor will make a $16 profit, which is equivalent to a $16 loss for the bookmaker.

So, almost always, the odds given by a bookmaker are slightly higher than the true odds and total more than 1.0. That allows the bookmaker to make a profit and prevents a situation where he or she is guaranteed a loss.

B.2   Expected Value

In his book *The Signal and the Noise*, the political forecaster Nate Silver describes a bet made by a Canadian college student who also worked as a skycap at the Winnipeg International Airport. Bob Voulgaris had saved $80,000 and, a few weeks after the

Table B.2

A single bettor puts $64 on horse 1, $60 on horse 2, and $20 on horse 3. If horse 1 wins, then for every $2 she bet on horse 1, she gets $3 (and she gets her stake back). Having bet $64, she gets $96—her winnings—plus the $64, for a total of $160. Since all three of her bets only totaled $144, she makes a $16 profit. Similarly, if either of the other two horses win instead, she will make a $16 profit.

	Odds	Probability	Amount bet ($)	If that horse wins	
				Winnings ($)	Total payoff ($)
Horse 1	3 to 2	.40	64	$^{64}/_2 \times 3 = 96$	160
Horse 2	5 to 3	.375	60	$^{60}/_3 \times 5 = 100$	160
Horse 3	7 to 1	.125	20	$^{20}/_1 \times 7 = 140$	160
Totals		.90	144		

1999–2000 NBA season began, he bet it all on the Los Angeles Lakers to win the NBA championship. Silver writes,

> The Vegas line on the Lakers at the time that Voulgaris placed his bet implied that they had a 13 percent chance of winning the NBA title. Voulgaris did not think the Lakers' were 100 percent or even 50 percent—but he was confident they were quite a bit higher than 13 percent. Perhaps more like 25 percent, he thought. If Voulgaris's calculation was right, the bet had a theoretical profit of $70,000.[2]

If the Lakers won the championship, Voulgaris would get $520,000. If they lost, then he would lose his $80,000. So, +$520,000 or –$80,000. Where does $70,000 come from?

With respect to Voulgaris's bet, there are only two events that matter: (1) the Los Angeles Lakers win the NBA championship, or (2) the Los Angeles Lakers lose the NBA championship. For Voulgaris, the value of *the Lakers win* is $520,000. But what's really important is the *weighted* or *expected value* of this event. That's the probability that it will happen multiplied by the $520,000:

$$.25 \times \$520,000 = \$130,000 \tag{B.4}$$

Likewise for *the Lakers lose*:

$$.75 \times -\$80,000 = -\$60,000 \tag{B.5}$$

---

2. Nate Silver, *The Signal and the Noise* (New York: Penguin Press, 2012), 237.

The expected value of the bet itself, then, is the expected value of *the Lakers win* plus the expected value of *the Lakers lose*.

$$E(bet) = \$130,000 + (-\$60,000) = \$70,000 \tag{B.6}$$

Of course, Voulgaris would never get $70,000. It's $520,000 or –$80,000. But often the expected value is useful when making a decision. Voulgaris's decision was between placing the bet or not placing the bet. The expected value of the latter is simply

$$E(no\ bet) = (.25 \times \$0) + (.75 \times \$0) = \$0 \tag{B.7}$$

Since placing the bet has a higher expected value, it is—or, at least, might be—considered the better choice. Voulgaris went with it, and at the end of the season

> the Lakers disposed of the Indiana Pacers in efficient fashion to win their first NBA title since the Magic Johnson era. And Bob the skycap was halfway to becoming a millionaire.[3]

Another example is in table B.3. There, a choice has to be made between betting that a red marble will be drawn and betting that a blue marble will be drawn. If a red marble is drawn from the jar, the payoffs are $7 and –$3, depending on which bet was made. If a blue marble is drawn, the payoffs are –$4 and $9. Just looking at these numbers, *bet on blue* looks like the better choice. The positive payoff is higher than it is for bet on red ($9 versus $7), and the negative payoff is also higher (–$3 instead of –$4).

But since the probability of a red marble being drawn and the probability of a blue marble being drawn are known, it's worth finding the expected value of each option.

$$E(bet\ on\ red) = (.60 \times \$7) + (.40 \times -\$4) = 4.20 + (-1.60) = \$2.60$$
$$E(bet\ on\ blue) = (.60 \times -\$3) + (.40 \times \$9) = -1.80 + 3.60 = \$1.80 \tag{B.8}$$

Table B.3
One marble will be selected from a jar that contains 60 percent red marbles and 40 percent blue marbles. The amount paid to make the bet, whatever it is, and the winnings (or lack there of) are combined into one value for each possible outcome.

	$P(R) = .60$	$P(B) = .40$
	Red is drawn	Blue is drawn
Bet on red	$7	–$4
Bet on blue	–$3	$9

3. Silver, *The Signal and the Noise*, 237.

Bet on red has a higher expected value, and so most people would agree that it's actually the better choice. The benefit of using the expected values to make a decision is pretty straightforward. The probabilities are extra information, and the expected value for each option combines the possible payoffs and the probabilities for each payoff into one number, which can then be compared to the expected value of the other option or options.

In some cases, however, many people would be wary of making a decision based on the expected values. Consider the choice between lottery A and lottery B in table B.4. This quick calculation shows that the expected value of lottery B is higher, and intuitively that seems like the better choice:

$$E(\textit{lottery A}) = (.01 \times \$100) + (.10 \times \$100) + (.89 \times \$100) = \$100$$
$$E(\textit{lottery B}) = (.01 \times \$0) + (.10 \times \$500) + (.89 \times \$100) = \$139$$

(B.9)

The two lotteries in table B.5 have the same format and the expected values work out the same way, just with more zeros.

$$E(\textit{lottery A}) = (.01 \times \$1,000,000) + (.10 \times \$1,000,000) + (.89 \times \$1,000,000)$$
$$= \$1,000,000$$
$$E(\textit{lottery B}) = (.01 \times \$0) + (.10 \times \$5,000,000) + (.89 \times \$1,000,000)$$
$$= \$1,390,000$$

(B.10)

Now, however, many people will—very reasonably, it seems—ignore the expected values and make a decision based on just the payoffs. The guarantee of $1 million that comes with choosing lottery A looks a lot more appealing than choosing lottery B and taking a small chance at getting $0. The example just shows that, while often the expected value is important for understanding the value of an option, it's not, for everyone, always going to be the basis for making a decision.

Table B.4

A choice between two lotteries. Lottery A and lottery B have the same format. For each, there are 100 tickets, and one ticket will be drawn. The only differences between the two lotteries are the payoffs for tickets 1 – 11.

	P = .01	P = .10	P = .89
	Ticket # 1 is selected	A ticket # 2 – 11 is selected	A ticket # 12 – 100 is selected
Lottery A	$100	$100	$100
Lottery B	$0	$500	$100

Table B.5

A choice between two lotteries. These lotteries are identical to the ones described in table B.4 except that the payoffs are increased 10,000-fold.

	P = .01	P = .10	P = .89
	Ticket # 1 is selected	A ticket # 2 – 11 is selected	A ticket # 12 – 100 is selected
Lottery A	$1,000,000	$1,000,000	$1,000,000
Lottery B	$0	$5,000,000	$1,000,000

B.3   Where Do Probabilities Come From?

The probabilities that were used in chapter 6 were taken directly from the proportions of the populations. Often, however, probabilities are used when there are not any populations available. For example,

- There is a 15 percent chance that the Philadelphia Phillies will win the next World Series.
- There is a 4 percent chance that there is other life, of some kind, in our solar system.
- There is a 60 percent chance that it will rain tomorrow.

In all of these cases, a probability has been established without reference to a proportion of a population. This section explains—in a very nonrigorous manner—three different ways of establishing probabilities, two of which can be used without having a population. What probabilities are and the most basic or fundamental way of establishing them are interesting philosophical questions, but they are beyond the scope of what will be addressed here.

B.3.1   Proportion of a Population

Although using the proportion of a population to find a probability has been covered, a couple of relevant points were not discussed in chapter 6. First, when a probability is derived from the proportion of a population, the process is actually just an application of the proportional syllogism. For example,

> P1   90 percent of the marbles in the jar are red.
>
> P2   One marble is about to be selected from this jar.
>
> C   The probability is .90 that the selected marble will be red.

Recall from chapter 6 that the conclusion can also be stated this way, which is exactly the probability that is needed:

> C   P(the selected marble will be red) = .90

This way of assigning probabilities is used any time there are a certain number of outcomes and each is equally likely. For instance, when one die is rolled, there are six possible outcomes. Presuming that the die is fair, each outcome is equally likely, and so to each number—one through six—the probability $1/6$ (or .167) is assigned.

B.3.2 Frequency

While in many cases a population is not available, there often are observed relative frequencies. These frequencies can be used as the basis for establishing a probability, but this must be done with some care.

Imagine that you have a coin and you want to know if it is fair—that is, if the probability of getting heads is .50. You toss it ten times and get six heads. Maybe it's not a fair coin. But even if it is perfectly fair, you had a 21 percent chance of getting six out of ten heads. You toss it another 90 times. Now, out of the 100 times that you've tossed it, you've gotten heads 56 times. Again, even if it is a fair coin, there was a 3.9 percent chance that you would get heads 56 out of 100 times—and there was only an 8 percent chance of getting exactly 50 percent heads. But this is all just a review of chapter 7.

The only way to get useful information is to toss the coin many, many times. Let's say you toss it 10,000 times. Even if the coin is fair, you probably won't get exactly 5,000 heads—in fact, it's very unlikely that you will get that number. But whatever you get is going to be pretty close to the coin's "true nature." A better way to proceed, however, is to find 1,000 people and have each one of them flip the coin 100 times. Now there are 100,000 flips to work with, and we can look at the information gathered in a different way.

Assuming that the coin is fair, some of these people will get exactly 50 percent heads. Some will get 49 percent heads; some will get 54 percent heads. Probably some—although not very many—will get heads on only 35 of their 100 flips. And so on. If these results are plotted, then the graph will look like the one in figure B.1, although not as perfectly bell shaped.

This graph is similar to, but not the same as, the ones in chapter 7. Here, the percentages of people who have gotten different proportions of heads are on the y-axis (i.e., around 8 percent will get 50 percent heads; a little less will get 49 percent heads; etc.). Even if the data do not form a perfect bell shape, it can be smoothed out, and the peak of the bell will correspond to the probability of getting heads with this coin.

Why does this work? Well, it's not too likely that anyone will get exactly 50 percent heads, but, if the coin is fair, that is the most likely result. Hence, more people should get that than any other single percentage of heads. Getting 49 percent and 51 percent heads on the 100 flips (which are equally likely) should have the next biggest groups, and so on. The bell curve is created, and the probability is identified.

B.3.3 Betting

Setting up a choice between two options and giving a decision maker an incentive to make the best choice is another way of establishing a probability. For instance, there is some probability that the Los Angeles Lakers will win the next NBA championship, but this probability can't be found by either of the two methods just discussed.

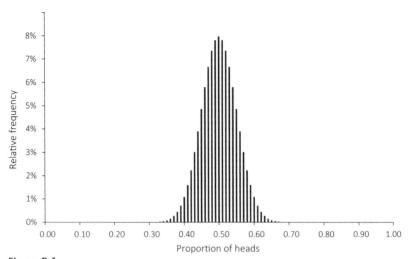

Figure B.1
One thousand people each flip a coin 100 times. The relative frequency (on the y-axis) is the percentage of people who get each possible proportion of heads on their 100 flips. For instance, around 8 percent of the people will 50 percent heads, a little bit less will get 49 percent heads, and so forth.

Here is a method for assigning a probability to such an event. Imagine that you have to choose either (a) and (b).

(a) The Los Angeles Lakers will win the next NBA championship.

(b) A red marble will be randomly selected from a jar that contains 50 percent red and 50 percent nonred marbles.

If your choice turns out to be correct, then you get $500. This amount of money should give you an incentive to choose the one that you think is the most likely to be true. Since the probability of (b) being true is 50 percent, if you choose (a), then that means that you think the probability that the Lakers will win the next NBA championship is higher than 50 percent. If you choose (b), that means that you think the probability that the Lakers will win the next NBA championship is lower than 50 percent.

You make a choice. Let's say that you chose (b). You think the probability that the Lakers will win the next NBA championship is less than 50 percent. The next step is not to figure out if your choice is correct (and we're not going to give you the $500). Rather, the percentage of red marbles in the jar is changed and you choose again. Now you are offered these two choices:

(a) The Los Angeles Lakers will win the next NBA championship.

(b) A red marble will be randomly selected from a jar that contains 40 percent red and 60 percent nonred marbles.

This is repeated until we find the point where you are indifferent between (a) and (b)—that is, the point at which you would be equally happy taking either (a) or (b). You would even be willing to let someone else choose for you because you don't care which one you get. When you reach that point, you believe that the probability of the two events is the same.

Let's say that you would take either of these for the $500, you don't care which:

(a) The Los Angeles Lakers will win the next NBA championship.

(b) A red marble will be randomly selected from a jar that contains 25 percent red and 75 percent nonred marbles.

If you think (a) and (b) are equally likely to be correct, then you believe that the probability of the Lakers winning the next NBA championship is .25.[4]

For the probability that is established by this method to be really meaningful, the person going through the process should be pretty well informed about the event that is stated in (a). The person also has to answer honestly and desire the $500 (although any other amount can be offered). To be certain that the person making the choices is invested, real money can be used, but, generally, it is thought that going through this process hypothetically (without actually having $500 to give) is sufficient, and as long as the person makes honest choices, then the process will work. Nonetheless, this method is more subjective than the other two methods. Being subjective does not mean that the process is random, but it does mean that the probability that results is tied to the person who has made the choices.

B.4 Exercises

For exercises 1 to 5, identify the probability represented by each of the odds. In some cases, the odds ratio (i.e., *a* to *b*) is written as *a*–*b* or as *a*/*b*.

1. Powered by Stephen Curry's 37 points in Game 5 Sunday, the Golden State Warriors are one game away from capturing their first NBA title in four decades. And odds makers like their chances even if the series goes a full seven games. According to the latest odds from Sportsbook.ag, the Warriors are favored to sew up the title in Tuesday night's Game 6 with ... a –185 money line. A Cleveland money line victory is at +160.

   The Warriors are also –1100 favorites to beat the Cleveland Cavaliers should these NBA Finals go the distance. ... After enduring a difficult 104–91 loss in Game 5, forward LeBron James and the Cavs are now a huge +700 underdog [to win the seven game series], with Golden State owning the right to host a potential Game 7.

---

4. At the beginning of the 1999–2000 NBA season, Bob Voulgaris, the gambler from the section on expected value, believed that (a) and (b) were equally likely.

2. Cheer up, Cleveland—the Cavaliers are the clear-cut favorites to win next year's championship. The Golden State Warriors outlasted the depleted Cavaliers on Tuesday, clinching this year's championship with a 105–97 win in Game 6 of the NBA Finals. But the Westgate Las Vegas SuperBook made Cleveland the early 9–4 [i.e., 9 to 4] favorite to win the 2016 NBA title. Golden State and the Oklahoma City Thunder are next at 5–1, followed by the Los Angeles Clippers (10–1), San Antonio Spurs (12–1) and Chicago Bulls (12–1). A lot could change during the offseason, with a plethora of big-name free agents possibly on the move.

3. Mitt Romney brought his campaign for the White House back to life today with a surprise victory over Barack Obama in their first live TV debate. His spirited, pugnacious performance was seen to have earned a clear win over the President, who appeared listless, disengaged and lacking in any killer lines. The 90-minute debate, watched by 60 million people, had an immediate impact on betting, with bookmakers slashing the odds on a Romney win from 5/1 [i.e., 5 to 1] to 11/4 in hours. The rival camps will now be waiting tensely to see if the opinion polls also shift.

4. Which actor will play the lead role in the next James Bond movie? Damian Lewis is the current odds-on favorite. According to oddsmakers from online sports book Mybookie.ag, Lewis is the favorite at +150 odds to play the next James Bond. Lewis is best known for portraying U.S. Marine Sergeant Nicholas Brody in the Showtime series *Homeland*, which earned him a Primetime Emmy Award and a Golden Globe.

   The actor with the next best odds is Tom Hardy, who is 2/1 [i.e., 2 to 1] to play the next James Bond. Hardy is a versatile English actor who starred as Bane in the superhero film *The Dark Knight Rises* and also portrayed "Mad" Max Rockatansky in the post-apocalyptic film *Mad Max: Fury Road*. Other actors with realistic odds to play the next James Bond [are] Idris Elba at 3/1, Henry Cavill at 4/1, and Michael Fassbender at 9/2. A complete list of odds from Mybookie.ag can be found below.

   Daniel Craig, who has successfully portrayed Bonds for four movies including 2015's *Spectre*, has decided to step away from the Bond series. There's always a chance that he could change his mind but for now, let the speculation on the new Bond commence.

   Who will play the next James Bond?

   . . . Orlando Bloom +1200, Tom Hiddleston +1000, Richard Armitage +1100, Dan Stevens +1500, Andrew Lincoln +1400, Jamie Dornan +1000 . . .

5. Worried about a Greek exit from the euro region ruining your summer vacation plans? Fret no more, it isn't going to happen. At least that's what bookmakers say. Betfair Group Plc puts the odds of Greece not leaving the euro zone this year at 1/5. . . . William Hill Plc is offering 1/4 Greece will stay in the euro area in 2015. "We've seen optimism come and go but at this stage, it's looking like a certainty that they will stay, at least for this year," said Graham Sharpe, a spokesman for William Hill.

Betting markets can provide clues to the direction of events. So certain was Betfair of the outcome of the Scottish independence referendum last year, it paid out on a "no" vote two days before the ballot, even after polls suggesting a tight contest had sent the pound tumbling. . . .

Paddy Power Plc, Ireland's largest bookmaker, puts the odds of Greece adopting an official currency other than the euro by the end of 2017 at 4/6, meaning a 6 euro bet wins 4.

6. Jeff and Claire are betting on the outcome of a baseball game between the Philadelphia Phillies and the New York Yankees. The bookmaker has the odds of the Phillies winning at 5 to 4 and the odds of the Yankees winning at 4 to 5. Jeff bets $4 on the Phillies to win, and Claire bets $5 on the Yankees.

What, according to these odds, is the probability of the Phillies winning? What is the probability of the Yankees winning? If the Phillies win, what is Jeff's payoff? (That is, how much, total, will the bookmaker give him?) If the Yankees win, what is Claire's payoff? Assuming that Jeff and Claire are the only ones who made bets, how much does the bookmaker gain or lose if the Phillies win? If the Yankees win?

How can the bookmaker change the odds so that when Jeff bets on the Phillies and Claire bets on the Yankees (and each bets the second number in the odds ratio), the bookmaker makes a profit?

For exercises 7 to 12, calculate the expected values for each option.

7. One marble is about to be selected from a jar that contains 45 percent red marbles and 55 percent blue marbles. Given the possible payoffs in table B.6, what is the expected value of *bet on red*? What is the expected value of *bet on blue*?

8. One marble is about to be selected from a jar that contains 90 percent white marbles and 10 percent black marbles. See table B.7 for the payoffs. What is the expected value of *deal one*? What is the expected value of *deal two*? Based on the expected values, which is the better choice?

9. A jar contains 25 percent red marbles, 35 percent blue marbles, and 40 percent green marbles. The options are *bet on red, bet on blue*, and *bet on green*. If someone bets on red and a red marble is drawn, the payoff is $20. If someone bets on blue and a blue marble is drawn, the payoff is $15. And if someone bets on green and a green marble is drawn, then the payoff is $13. In all other cases, the payoff is –$2.

Table B.6

	P(R) = .45	P(B) = .55
	Red is drawn	Blue is drawn
Bet on red	$12	–$3
Bet on blue	–$3	$10

Table B.7

	P(W) = .90	P(B) = .10
	White is drawn	Black is drawn
Deal one	−$15	$100
Deal two	−$30	$250

Table B.8

	P(A) = .03	P(no A) = .97
	Accident	No accident
Buy car insurance	−$700	−$200
Don't buy car insurance	−$10,000	$0

Calculate the expected value of each bet. Based on the expected values, which is the best bet?

10. Larry is planning to sell his car at the end of the month, and he has to decide if he wants to extend his car insurance for this last month that he will have the car. Using the information in table B.8, calculate the expected value of *buying car insurance* and the expected value of *not buying car insurance*. Based on the expected values, which should he choose?

11. Kate and Amy are selling raffle tickets for two separate raffles. The cost to enter either raffle is the same. In both raffles, there are 100 tickets.

    In Kate's raffle, first, 80 of the 100 tickets will be selected, and each of those ticket holders will get $2. Then, five more tickets will be selected, and each of those ticket holders will get $20. The remaining ticket holders will not get anything. In Amy's raffle, 80 tickets will be selected, and those ticket holders will also get $2. Next, fifteen tickets will be selected, and those ticket holders will get $4. The remaining five ticket holders will each get $5.

    Ignoring the cost of entering the raffle (which isn't given), what is the expected value of participating in Kate's raffle? What is the expected value of participating in Amy's raffle? Which has the higher expected value?

12. In the movie *Fight Club* the narrator (played by Edward Norton) explains to the woman sitting next to him on an airplane,

    A new car built by my company leaves somewhere traveling at 60 miles per hour. The rear differential locks up. The car crashes and burns with everyone trapped inside. Now, should we initiate a recall? Take the number of vehicles in the field, A. Multiply it by the probable rate of failure, B. Then multiply the result by the average out-of-court settlement, C. A times B times C equals X. If X is less than the cost of a recall, we don't do one.

Assume that the probable rate of failure is 1 in 10,000 (that is, .0001), the average out-of-court settlement is $250,000, and the cost of the recall is $100 per vehicle.

Don't worry about the number of vehicles in the field. That figure won't change the outcome. (So, the result will be the expected value per car.) Also, don't figure in the cost of the first accident that precipitates the choice between *recall* or *no recall*. If there is a recall, then assume that there are no out-of-court settlement costs.

What is the expected value of *doing a recall*? What is the expected value of *not doing a recall*? Would the narrator's company do a recall?

Sources

Greg Price, "NBA Finals 2015 Betting Odds: Golden State Warriors or Cleveland Cavs Pick to Win Game 6?" *International Business Times*, June 15, 2015.

David Purdum, "Cavaliers Favored by Las Vegas to Claim 2016 NBA Championship." *ESPN.com*, June 17, 2015 (http://espn.go.com/chalk/story/_/id/13096380/).

David Gardner and Guy Adams. "Mitt Romney Odds Slashed as He Mauls Barack Obama in Their First Live TV Battle," *London Evening Standard*, October 4, 2012.

Anthony Rome, "Who Will Be the Next James Bond? Damian Lewis Is the Current Favorite." *TheSpread.com*, December 16, 2015 (http://www.thespread.com/blog/121615).

Dara Doyle, "Greece 'Certain' to Stay in Euro Region This Year, Odds Signal." *Bloomberg Business*, June 22, 2015 (http://www.bloomberg.com/news/articles/2015-06-22/greece-certain-to-stay-in-euro-region-this-year-odds-signal).

B.5 Answers

1. The probability of the Golden State Warriors winning game six of the NBA finals, according to Sportsbook.ag, is 65 percent. The probability of the Cleveland Cavaliers winning game six is 39 percent.

$$\frac{185}{100 + 185} = .649 \tag{B.11}$$

$$\frac{100}{160 + 100} = .385 \tag{B.12}$$

If "these NBA finals go the distance"—that is, go to a game seven in the best of seven series—the probability of the Golden State Warriors winning that game is 92 percent. The probability of the Cleveland Cavaliers winning the seven-game series is 13 percent.

$$\frac{1100}{100 + 1100} = .917 \tag{B.13}$$

$$\frac{100}{700 + 100} = .125 \tag{B.14}$$

2. The probability of the Cleveland Cavaliers winning the 2016 NBA title is 31 percent, according to the Westgate Las Vegas SuperBook. For the Golden State Warriors and the Oklahoma City Thunder, the probability is 17 percent. The probability of the Los Angeles Clippers winning the 2016 NBA title is 9 percent; the probability of the San Antonio Spurs winning is 8 percent; and the probability of the Chicago Bulls winning is also 8 percent.

$$9 \text{ to } 4: \quad \frac{4}{9+4} = .308 \tag{B.15}$$

$$5 \text{ to } 1: \quad \frac{1}{5+1} = .167 \tag{B.16}$$

$$10 \text{ to } 1: \quad \frac{1}{10+1} = .091 \tag{B.17}$$

$$12 \text{ to } 1: \quad \frac{1}{12+1} = .077 \tag{B.18}$$

3. Before the debate, the probability of Romney winning the election—according to bookmakers—was 17 percent (that is, $1/(5+1) = .167$). After the debate, that probability rose to 27 percent ($4/(11+4) = .267$).

4. According to Mybookie.ag, the probability of Damian Lewis taking the role of James Bond is 40 percent ($100/(150+100) = .40$). The probability of Tom Hardy taking the role is 33 percent ($1/(2+1) = .33$).

   For Idris Elba, the probability is 25 percent ($1/(3+1) = .25$). For Henry Cavill, it's 20 percent ($1/(4+1) = .20$), and for Michael Fassbender, it's 18 percent ($2/(9+2) = .182$). For the other actors, the probabilities are listed in table B.9.

5. According to Betfair Group Plc, the probability of Greece staying in the euro zone in 2015 is 83 percent ($5/(1+5) = .833$). According to William Hill Plc, the probability is 80 percent ($4/(1+4) = .80$). On the other hand, the probability of Greece leaving the euro zone—i.e., adopting a currency other than the euro—by the end of 2017 is 60 percent ($6/(4+6) = .60$) according to Paddy Power Plc.

6. The probability of the Phillies winning is 44 percent ($4/(5+4) = .444$). The probability of the Yankees winning is 56 percent ($5/(4+5) = .556$). If the Phillies win, Jeff

Table B.9

	Money line	Probability
Orlando Bloom	+1200	$100/(1200+100) = .077$
Tom Hiddleston	+1000	$100/(1000+100) = .091$
Richard Armitage	+1100	$100/(1100+100) = .083$
Dan Stevens	+1500	$100/(1500+100) = .063$
Andrew Lincoln	+1400	$100/(1400+100) = .067$
Jamie Dornan	+1000	$100/(1000+100) = .091$

will get $5 plus the $4 that he bet for a total of $9. If the Yankees win, Claire will get $4 plus the $5 for a total of $9. Before the game, the bookmaker collected $9 ($4 from Jeff and $5 from Claire). Whichever team wins, the bookmaker pays out $9, and so his or her profit is $0.

To make a profit, the bookmaker has to change the odds so that the corresponding probabilities total more than 1.0. Recall the relationship between odds and probability:

$$a \text{ to } b = \frac{b}{a+b} = probability \tag{B.19}$$

Thus, to increase the probability, either a must be lowered or b must be raised. If the number on the left side of the ratio (the a value) is lowered so that the odds of the Phillies winning is 4 to 4—even odds—and the odds of the Yankees winning is 3 to 5, then the corresponding probabilities are .50 and .625. In this case, when Jeff bets $4 on the Phillies and Claire bets $5 on the Yankees, the bookmaker will make $1 no matter which team wins.

If the odds are changed to 5 to 5 and 4 to 6, then the probabilities are .50 and .60. In this scenario, when Jeff bets $5 on the Phillies and Claire bets $6 on the Yankees, the bookmaker will, again, make $1 no matter which team wins. (The information for both of these scenarios is in table B.10.)

7. The expected value of *bet on red* is $3.75, and the expected value of *bet on blue* is $4.15.

$$E(bet \; on \; red) = (.45 \times \$12) + (.55 \times -\$3) = 5.40 + (-1.65) = \$3.75$$
$$E(bet \; on \; blue) = (.45 \times -\$3) + (.55 \times \$10) = -1.35 + 5.50 = \$4.15 \tag{B.20}$$

8. The expected value of *deal one* is –$3.50, and the expected value of *deal two* is –$2.00. So, deal two is the better choice.

$$E(deal \; one) = (.90 \times -\$15) + (.10 \times \$100) = -13.50 + 10.00 = -\$3.50$$
$$E(deal \; two) = (.90 \times -\$30) + (.10 \times \$250) = -27.00 + 25.00 = -\$2.00 \tag{B.21}$$

Table B.10
The original odds (which were the true probability of each team winning) were 5 to 4 on the Phillies winning and 4 to 5 on the Yankees winning.

	Odds	Probability	Amount bet ($)	Phillies win ($)	Yankees win ($)	Bookmaker ($)
Jeff	4 to 4	.50	4	8	0	1
Claire	3 to 5	.625	5	0	8	1
Jeff	5 to 5	.50	5	10	0	1
Claire	4 to 6	.60	6	0	10	1

Table B.11

	$P(R) = .25$	$P(B) = .35$	$P(G) = .40$
	Red is drawn	Blue is drawn	Green is drawn
Bet on red	$20	–$2	–$2
Bet on blue	–$2	$15	–$2
Bet on green	–$2	–$2	$13

9. *Bet on green* has the highest expected value, $4.00, so that is the best choice.

E(*bet on red*) =

$\quad (.25 \times \$20) + (.35 \times -\$2) + (.40 \times -\$2) = 5.00 + (-0.70) + (-0.80) = \$3.50$

E(*bet on blue*) =

$\quad (.25 \times -\$2) + (.35 \times \$15) + (.40 \times -\$2) = -0.50 + 5.25 + (-0.80) = \$3.95$

E(*bet on green*) =

$\quad (.25 \times -\$2) + (.35 \times -\$2) + (.40 \times \$13) = -0.50 + (-0.70) + 5.20 = \$4.00$

$$\text{(B.22)}$$

10. The expected value of *buying car insurance* is –$215, and the expected value of *not buying car insurance* is –$300. Since buying car insurance has the higher expected value, that is the better choice for Larry.

E(*buy car insurance*) = $(.03 \times -\$700) + (.97 \times -\$200) = -21 + (-194) = -\$215$

E(*don't buy car insurance*) = $(.03 \times -\$10,000) + (.97 \times \$0) = -300 + 0 = -\$300$

$$\text{(B.23)}$$

11. Participating in Kate's raffle has a higher expected value.

E(*Kate's raffle*) = $(.80 \times \$2) + (.15 \times \$0) + (.05 \times \$20) = \$2.60$

E(*Amy's raffle*) = $(.80 \times \$2) + (.15 \times \$4) + (.05 \times \$5) = \$2.45$

$$\text{(B.24)}$$

Table B.12

	P = .80	P = .15	P = .05
	80 tickets	15 tickets	5 tickets
Kate's raffle	$2	$0	$20
Amy's raffle	$2	$4	$5

Table B.13

	P = .0001	P = .9999
Recall	$100	$100
No recall	$250,000	$0

12. Doing a recall has only one outcome and the probability of that outcome is 1.0. Thus, the expected value of *doing a recall* is simply $100; that is, E(*recall*) = 1.0 × $100 = $100. A table with both options listed, however, looks like table B.13. The corresponding calculation, then, is in equation B.25. The expected value of *not doing a recall* is $25. That is less than the expected value of the recall and so, according to the narrator, "we don't do one."

$$E(recall) = (.0001 \times \$100) + (.9999 \times -\$100) = .01 + 99.99 = \$100$$
$$E(no\ recall) = (.0001 \times \$250,000) + (.9999 \times \$0) = 25 + 0 = \$25$$

(B.25)

Index